Erased

Marilee Strong

with Mark Powelson

—⁓— Erased

Missing Women, Murdered Wives

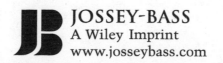

JOSSEY-BASS
A Wiley Imprint
www.josseybass.com

Published by Jossey-Bass
A Wiley Imprint
989 Market Street, San Francisco, CA 94103-1741—www.josseybass.com

Readers should be aware that Internet Web sites offered as citations and/or sources for further
information may have changed or disappeared between the time this was written and when it is read.

Jossey-Bass books and products are available through most bookstores. To contact Jossey-Bass
directly call our Customer Care Department within the U.S. at 800-956-7739, outside the U.S.
at 317-572-3986, or fax 317-572-4002.

Jossey-Bass also publishes its books in a variety of electronic formats. Some content that
appears in print may not be available in electronic books.

Library of Congress Cataloging-in-Publication Data

Strong, Marilee.
  Erased : missing women, murdered wives / Marilee Strong, with Mark Powelson.—1st ed.
     p. cm.
  Includes bibliographical references and index.
  ISBN 978-0-7879-9639-0 (cloth)
  ISBN 978-0-470-44252-4 (paperback)
  1. Uxoricide—United States—Case studies. 2. Pregnant women—Crimes against—United
States—Case studies. 3. Murderers—United States—Psychology. I. Powelson, Mark. II. Title.
  HV6542.S77 2008
  364.152'3—dc22

                                                                          2007041054

Printed in the United States of America
FIRST EDITION
PB Printing   10 9 8 7 6 5 4 3 2 1

~~~ Contents

*To all the women still missing, may they yet be found,
and to the living victims who seek justice in their name*

∼∼∼ Acknowledgments

I could not have written this book without the love, support, advice, and assistance of Mark Powelson, who constantly challenged me to go deeper than I thought I could go. His help in shaping the central idea of this book was invaluable, as were his magnificent research abilities and editing skills. He is a true partner in every sense of the word.

My friend and agent, Amy Rennert, set me on the path that led to this book. Her unwavering belief and support carried me through the darkest days of a long and arduous journey, and I owe her more than I can ever say. In the increasingly commercial world of book publishing, her commitment to ideas and her willingness to go the distance for her writers are both remarkable and rare.

My editor, Alan Rinzler, embraced the concept I envisioned for this book from our very first conversation and pushed me to take it even further. Every writer should be so lucky to have the opportunity to work with such a gifted and enthusiastic editor.

I am indebted to countless people who generously shared their time and insights with me during the reporting of this book, including Jim Anderson, Ron Arias, Anne Bird, Martin Blinder, Lisa Borok, Howard Breuer, Jacquelyn Campbell, Paula Canny, Michael Cardoza, Jason Dearen, Candice DeLong, Thomas DiBiase, Stacy Finz, Victoria Frye, Ann Goetting, Stan Goldman, Gloria Gomez, Gary Greene, Jim Hammer, Jodi Hernandez, Miriam Hernandez, Daniel Horowitz, Dean Johnson, Mark Klaas, Dennis Mahon, James Murphy, Alan Peacock, Delroy Paulhus, Dan Saunders, Garin Sinclair, Stan and Denise Smart, Chuck Smith, Kevin Smith, Vince Sturla, Robert Talbot, Diana Walsh, Janelle Wang, Neil Websdale, Chris Weicher, and Irwin Zalkin.

I am also grateful to the following people for the access and assistance they provided to me during the legal proceedings in the Scott Peterson case: Peter Shaplen, Judy Lucier, Carol Hurst,

Jenne Carnevale, Mike Orange, Doug Ridenour, Kelly Huston, Tom Letras, and, most especially, the Honorable Alfred A. Delucchi, an extraordinary human being and a judge of incomparable intelligence, patience, fairness, and compassion.

I kiss'd thee ere I kill'd thee.

—*William Shakespeare,* Othello

Erased

Introduction

A Crime Without a Name

The long road that led to this book began for me with the disappearance of Laci Peterson. From the first bewildering reports that a young pregnant woman had vanished from her home on Christmas Eve 2002 in a town in California's Central Valley, I sensed that something greater and even more disturbing was at play than an already overwhelming individual tragedy, although at the time I could not identify exactly what that was. The initial reports seemed to point to a stranger abduction, but the facts as they began to unfold did not cleanly fit the pattern that such a crime normally leaves behind.

Trained as a journalist in the South Bronx in the 1980s, I was well acquainted with violent crime in all its terrible manifestations. More recently I had become painfully familiar with the often-unending horror of stranger abduction while covering a string of child kidnappings in the San Francisco Bay Area. Although it's no guarantee of a positive outcome—none of the missing little girls I wrote about has ever been found—I saw how aggressive reporting was essential

1

to keep police and the public focused on these cases to provide any hope of a resolution to the mystery of their disappearances.

I also learned how much the ability to solve this kind of crime depends on rapid police response and the complete cooperation of those closest to the victim—especially whoever was the last to see the missing person. For the detectives on such cases, the clock begins ticking from the moment the person vanishes, as the chances of recovering the victim alive fall dramatically after the first twenty-four to forty-eight hours. I could see firsthand how, as more and more time passed, feelings of helplessness, self-blame, and intractable grief take an immeasurable toll on the family of the missing, just as frustration and irresolution eat away at the detectives searching in vain for their loved ones.

When the trail grows cold—when the hundreds or thousands of tips, leads, sightings, interviews, and alibi checks all come up dry—the case remains officially open. But, in a sense, a curtain is drawn around an ongoing tragedy.

In this type of crime, where a beloved family member has disappeared and no hint of evidence remains, someone has been able to commit what is, in effect, personal terrorism against everyone who knew and loved the missing person, and has literally gotten away with murder. By leaving no trace and no trail, no usable evidence or clues, the murderer faces fewer personal consequences than the average citizen might face from a minor traffic violation. There is no arrest, no hearing, no trial, no justice, and no answers. There is no body to recover, no funeral, no burial, no headstone.

Whereas most of the public is cognizant only of the few weeks or months when the search for a missing person is at its zenith, those who have been close to these crimes have seen the unresolved grief, the wrenching apart of families, the pained expressions on the faces of investigators. These cases are never formally closed, but they fall into a horrible state of limbo where hope is squeezed beyond human endurance.

When I first heard about the disappearance of Laci Peterson and the allegations that someone had abducted a pregnant woman as she walked her large and protective dog in a heavily utilized city park, my instincts as a reporter told me that something was off. Within a week of her disappearance, I began reporting on the story, making the first of many trips to her hometown of Modesto, walking where she was said to have walked that day, visiting the places and people that were pivotal to understanding this crime. I would go on to follow the case through to its resolution, attending every day of the nearly yearlong trial of her husband, Scott, for the double murder of his wife and unborn son. I was driven, like so many millions of other people, by compassion for this vital young expectant mother but also by a growing sense that a larger story was still unrecognized.

As is now well known, the kidnapping scenario advanced by Scott Peterson was simply an elaborate ruse—a complete fabrication in a profoundly Machiavellian plot. The ugly truth that emerged at trial was that Laci had been murdered by her own husband, a seemingly normal, well-functioning man—a young man with a college education and an apparently good upbringing, who held a job and managed the responsibilities of adult life, and who had no criminal background whatsoever. The murder occurred without warning, without any prior history of abuse in the marriage.

Furthermore, this "normal" young man took the extraordinary risks involved in "staging" a phony crime, to use the technical term that forensic investigators use when a crime or crime scene is made to seem like something other than what it was, and disposing of his dead wife's body in broad daylight ninety miles away in the middle of San Francisco Bay. He was then able to maintain utter calm and put on an at least quasi-believable demeanor as he told lie after lie to conceal the truth from his wife's concerned family as well as his own, dozens of friends, a girlfriend who had no idea she was a married man's mistress, an array of very shrewd police investigators, and, much to Scott's surprise, an ever-increasing media contingent.

What puzzled so many people who attempted to analyze the Peterson story was that Scott did not fit the well-known profile of a wife-killer. Usually domestic homicides are preceded by years of physical abuse, incidents known to family and friends and often documented by police. I had some familiarity in this area as well, having worked the crisis hotline at a shelter for battered women and at a legal clinic assisting women in obtaining restraining orders against their abusers. I had heard enough stories from victims who had faced every imaginable kind of abuse to see that the marriage of Scott and Laci Peterson did not fit this particular pattern, even if in the end Scott was capable of the consummate act of domestic violence. Something else was going on here, but what?

After a number of other incidences of mysteriously disappearing women broke into the headlines, I began to see a connection. At first the similarities between these new stories and the Peterson case just seemed like strange coincidences. Nineteen months after Laci's disappearance, Lori Hacking—another young pregnant woman in what had appeared to be a loving relationship—went missing in Utah. Lori's husband, who everyone believed to be an honest, hard-working, religious man, seemed almost to have taken notes from Scott Peterson's playbook in an effort to pull off a perfect murder. Hacking had set the scene so that it appeared his wife had gone jogging in a quiet park on the mouth of a canyon, thus putting her well outside the home and into an area where, conceivably, something bad but unknown could easily have happened to her.

Although Mark Hacking stuck to his very simple and straightforward story, police quickly uncovered a series of lies not directly linked to Lori's disappearance, but which cast grave doubt on the young man's honesty. Mark Hacking had been leading a double life—not the kind of stylish and seductive double life one sees so often in fictional portrayals of spies or sophisticated con artists, but a strangely sad double life in which he spent all his time and effort pretending that he was a nose-to-the-grindstone premed student when he was nothing of the sort.

Learning the details of the Hacking case sent me back to my files and detailed notes covering some seemingly minor facts about Scott Peterson. In addition to the obvious lies Scott had told to cover up his murder, and the whopper he had told his girlfriend and others in claiming not to be married, there was an eerie parallel here. I knew through a series of sources how Scott would "innocently" but frequently introduce lies about himself whenever he had the chance to inflate his own image. Rather than being a married fertilizer salesman who worked for a subsidiary of a European corporation, he portrayed himself as an international business owner and globetrotting playboy. When he was away from anyone who actually knew him, his wealth, accomplishments, and prowess all increased dramatically.

This tendency toward extravagantly embroidered mendacity seemed to reflect two distinct but interrelated psychological characteristics. Peterson and Hacking appeared to be compulsive liars—although they both had the ability to modulate their lies in situations where they knew they might get caught. But even more interesting was the complex pattern of their lying, especially to their wives—lies told, maintained, and elaborated over long periods of time—in order to cover the fact that they were leading secret lives.

Scott Peterson's other, more glamorous life was that of a randy bachelor; he was able to take advantage of a surprising number of nights "away on business" to pursue his compulsive need to romance other women. Mark Hacking's secret life was far less exciting. His studious façade masked a kind of aimless slacking, like that of a boy who didn't want to grow up.

Then one day when I was researching the legal issue at the very center of the Peterson case—whether murder can be proved by purely circumstantial evidence—I stumbled unexpectedly on details of another case that led me to believe that some of the key psychological factors being exhibited by these unusual killers were more than a coincidence and might, in fact, provide essential clues to the real motivation and makeup of these men.

That third case involved an urbane lothario named L. Ewing Scott, who killed his wife more than fifty years ago. Although no trace of Evelyn Scott was ever found, her husband was found guilty of killing her—the first time in U.S. history that someone was convicted of murder without a corpse or without any physical proof of death whatsoever. The case established clear legal precedent—not only that murder can be proven without a body but also that circumstantial evidence can be given just as much weight as eyewitness testimony or other forms of evidence.

However, for reasons that will be explored in this book, bodiless murder convictions remain relatively rare. The odds of getting away with murder by erasing the victim are astonishingly good a full half-century after the L. Ewing Scott decision.

As I looked into more and more of these "missing wife" cases, it became clear to me that "getting away with murder" was an essential force, but not the only force, driving these killers. One might assume that every killer, every criminal of any sort, wants to get away with his crime. But most domestic homicides are not planned, not carefully calculated and covered up. In fact, most intimate partner killers make no attempt to hide their identity.

Then a case broke into the news that seemed like a variation on this type of hidden domestic homicide, involving an even more audacious ruse than a faked missing person scenario. Dr. Barton Corbin, a successful dentist who lived in a suburb of Atlanta, was indicted in December 2004 for the death of his one-time girlfriend fourteen years earlier, and two weeks later he was indicted for the murder of his current wife.

Both women had been found dead under nearly identical circumstances: looking as though they had committed suicide, a gun by their side, their bodies both in very similar postures. Although friends of the first dead woman were highly suspicious of the coroner's finding of suicide, Corbin had not been charged with anything and had simply gone on to build a flourishing dental practice and find a new woman to love him . . . until he was through with her, too. Although Corbin used a different strategy to rid himself of a partner for whom he no longer had any use, he seemed a close cousin to the Scott Peterson type of killer. Corbin's crimes were just as carefully planned and premeditated as Peterson's, but instead of disappearing his victims and leaving what happened to them an open-ended mystery, he created a staged crime scene to account for each woman's death in a way that seemed to clear him of any involvement—in fact, made the victims appear not to have been murdered at all. And he did such a convincing job of it that he only tipped his hand when he had the temerity to try it a second time.

Both Peterson and Corbin were confident, intelligent, educated men who appeared to be unblinking in the face of enormous pressure from the police, the media, and the families of their loved ones. In both cases there was almost no physical evidence linking the killer to the crime. In fact, both men had gone to an unusual amount of effort to eliminate any sign that their victims had struggled for their lives, to time their crimes such that there would not be eyewitnesses, and to erase forensic evidence that might betray their actions. And both men concocted scenarios that, if believed, would leave them in the clear. Whereas Scott Peterson made his wife's pregnant body disappear, Barton Corbin left his wife's dead body in plain view but made his own actions and involvement "disappear."

Yet unlike Scott Peterson, Corbin gave no media interviews, refused to speak even to police, and, to use cop terminology, "lawyered up" within hours of his wife's death, even though he was maintaining that it was just a tragic suicide. I suspected at the time that Corbin—who committed his second murder in the waning days of the Peterson trial—was learning from the Peterson case and was trying to avoid the mistakes that Scott had made by not saying anything that could possibly be used against him.

In her book on the Corbin case, *Too Late to Say Goodbye*, crime writer Ann Rule confirmed the fact that Corbin had followed the Peterson trial avidly. His sister-in-law remembered Barton remarking one day that Peterson got caught "because he couldn't keep his mouth shut."

Around this same time, a thirty-seven-year-old Alabama man named Thomas Lane broke into the home where his estranged wife was staying and drowned her while she was taking a bath, holding her down under the water with his foot until she stopped breathing. He then took some money and jewelry to make it appear that his wife had been killed when surprised by a burglar.

Lane murdered his wife of eight years, Teresa, a "mail-order bride" from the Philippines, not because she was attempting to leave him. It was Thomas who wanted out of the marriage, telling friends and neighbors even before he killed Teresa that he was planning to replace her with a younger model he had already "bought and paid for." He even showed them pictures of his new bride-to-be, a woman he met on the Internet, bragging that she was just thirteen or fourteen years old.

Like Scott Peterson and so many of the other killers I was beginning to research, Lane seemed to have no emotional attachment to his wife whatsoever. In his mind, she was nothing more than a commodity he had purchased, and he had the right to an upgrade whenever he saw fit. Tragically, he believed that once she was of no further use to him, she had no right to go on living.

At trial his father revealed how Lane was directly inspired by Peterson, whom he saw as offering a solution to his own marital woes.

"If I could do what Peterson did and get away with it, I'd kill her," Thomas Lane told his father three weeks before the murder.

It was chilling to see that the killers themselves were making the connection between these crimes, regardless of the specific modus operandi employed. Whether they chose to disappear the victim or the crime itself by staging the death as a suicide or some other event, it was clear that these were simply two sides of the same coin. The meticulous planning and supreme self-control exhibited both before and after the crimes I was investigating and beginning to link together seemed to be a significant aspect of these men's characters, far beyond the murderous aspect of their personalities. The expertise at lying and manipulation that is needed to successfully lead a double life is indicative of a high degree of Machiavellian thinking and behavior. Whereas political scientists and others sometimes use the term *Machiavellian*, psychologists have developed a formal category and accompanying tests and measures for people whose psychological makeup ranks high in such traits.

Other malignant personality characteristics seemed to be involved as well, from cold-blooded psychopathic tendencies to extreme degrees of narcissism. But there was something else curious about these men's characters. Erasing their victims appeared to be not just a means to an end but an end in itself. Once they made the decision to kill, they began purging all traces of the victim's existence in their lives. Many began getting rid of the woman's possessions within days of her disappearance, pulling up stakes, changing their lifestyles dramatically. Some immediately replaced their missing wives or girlfriends with other women—sometimes with look-alikes for the disappeared. And, most shockingly, some later attempted to get away with murder again, erasing another wife or girlfriend, sometimes, as in Corbin's case, in exactly the same manner as their first crime.

Many put an extraordinary amount of thought into their crimes, researching methods of killing and means of body disposal, and boning up on investigatory and forensic techniques. They also seemed to look to and learn from each other as models, noting what worked for other killers and what pitfalls to avoid.

For example, I believe that Scott Peterson based his plan on a number of highly publicized prior disappearances, most notably of several coeds during his college years in San Luis Obispo. One of these young women, Kristin Smart, remains missing more than a decade later. Even though police believe they know who killed her, no one has ever been charged.

The Smart case is an almost textbook example of how easy it can be to get away with murder. I believe Scott learned from this case how oversights and inaction in the crucial first days of a disappearance may prevent a killer from ever being charged, much less convicted. I think he relied on assumptions about police investigation that he drew from this case in conceiving his own murder plan—for example, choosing to carry out the crime and report his wife missing on Christmas Eve. He assumed, wrongly, that no experienced detectives would even begin looking into his wife's disappearance for several days, enough time for the trail to grow stale and for him to thoroughly cover his tracks. He believed that if a body was never found and the suspect refused to confess, he would never be charged—something the police publicly declared in the Smart case.

—᠕᠕᠊—

The concept of serial murder has only been recognized as a distinct category of crime for a few decades, even though serial killers have been making headlines at least as far back as "Jack the Ripper." For nearly a century, the notorious slayer who terrorized Victorian London was viewed as a criminal freak of nature, even though other serial killings during the same historical period were soon reported from Sweden to San Francisco. Then, in the late 1970s and early 1980s, forensic psychologists in the FBI's now famous Behavioral Science Unit began assembling common characteristics from interviews and case files of killers who now bear this moniker.

Although experts may disagree on what precisely is and is not a serial homicide, naming and defining the crime opened the door to serious research, which has led to hundreds of studies of these type of killers by psychologists, sociologists, criminologists, and other scientists.

Identifying a new crime category is a bit like discovering a new or previously misunderstood disease: everything changes when the phenomenon has a name. New syndromes in the medical field, first noticed as a seemingly unrelated collection of problems and symptoms, are often initially treated with shame and derision—from alcoholism to posttraumatic stress disorder, anorexia and bulimia to chronic fatigue syndrome. Giving them a name is the first step toward serious scientific study and public awareness.

—᠕᠕᠊—

• This book sets forth a profile of what I call eraser killing: a form of intimate partner (or domestic) homicide that is committed almost exclusively by men, done in a carefully planned manner, often through bloodless means known as a "soft kill" (such as smothering, suffocating, or strangling) so as to leave behind as little evidence as possible or with the crime scene thoroughly cleaned up. To further cover his tracks, the eraser killer disposes of his victim's body by some means meant to ensure that it will never be found, or erases anything that links him to her death by "staging" the murder as something completely different—an accident, a suicide, or a crime committed by a total stranger, such as mugging, carjacking, or other random crime of opportunity.

• On the basis of five years of investigation into hundreds of killings that I believe fit this profile, I will explain what is truly going on behind the stories of missing women that have dominated the news since the disappearance of Laci Peterson six years ago, identifying the hidden pattern among cases that the media has simply presented as mystery after unrelated (and often unresolved) mystery.

• Using new research on the psychology of dark criminal impulses in otherwise high-functioning men, I will also offer a psychological profile of the factors I believe explain and drive this curious breed of killer—men who live behind a mask of normality, who seem incapable of violence to most of those who know them, who lead productive and often quite accomplished lives right up until the minute they kill the ones they supposedly love.

• This book will examine more than fifty eraser killings, some just recently in the headlines, some dating back a century, challenging some of the well-honed myths about domestic violence and domestic homicide. For eraser killers are not like ordinary killers, nor are they even like more typical wife- or girlfriend-killers. These men do not commit their crimes in the "heat of passion" or in a moment of out-of-control rage. Their crimes are not hot-blooded but cold-blooded, arrived at after much thought and carried out with meticulous care. Because these men premeditate and plan their killings with inordinate stealth and cunning, because they are fearless and expert at manipulating and deceiving those around them, because they hold nearly everything that is true about them in complete secrecy, the women in their lives often have no idea they are in mortal danger until it is too late.

• The motive behind these killings is something else that has been widely misunderstood and misrepresented both in the media and in the courtroom. Fundamentally, eraser killers do not kill for the reasons normally ascribed to murderers, such as greed, sex, or jealousy. They eliminate the women, and sometimes children, in their lives because their victims no longer serve any "purpose" in the emotionally desolate world of the eraser killer, or are seen as impediments to the kind of life they covet and fantasize for themselves. In the mind of this type of murderer, it is better, easier, and more satisfying for him to kill than simply to get a divorce.

• Eraser killers often go to extraordinary lengths not just to manipulate a crime scene or make a woman disappear but also to manipulate the police, the courts, and justice itself as part of their high-stakes game. This manipulation, I believe, is something that is also key to the nature of the eraser killer and becomes almost an end in itself—an enjoyable battle of wits in which he is sure he will always come out on top.

• In a kind of Catch-22 that is built into the American criminal justice system and its reliance on antiquated and faulty assumptions about this type of intimate homicide, police and prosecutors are very often sandbagged before they can even launch a homicide case. This book will provide several illuminating stories that expose the unintentional loopholes that both encourage eraser killers to believe that they can get away with murder and very often make it possible for them to do just that.

For example, eraser killers have used constitutional protections against search and seizure to seal off the scene of their crimes, usually in the victim's own home, and prevent police from entering by staging the crime to appear to have happened elsewhere. Investigators are forced to wait sometimes for weeks, sometimes years before the actual murder scene can be searched and forensically examined, thus giving a killer as much time as he needs to completely erase all the evidence.

Murder is much harder to prove when the killer takes pains to leave no physical evidence behind. Someone clever enough to make sure his victim's body remains hidden stands a good chance of never being charged with murder, much less convicted. Eyewitness testimony, the only purely direct evidence other than a confession, is notoriously unreliable. (Groups like the Innocence Project are regularly getting rape convictions overturned after DNA tests prove that the victim identified an innocent man.) Yet most jurors buy into the popular stereotype that circumstantial evidence is not proof, a sometimes insurmountable burden even when the body is not hidden.

"They couldn't put the gun in his hand," jury foreman Thomas Nicholson declared after acquitting *In Cold Blood* star Robert Blake of killing his wife, Bonny Lee Bakley—in spite of the fact that Blake openly hated his wife and that two men testified that he had attempted to hire them to "whack" her. (Bakley was ultimately shot to death as she waited for Blake in his car outside a restaurant where the two had just dined together, Blake claiming that at the time the shooting occurred, he had gone back inside to retrieve a gun he had inadvertently left behind.)

Prosecutors are often loath to take on no-body cases, knowing that if a defendant is acquitted, there will be no second chance to convict him even if the victim's remains are later found right in the defendant's backyard. Jurors erroneously but almost uniformly view circumstantial evidence as a weak form of proof, internalizing an attitude, often expressed in the popular media, that a case is "merely circumstantial." Nearly every one of the sixteen hundred potential jurors who were queried to serve on the Peterson case initially expressed qualms about circumstantial evidence, believing it was not "real" evidence—or, as one put it, "My understanding is circumstantial evidence is what you *can't* prove."

Peterson juror John Guinasso said he would not have voted to convict if the bodies had not washed up where they did—on the shore of San Francisco Bay ninety miles from the Peterson home in Modesto, California, and within about a mile of the exact spot where Scott told police he had spontaneously decided to go fishing the day his wife disappeared.

In exploring these and other issues, I draw sometimes heavily on my investigation and analysis of the Scott Peterson case, which I believe to be a quintessential eraser killing, and which can shed more light on the phenomenon than perhaps any other single case. Although many feel that they already know this case quite well, I believe that this book breaks new ground by

- Exploring the real motive behind Peterson's murder of his pregnant wife, something even the jurors who convicted him did not seem to fully understand

- Explaining how the death of his unborn son, Conner, was not simply an unfortunate by-product of his decision to kill his wife but represented a pivotal aspect of his motivation

- Offering the first comprehensive psychological portrait of Scott Peterson and explaining how different and competing aspects of his personality made him believe he could commit the perfect murder but also caused him to make fatal errors that got him convicted

- Revealing many new and disturbing facts about the case, including an alternative plan Peterson may have been considering for disposing of his wife and child that would have prevented their bodies from ever being found and all but ensured that he would never have been charged with their murders

I do not believe Scott Peterson killed his wife in order to be with another woman or to collect on the substantial inheritance his wife had coming. That he was having an affair and that he was living beyond his means, spending recklessly on such luxuries as an expensive golf club membership in the weeks before his first child was to be born, are important clues into his psyche. But they do not, in and of themselves, constitute motive. They are ultimately what film director Alfred Hitchcock called MacGuffins, red herrings that obscure rather than reveal the darker machinations of the plot.

Clearly there is something very disturbed in the psychological makeup of a man who could coldly plan a murder, but was unable or unwilling to face a divorce; who could strangle or smother his pregnant wife to death but could not displease her by maintaining that he did not want children; who could turn on his fourteen-carat charm to woo a new lover, but was unable to use that charm and power of persuasion to succeed in his job as a salesman; who believed himself fully capable of outfoxing the police, never doubting his ability to fearlessly win every nerve-wracking encounter, but whose fragile ego was threatened by the rapidly approaching responsibilities of fatherhood.

The Peterson case is rife with these seeming contradictions, which no one has yet been able to explain. I believe that they are not actually contradictions, but instead are part and parcel of the peculiar psychology of eraser killers. The strange and unstable mixture of pathologies that drives these killers explains not only their criminal success but also the mistakes and contradictions that sometimes get them caught.

When I began covering the Peterson case, the facts were so horrific that I wanted to believe that it was an anomaly. Unfortunately for the score of "missing" women who have since made headlines—and many more whose stories did not make national news but were no less tragic—the Peterson case turned out not to be singular at all. Whereas part of the media—led by the more innovative and less tradition-bound producers in cable television—covered these stories intensively, many editors, news anchors, and print columnists simply scoffed at such coverage. Some even extended their derision beyond media outlets they dislike to an unseemly attack on the victims themselves.

My own belief is that the recent flood of such seemingly inexplicable stories makes many people uncomfortable. Perhaps the betrayal at the heart of these crimes is too unsettling, too challenging to the illusion of safety we cling to in the sanctuary of our own home.

Those who dismiss news coverage (and books) focusing on this kind of crime have never sat down with the shell-shocked family members of women who have never been given even the dignity and validation of a trial. The most tragic eraser killings are those in which there is no arrest, no arraignment, no trial, no justice, no body recovered, no funeral, no burial, no headstone—no answers or resolution of any kind.

I have written this book so that all of us may start to understand a type of crime that has been right in front of us but obscured from view, just as its perpetrators have intended. My hope is to cast light on the shadows where the killers have hidden their faces from us. It is an attempt, however inadequate, to give voice as best I can to these women whose deaths have left them voiceless, for erased women are truly silent victims. They cannot call out for justice. They cannot point a finger at their killer, whose true face they may have recognized only at the moment of their death.

PART ONE

Eraser Killing

The History and Psychology of
a New Criminal Profile

CHAPTER ONE

Out of the Shadows

A new type of killer is wreaking havoc across America and around the world. He has made countless headlines in recent years, but until now his core identity has been hidden. He is not driven by rage or lust. His conscience is not set loose by drugs or alcohol—the deadly fuels that can turn some men into momentary killers. Unlike most other murderers, he very often has no criminal record and sometimes no history of violence whatsoever. He is an intelligent, careful, methodical killer.

He is also someone who has always been a fabricator of reality. He is not your harmless garden-variety fibber but a compulsive, pathological liar whose lies are meant to get a reaction out of others: to inspire their admiration, to evoke their sympathy, to get him exactly what he wants. He makes up stories big and small, often lying about things for no readily apparent reason. But he is especially practiced at deceiving others about who he really is.

He fabricates evidence to exaggerate his accomplishments, wealth, success, social standing. Sometimes he proudly displays phony business cards or diplomas, awards from military service he never earned, and other "proof" he needs to create the impression that he craves. He knows how to use words, lies, and actions to manipulate others. Manipulation—either subtle or overt—is a core feature of how he interacts with others.

He leads what appears to be a normal and productive life and is often considered to be an exemplary citizen. But quietly, beneath the surface, unbeknownst to almost anyone, he has used all his well-honed abilities to lie, manipulate, and fabricate reality in order to commit the crown jewel of crimes, the perfect murder.

His goal is to erase his victim—be it his wife, ex-wife, girlfriend, or lover—to expunge her from the record of his life. If she is pregnant with a child he does not want—and an unwanted pregnancy is an alarmingly common motive for eraser killings—he is killing two birds with one stone, eliminating what he views as dead weight dragging him down. In his mind, he is not really murdering a human being; he is simply rearranging the world to better suit his needs, to remove a major annoyance or let him make a fresh start of things.

He harbors a cluster of psychological traits very unusual in the general public. He does not experience the almost universal psychological reaction called fear. It is not that he is uncommonly brave or that he has "conquered" fear. He does experience an abstract, emotionally colorless sensation when put under great stress—especially if he feels caught in a situation he is not confident he can talk his way out of, when he is no longer in control of everyone around him. Most of the time, any sense of truly being afraid is more like a thought than a feeling. His heart does not beat faster, and he shows few if any signs of the *emotion* of fear. He knows about fear a bit like a colorblind person is aware of color: it is visible, but only as another shade of gray.

Eraser killers employ cunning, stealth, and often meticulous planning to overcome their trusting prey, frequently employing the agonizingly slow and terror-inducing method of suffocation or strangulation in order to minimize the type of messy crime scene evidence that could get them caught.

These killers represent a previously unrecognized subset of intimate partner murderers, different in distinct ways from other domestic killers:

- Their killings are not committed in the violent rage or sudden loss of control that characterizes more classic domestic homicides. On the contrary, they kill with total calm, total control. If they leave behind any crime scene at all, it will be what criminal profilers refer to as "organized"—just the kind of crime scene investigators do not expect to see when a domestic homicide is involved, for that is supposed to be the most "hot-blooded," disorganized, and messy of crimes.

- The eraser killer is a master of deceit and an expert manipulator. His killing is carried out in total secrecy (unlike many domestic homicides, which often are committed even though there are witnesses present) and then very highly "staged," to use the investigators' term for a crime scene that is arranged like a stage set to create an illusion intended to confuse the police and send them down a wrong trail.

- Most domestic homicides involve jealousy, money, another woman, or explosive and vengeful rage felt by the killer because the woman is planning to leave him. Although there are sometimes subsidiary motives involving monetary gain or other women, the eraser killer is not "driven" by these things. His real motivations stem from the unique psychology of men with a particular set of dangerous traits that psychologists have recently named "the Dark Triad" of personality.

- He is killing because the woman in question has become inconvenient. In his eyes, she no longer meets his needs, or she stands in the way of something he wants. She is not allowed to leave him or take away anything he holds dear, be it a home or children or the lifestyle he has come to enjoy. He will only let her go on his deadly, unilateral terms.

- He plans his killing well in advance, once again distinguishing him from the standard wife-killer. Far fewer than half of all wife-killings are actually planned in advance of the final encounter, according to available research.

- The eraser killer will exhibit neither mourning nor real signs of emotional loss, and will almost always exhibit strangely inappropriate behavior and speech after the mysterious death of his wife or girlfriend. (Sometimes he even starts speaking about her in the past tense *before* he has killed her.) Although he may actively participate in the search for a missing loved one, he will be using his full array of skills to direct any inquiries or police investigation toward fictitious threats and other suspects and away from himself.

- He may have hidden his contempt for the object of his enmity, especially if doing so gives him tactical advantage when the moment of attack arrives. But once he makes up his mind to erase his victim, his determination is all-consuming. When the act begins—once he puts his hands around her throat or strikes her with a heavy object as she sleeps—there is no twinge of conscience or compassion.

- He is generally intelligent, though he also greatly overestimates his talents. He believes he is smarter and better than the rest of us, certainly smarter than the police and more deserving in all ways than his victim. He often has considerable familiarity with the law and with how the police work. He may have read up on these matters diligently to help him with his plan. Or he may have used his unusual ability for absorbing things around him, observing with the cold eye of a lizard in the desert how other predators kill and get away with it, because getting away with murder is his goal.

- To achieve that goal, he may follow one of two distinct strategies. Either he can erase the victim's body by destroying it entirely or secreting it where it won't be found, or he can rearrange the crime or stage a wholly false scenario to erase all connection between himself and any criminal act. Either way, he appears to remain free and clear of any involvement in a dastardly act.

Although men have been carrying out this kind of crime for centuries, it is only now that the extraordinary glare of television lights and an almost "shock-and-awe" level of news coverage are beginning to drive him out of the safety of the darkness. But without an actual name for this crime and for this killer, it is still hard for us to make sense of these crimes, to find the hidden clues, and solve what too often and quite tragically remain unsolved mysteries. As criminal profilers have discovered, truth and resolution can be found only by ferreting out the unseen links and connections between these seemingly disparate cases.

I believe these killers are best described as *eraser killers*, because that term describes simply and succinctly both their motive and their methods. Their victims are not "missing women" or "vanished wives." They are women who have been erased, just as repressive political regimes have used the method of "forced disappearances" to dispose of their enemies and strike terror into all those who oppose them. The impact of so many women being "erased" or "disappeared" from our very midst, from communities or homes we have assumed to be "safe," is overwhelming in its magnitude and undermines so many of the fundamentals on which our sense of trust and security is based. These eraser killers exploit the safeguards built into our legal system—principles enshrined in our constitution to protect honest citizens from unreasonable searches of their property and from being forced or coerced into making a false confession—as if those honored protections were simply escape hatches built to provide safe haven for someone capable of pulling off an expert murder.

By following a series of threads, beginning with Laci Peterson and then going back and forth in time to hundreds of other instances of mysteriously disappeared women, I discovered that most of the cases fit a distinct pattern or profile of a startlingly prevalent type of murder, yet one that had never been identified because we have tended to look at each case in a vacuum.

Most were not missing persons cases in any strict sense of the word, but elaborately planned and premeditated domestic homicides disguised to appear to be mysterious vanishings. Invariably, the person responsible for the woman's disappearance was her current or former husband or boyfriend. Although some recent killers even cited Scott Peterson as their inspiration, he was hardly the first to come up with such an idea. Looking back in time, I traced the same pattern back a century to the murder that inspired Theodore Dreiser's literary classic, *An American Tragedy*.

Although the essential facts of these cases bear a striking similarity, the outcomes vary widely. Many "disappeared" women are never found, and no one is ever held to account for what happened to them. A few victims—the "lucky" ones, in a manner of speaking—are eventually discovered, often by pure chance or an act of nature. Their families get a chance to bury their loved ones, or what is left of them, and sometimes their killers are brought to justice. A small number of presumed killers are tried and convicted in the absence of a body; others are acquitted with or without a body because there is not enough evidence to convince a judge or jury beyond a reasonable doubt that a murder occurred, much less that the woman's intimate partner was the one responsible.

The victims of these killers are women of all races and social classes, from all parts of the country (and around the world as well). Whereas some have been the subject of intensive media coverage, others are all but unknown beyond their closest loved ones.

All the women listed here are dead or presumed to be dead. All were murdered or are believed by authorities to have been murdered by a husband or boyfriend, falling victim precisely because of their physical and emotional vulnerability to their killer. All "went missing" under mysterious circumstances, but none of these women was ever truly lost. They didn't wander off, run away from home, suffer amnesia and forget where they belonged. They were deliberately "disappeared" by someone who had good reason to try to make sure they would never be found, someone who wanted to erase them from the face of the earth.

———

• Hattie "Fern" Bergeler, fifty-seven, was found floating in the bay near her Florida home in August 2002 with a bedsheet wrapped around her head and cinderblocks tied to her neck and ankles. Her multimillionaire husband, Donald Moringiello, a retired aerospace engineer, claimed the two had lost sight of each other while driving in separate cars to visit his children. But he had still not reported her missing by the time her remains were identified—a month after he claimed to have lost her in traffic. Despite a wealth of physical evidence—the sheet, rope, and cinderblocks and the gun used to kill Fern, also fished from the water behind their Fort Myers Beach home, were all tied to her husband, and cleaned-up blood was found in the house—it took two trials to convict him of second-degree murder. A man of Moringiello's intelligence and character would never have made so many stupid mistakes, his attorney had argued.

• Isabel Rodriguez, thirty-nine, vanished in November 2001 two weeks after seeking a protective order against her estranged husband, Jesus, who she said threatened to kill her if she was awarded any money from him in their divorce. In the days before her disappearance, her husband ordered ten truckloads of dirt and gravel delivered to his five-acre farm on the outskirts of the Florida Everglades. On the day she went missing, a witness saw a fire burning for hours on the property. Jesus had told all his farmhands not to come to work that day, explaining to one that he was planning a Santeria "cleansing" ritual on the property. Police believe he killed his wife that day, burned her corpse on the farm, and scattered the ashes under the dirt and gravel. He claims she returned to her native Honduras, abandoning their two children, but there is no record of her leaving the United States or entering Honduras. Not long after his wife disappeared, he began seeing another woman, who looks uncannily like his missing wife and whose name even happens to be Isabel. At the time this book was written, prosecutors were preparing for a third trial after two previous efforts ended in mistrial.

• Kristine Kupka, twenty-eight, was just two months away from graduating with a degree in philosophy from Baruch College in New York City when she vanished without a trace in 1998. She was also five months pregnant by one of her professors, Darshanand "Rudy" Persaud, who did not confess to her that he was married until after she became pregnant. He was so adamant that she get rid of the baby that she began to fear he might hurt her. Kupka left her apartment with Persaud on the day she disappeared. Although he admits seeing her that day, he denies harming her or having any knowledge of her whereabouts, and no charges have ever been brought against him or anyone else.

• Lisa Tu of Potomac, Maryland, a forty-two-year-old Chinese immigrant caring for two teenagers and her elderly mother, disappeared in 1988. Tu's common-law husband, Gregory, a Washington, D.C., restaurant manager heavily in debt from business failures and gambling losses, said she never returned from a trip to San Francisco to visit a sick friend. But police believe he killed her as she slept on their couch, then attempted to assume a new identity, traveling to Las Vegas, forging checks under her name, stealing from her son's college fund, and enjoying the services of prostitutes. A first-degree murder conviction was overturned when an appeals court ruled that evidence seized from his Las Vegas hotel room was improperly admitted. In the retrial, he was found guilty of second-degree murder.

• Pegye Bechler, a physical therapist and mother of three, disappeared in 1997 while boating off the Southern California coast with her husband to celebrate their fifth wedding anniversary and her thirty-eighth birthday. Eric Bechler claimed she was piloting a rented speedboat and towing him on a boogie board when she was washed overboard by a rogue wave. Although Pegye was an expert swimmer who completed in triathlons, Bechler claimed she never surfaced, and no sign of her has ever been found. After sobbing for the cameras about his devastating loss, Bechler took up with another woman just three months after his wife's disappearance, an actress and lingerie model; she agreed to wear a wire for police. Having been recorded describing how he bashed his wife over the head with a barbell, then attached the weights to her body and dumped her at sea, he was convicted of first-degree murder.

• Lisa Thomas's rocky marriage turned strangely amicable in the summer of 1996 when she and her husband of eight years finally agreed to divorce. Then the thirty-six-year-old mother of two vanished on the same weekend she planned to begin looking for her own place to live. Her husband, Bryce, seemed remarkably nonchalant about the fact that his wife was missing, and refused to allow police into their Bakersfield, California, apartment. Lisa's frantic twin sister, Theresa Seabolt, broke in and found the underside of the couple's mattress, which had been flipped, soaked in blood. Only then did Lisa's husband move into action, setting up a tip line and pleading for the public's help in finding his wife. Although Lisa's body was never found, a jury convicted her husband of second-degree murder. But the verdict was almost immediately thrown into question when one of the jurors accused fellow panelists of not following the judge's instructions. Facing the possibility of a new trial, Bryce Thomas attempted to hire a hit man (who was actually an undercover sheriff's investigator) from his jail cell to eliminate his wife's twin, the woman he believed responsible for putting him behind bars. Dictating a scenario identical to the one he carried out against his wife—presumably in the hope that it would appear that the same person killed both sisters—he asked the purported hit man to kill his sister-in-law in her sleep, then make her body disappear, leaving just a little trail of blood "because that's similar to what happened to the one I'm accused of murdering." Ultimately, the trial judge allowed the conviction for killing his wife to stand, and handed down a sentence of fifteen years to life. He was subsequently convicted and sentenced to another twelve years for trying to arrange the murder of Theresa Seabolt.

• Jami Sherer, twenty-six, mother of a two-year-old son, disappeared in Redmond, Washington, in 1990 the day after telling her husband, Steven, that she wanted a divorce and was moving back in with her parents. At her husband's insistence, she had gone to meet him one last time, but never returned. Within hours of that meeting, days before her car was discovered abandoned with her packed suitcase still inside, Sherer began telling family members that his wife was "missing." Ten years later, still maintaining that his missing wife was alive somewhere as a jury found him guilty of murder, he lashed out at his wife's family: "When Jami does turn up, you can all rot in hell!"

• Peggy Dianovsky, twenty-eight at the time of her disappearance, vanished from her suburban Chicago home in 1982, leaving no trace of her existence. Her husband, Robert, admitted striking her during an argument with enough force to splatter blood on a stairway in the couple's home. But he insisted that she packed a bag and left that night, never to be seen again—without taking her car or her three children. Twenty-two years later, he was acquitted of her murder in a bench trial, despite testimony from two of her now grown sons, who said they witnessed their father hit their mother and hold a knife to her throat in the hours leading up to her disappearance. A family friend also testified that several months before Peggy went missing, Robert Dianovsky asked him to help dispose of his wife's body and outlined a plan to make her killing look like suicide. The friend declined to participate in Dianovsky's schemes, telling him that he would never get away with it—an incorrect assumption, as it would turn out.

The sheer callousness of eraser crimes is breathtaking, not just the murders themselves but the actions taken after the fact to cover them up. As if taking the life of women they were supposed to love is not cruel enough, these killers afford their victims no solace or dignity even after death.

• Stephen Grant, who reported his wife missing on Valentine's Day 2007, strangled thirty-four-year-old Tara, hacked her body into pieces at the tool-and-die shop where he worked, then buried the pieces in a Michigan park. He was caught three weeks later when he retrieved the largest portion of his wife's remains, her torso, and brought it back to his home for safekeeping after learning police were searching the park. Grant, who ghoulishly used his children's sled to haul the body parts into the snow-covered woods, was convicted of second-degree murder and sentenced to a minimum of fifty years behind bars.

• Thomas Capano, one of Delaware's most prominent attorneys, a former prosecutor, mayoral chief-of-staff, and an chief legal counsel to the state's governor, shot his girlfriend, Anne Marie Fahey, to death in 1996, then dumped her body sixty miles out to sea inside a giant Igloo cooler. When the ice chest failed to sink because of its natural buoyancy, he pulled her out, wrapped chains and boat anchors around her, and sank her to the bottom of the Atlantic. Although no body was ever found, Capano's younger brother, who drove him out to sea that day in his boat, eventually admitted to police that he had seen the corpse sink below the ocean surface. He was convicted of first-degree murder in 1999 and sentenced to death, but the sentence was later reduced to life in prison.

• Robert Bierenbaum, a brilliant Manhattan surgeon and licensed pilot, is believed to have dropped the corpse of his wife, Gail, from a rented plane into the Atlantic Ocean in 1985. He was convicted of second-degree murder, but not until fifteen years after the crime.

• Ira Einhorn, a counterculture icon and widely revered peace and environmental activist, shattered the skull of his girlfriend, Holly Maddux, in 1977, then locked her—still alive—inside a steamer trunk in their apartment. When police finally gained access to the apartment a year and a half later and discovered her body, Einhorn insisted he had been set up by the CIA or possibly the KGB, that Holly's body was planted in a grand frame-up to silence him because of his radical views and research into "sensitive" areas. Ira was so well regarded in certain circles as the embodiment of peace that many influential acolytes bought that far-fetched story, lobbying for his release on bail and even posting his bond. Just before trial, he fled to Europe, where he managed to elude justice for a quarter century, living for much of that time happily and openly as a country gentleman in the south of France. After a long extradition battle, he was finally returned to the United States, where he was convicted in 2002 and sentenced to life in prison.

—*vvv*—

Eraser killings raise such disturbing questions—can we ever really know anyone, can we trust those closest to us?—that we have not wanted to ask them. We don't want to believe that someone we let into our heart or our bed could be capable of such monstrous cruelty. We cling to the illusion that danger is something outside ourselves, at a distance, easily identifiable, like the stranger in the alley we can avoid by being safe and prudent.

But the truth is that except in a few notorious cases involving serial killers or sexual predators, grown women are not stolen off the street or ripped from the safety of their own homes by perfect strangers, never to be seen again dead or alive. Despite what Scott Peterson's defense attorneys wanted us to believe, we need not live in fear of mysterious men in vans or homeless people or satanic cults. Young women, and especially young pregnant women, are most in danger from the men they love.

More than a thousand women a year are murdered in America by an intimate partner. Many of those women, about seven in ten, bear the scars of years of male rage directed at them precisely because of their proximity and vulnerability. Others trust their partners implicitly and have no inkling of what lies ahead.

In the last year for which statistics are available, eighteen hundred women in the United States were murdered by men, more than half of those by a current or former husband or boyfriend. Intimate partner homicide is a truly one-sided phenomenon, as less than 5 percent of male murder victims are killed by their wife or girlfriend.

One of the most disturbing and perplexing aspects of the Peterson case was the fact that Laci was nearly eight months pregnant at the time she was murdered. It was unthinkable to most people that a man could kill not only his wife but also his unborn son. Yet young women between the ages of twenty and twenty-nine—women in their prime childbearing years—are most likely to be killed by their partner. In fact, pregnancy may place them at greater risk of being murdered.

Recent studies from several states and cities across the country have found homicide to be the number one cause of death among pregnant women and that women continue to be at increased risk for being murdered for up to a year after giving birth.

An analysis of five years of death records in Maryland revealed that a pregnant or recently pregnant woman is more likely to die from homicide than any other cause whatsoever. Homicide was discovered to be the single biggest cause of injury-related death among pregnant and postpartum women in New York City and Cook County, Illinois, and among women up to a year after giving birth in the state of Georgia. Researchers reviewing eight years of autopsy records of reproductive-age women in the District of Columbia found murder to be the second most common cause of death among pregnant women, just one death behind medical complications related to pregnancy.

A 2005 study that attempted to look at the problem nationally found homicide to be the second leading cause of injury death in pregnant and postpartum women, behind motor vehicle accidents. But Isabelle Horon and Diana Cheng, authors of the Maryland study, believe that the national study seriously undercounted the number of pregnancy-associated homicides because it looked solely at voluntarily submitted death certificates for women who died during pregnancy or within a year of delivery.

In their own 2001 study, the two researchers from Maryland's state Department of Health found that only a small portion of pregnancy-associated deaths could be determined from death certificates. The rate of homicide reported in the national study was suspiciously low compared to the earlier regional studies, six times lower than what the Maryland researchers found in their state by using medical examiner and other records in addition to death certificates.

In any event, it is clear that the true number of pregnant or recently pregnant women who are murdered is higher than anyone has yet estimated, as pregnancy is not even looked for in all autopsies and may go undetected when women are killed in early stages of pregnancy. Nor are the numbers of "erased" women whose bodies are never found to be autopsied or to be issued a death certificate included in any of these studies.

Although murder is the most extreme form of a larger epidemic of domestic violence—an estimated two to four million American women are physically assaulted by their partner every year—the rate of homicide just within families in this country is higher than the total homicide rates in most other Western industrialized nations.

Eraser killers represent a small and highly pathological subset of the larger group of men who commit what is known as intimate femicide. Their means, methods, and motives are distinct in almost every way from those of the more "ordinary" spousal killer.

One of the most important differences is that many of the men who commit a more typical domestic homicide never even leave the crime scene or attempt to deny their culpability. Some call police immediately afterwards to turn themselves in, and a significant percentage take their own life as well (whether this is motivated by any genuine sense of remorse or merely by the fear of punishment is debatable). A recent Canadian study found that half of men who had killed their intimate partners contemplated killing themselves afterward, and up to 40 percent of the men claim they tried to kill themselves. Although the exact numbers vary, the surprisingly high percentage of men who commit suicide after killing their intimate partner is validated by numerous studies both in the United States and Canada.

Those who kill both their partner and their children, whom criminologists refer to as "family annihilators," very often take their own lives as well.

By contrast, true eraser killers hardly ever commit suicide. They feel no guilt for what they have done. In fact, they feel entitled to kill anyone who stands in the way of their happiness. And they do not fear punishment because they are thoroughly convinced they will never be held accountable. Only in the rarest of instances will they ever admit their crimes.

CHAPTER TWO

The Dark Triad

E raser killers often leave an unwitting trail of evidence that points to their secret motivations, a series of clues that can help us understand what really happened and why. The trail is fragmented and twisting, but the clues are intelligible once we find an appropriate key with which to decipher them.

The most damning evidence against Scott Peterson at his trial was the complete lack of concern he displayed toward his missing wife, captured most vividly in unguarded moments with Amber Frey—the girlfriend who turned against him when she discovered Peterson had not only a wife but a missing one, and agreed to surreptitiously tape her telephone conversations with him. Listening to the tapes from the first crucial days of Laci's disappearance, when Scott should have been consumed with worry but instead seemed to be a man without a care in the world, it is clear that Laci and Conner were dead to Scott long before he killed them.

Eraser killers are not driven by bloodlust, like sadists who claim they only feel alive when they are inflicting pain and terror on their victims. Nor are they clinically or legally insane, compelled by voices or visions that command them to hurt those around them. These men kill for sheer convenience. Their actions are dispassionate, almost businesslike, yet their crimes are unimaginably cruel. They know what they are doing is wrong, but they do it anyway because they believe that rules don't apply to them—not when it is something they really want.

Eraser killers like Scott Peterson feel no remorse either immediately after their crimes or during the protracted scrutiny of a police investigation, which can wear down criminals for whom toughness is only a front. They almost never show any emotion at trial, even when the most graphic evidence of their crimes is presented.

At moments in the Scott Peterson trial so wrenching that they brought nearly everyone in the gallery to tears—even hardened detectives and reporters—I was taken aback by the placidity on the defendant's face. Throughout the trial he listened with rapt, almost bemused attention to the evidence against him—no matter how painful, embarrassing, or incriminating—as if fascinated to be the center of so much attention.

He watched himself with cool regard, projected larger than life on a giant courtroom screen, as he told blatant lies on national television, claiming he informed police "that very first night" Laci went missing that he was having an affair with another woman.

He sat stoically through hours of secretly recorded audiotapes, listening to himself casually deceive everyone who knew and cared about him, including his own mother; kibitz for hours on end with his girlfriend about his favorite books and movies, his weight, and his New Year's resolutions while the rest of the world feverishly looked for his wife; and spin fantastical tales in which he claimed to be in Paris, watching fireworks explode above the Eiffel Tower with his friends Pasqual and François, when he was really in Modesto at a candlelight vigil for his missing wife, ducking the media and his devastated in-laws.

He looked with equanimity at gruesome photos of his wife's ravaged remains and listened dispassionately to the medical examiner describe the horrific facts of underwater decomposition—how barnacles were growing on Laci's exposed bones, how the only organ remaining in her body after four months in a bay teeming with sea life was her uterus.

During the three months of jury selection that preceded the trial, before his parents began attending, he laughed and joked with second-chair counsel Pat Harris and the defense jury consultant even while potential jurors were being grilled about prejudices they may have formed against him. When the trial began, he took on a more serious mien, a sphinxlike demeanor that was impossible to read but that at the same time, as juror Richelle Nice noted, "spoke volumes."

During the guilt phase of his trial, he shed a tear only on two or three occasions, such as when his mother took the stand and when a former buddy testified. Greg Reed met Scott through their membership in the Rotary Club, and their wives became friends as well. Greg's wife, Kristen, was pregnant at the same time as Laci, and the Petersons attended Lamaze class at the Reed home. Greg was one of Scott's closest friends, and as Reed described their mutual passion for hunting and fishing, their membership in the Del Rio Country Club, the party the couples had planned to attend together on New Year's Eve 2002, Scott seemed genuinely moved.

When psychopaths shed tears, they are almost always ones of self-pity. I suspect that at that moment, Scott was seeing not his friend but a mirror image of himself, Scott Uninterrupted, and the life he could have been enjoying if not for a cruel twist of fate. I believe he was mourning at that moment not the loss of a beloved wife and child but the chasm between the lifestyle he had when he was pals with Greg Reed and the one he now had behind bars.

He cried often during the penalty phase, when family members and other defense witnesses attested to his sterling character and insisted, despite the fact that he had now been convicted and his life hung in the balance, that he could not possibly have killed his wife and child. But when a show of sadness or regret for his actions might easily have made the difference between getting the death penalty and being sentenced to life imprisonment, he made not even a feint in that direction.

The total lack of normal human emotions exhibited by eraser killers is the hallmark characteristic of psychopaths. Although I believe that eraser killers have psychopathic tendencies, they do not appear to be typical psychopaths by all definitions of that term, nor do I believe that psychopathy is the only factor playing an important role in their psychology.

In common parlance, the terms "psychopath" or "sociopath" are names laypeople too often apply to those whose conduct they find morally and socially objectionable, whether it be a mass murderer or (as one recent documentary film argued) a corporation.

But for forensic psychologists, psychopathy has a distinct meaning and—with the cooperation of the subject and enough time and skill on the part of a qualified examiner—the degree of psychopathy in a particular personality can be measured and quantified. Because such cooperation is required, however, few if any of the world's most famous psychopaths—the classic type represented by Jeffrey Dahmer or Ted Bundy—have ever been formally tested for psychopathy using the recognized "gold standard" for diagnosis.

That test, the Psychopathy Checklist or PCL, has been developed over the course of at least three decades of investigation by the acknowledged leader in the field, Robert Hare, now professor emeritus of psychology at the University of British Columbia. Hare has spent his entire career trying to understand the minds of psychopaths, primarily studying those in prison for violent offenses. Hare based his body of work on the groundbreaking research done by the famous American psychiatrist, Hervey Cleckley. Cleckley wrote the first modern treatise on psychopaths, *The Mask of Sanity*, in 1941, a seminal work still used and referred to today.

Through trial and revision, Hare perfected a test that measures twenty key items to assess the presence and degree of clinical psychopathy. Eight of the items concern primarily psychological and interpersonal factors, which, for simplicity's sake, we can call the personality items:

1. Glibness and superficial charm
2. A grandiose sense of self-worth
3. Pathological lying
4. Conning and manipulation of others
5. Lack of remorse or guilt
6. An overall shallow affect
7. Callousness and lack of empathy
8. Failure to accept responsibility for one's own actions

The second axis of the checklist deals with lifestyle traits and criminal behavior, how psychopaths' lives are characterized by a high degree of social deviance—the constant breaking of rules, lack of an ability to control negative impulses, and inability to set and achieve goals. We can sum these up as the behavioral or antisocial lifestyle items:

1. Constant need for external stimulation and a tendency to become quickly bored without such stimulation
2. A parasitic lifestyle (sponging off or taking advantage of others)
3. The inability to control one's behavior
4. Behavioral problems early in life
5. Lack of realistic, long-term goals and instead having either no goals or wildly unrealistic ones
6. A high degree of impulsivity (for example, tending to do things to excess or without substantial thought, from high job turnover and relationship volatility to excessive spending, drinking, or gambling)
7. Irresponsibility (lack of trustworthiness, reliability, punctuality, and so on)
8. History of juvenile delinquency
9. Failure to adhere to the conditions of probation

There are three additional items that, according to established typologies, might fall into either the first or second categories:

1. Promiscuous sexual behavior
2. The tendency to have multiple short-term marital relationships
3. Criminal versatility (which means that one commits and is accomplished at not just one specialized kind of crime, such as forgery, but a wide array of crimes)

Having two or three traits in moderate levels from various parts of the checklist does not mean that someone is a psychopath. The testing procedure involves assigning a score from 0 to 2 on each item, then adding up the total, with a score of 40 being the highest possible. Those scoring 30 and over are generally regarded as clinical psychopaths, though some researchers set the cutoff at a lower level. When tests are done among large groups of prisoners, the average score is typically around 22, but different levels of prisons will yield different results. Testing of "normal" nonprison populations may yield an average of around 5.

Although all this sounds simple enough, the test for psychopathy was developed almost completely within the confines of the prison system and was originally used only to assess and study violent and career or recidivist criminals. Robert Hare is the first to admit that a much larger problem is the unknown number of still dangerous but much less obvious subclinical psychopaths running at large in society—people whose intimate partners are not armed the way prison guards are protected from these potentially violent individuals.

For those who have had no previous brush with the law, have held down jobs, have stayed married for a considerable period of time, and are generally "high-functioning" yet share many of the personality characteristics that define psychopathy, the test is not particularly useful because it was never designed for such people.

In the unvarnished Scott Peterson, the man captured in words on the Amber tapes and other wiretaps and in deed by his crime, we can see nearly all the personality traits associated with psychopaths: superficial charm, manipulativeness, pathological lying, self-centeredness, a lack of empathy, and an absence of remorse.

He does not, however, have the long documented history of lawbreaking and behavioral problems that would rank him in the highest levels on the PCL. Rather, Scott Peterson appears to be more typical of the high-functioning or subclinical psychopaths Hare and psychologist Paul Babiak refer to as "snakes in suits."

"The *real* Scott Peterson . . . can be appreciated by anyone who watched [his TV interviews] or listened to the taped phone conversations his girlfriend made," Hare and Babiak write in their 2006 book *Snakes in Suits*. "In these audio and visual documents, he shows no apparent concern, empathy, remorse, or even sadness at his wife's disappearance."

Peterson had no history of violence, had never even been in a fistfight, according to his family, yet was suddenly able to commit an extraordinarily heinous murder. He was fairly responsible, capable of holding down a job and achieving moderate success, although at the time of the killings he was not meeting the expectations his employer had set for him. He did not leech parasitically off of those around him. Other than being serially promiscuous, he did not engage in random thrill-seeking behavior.

If anything, Scott Peterson seemed pathologically overcontrolled and passive-aggressive, catering to his wife's every wish while meticulously plotting her demise. In many respects he was law abiding to a fastidious degree. How many full-blown psychopaths would go to the trouble of purchasing a fishing license and bringing along tackle and poles if the sole purpose of their boat ride on San Francisco Bay was to dump a body? How many would spend potentially their last precious hours of freedom—knowing two bodies had been discovered in the bay and that they might be arrested at any minute—preparing their tax return?

What we see in Scott Peterson is not the unrestrained psychopathy of a pure predator like Jeffrey Dahmer. He was capable of controlling his darker impulses in a way a more classic psychopath is not. On the surface, he was a veritable Boy Scout. His violence was channeled to a singular and specific goal, timed, planned, and well thought out, not driven by an animal-like frenzy. As the noose of apprehension drew tighter around him, he did not snap into the self-preservation-at-all-costs mode of a full-blown psychopath.

Scott's continued communication with Amber Frey is another example of behavior not consistent with a "classic" psychopath. Scott continued to call and romance Amber after his wife's disappearance, chatting with her for hours on end about nothing and everything but the fact that he was married and had a wife who was missing. When Amber discovered that her purportedly single boyfriend was at the center of a massive missing persons investigation, she contacted police and offered to help.

For a while, she played along, pretending not to know anything about Laci as Scott told her lie after lie, fantastical story after fantastical story about his exciting bachelor life. Eventually, at the direction of the police, she confronted him. Scott continued to call her on an almost daily basis—even after she was presented to the world at a press conference held by Modesto police, a plan detectives hastily conceived after learning that the media was about to reveal Amber's identity, hoping to turn the situation to their advantage by ratcheting up the pressure on their suspect.

A high-scoring psychopath would not have taken such news well. In fact, personal betrayal, whether real or imagined, is often a key triggering mechanism for psychopathic violence. A full-fledged psychopath would have immediately realized that Amber was working with the police and ceased contact with her to protect himself—just as his attorney ordered him to do. Scott kept right on talking to her, sending her gifts, talking of a future between them, all to his ultimate peril. Not very smart for a guy who prided himself on his intelligence.

Interestingly, he did experience a gut-level reaction to this unexpected development. But he immediately spun the momentary fear he felt into an attempt to continue manipulating Amber and to win back her trust. He told her the next day that as he listened to the press conference on his car radio, he had to pull over and throw up because he was so "proud" of her "amazing character." That wasn't pride—it was cold-sweat panic.

These kinds of anomalies are seen in other eraser killers. For example, Mark Hacking's strange but dogged pursuit of a "double life" as an imaginary doctor certainly involved pathological lying, conning others, and a failure to accept responsibility. "Classic" predatory psychopaths do not pretend to be doctors. They grab women off the street, hold up liquor stores and execute the compliant clerk for no reason, kill for laughs or to satisfy a $2 debt. Something more complex and more subtle had to be driving these very controlled and otherwise high-functioning eraser killers.

The puzzle of seemingly ordinary people who engage in bad acts but who do not have a history of easily identifiable antisocial behavior—the kind that would usually earn them a criminal record—is a problem that another research psychologist has been working on for many years.

Delroy Paulhus, a colleague of Robert Hare at the University of British Columbia, has been studying such behaviors as cheating, lying, and a phenomenon he calls overclaiming—a technique some people use to enhance themselves in the eyes of others by willfully exaggerating or fabricating their knowledge or experience. He believes that a combination of three closely related negative personality factors explains the behavior of a wide range of people who may never have been to prison but who consistently deceive, manipulate, and take advantage of others, and do so without any sense of guilt or shame.

Paulus has named the cluster of toxic traits—psychopathy, narcissism, and Machiavellianism—"the Dark Triad." Although the three personality constructs overlap a great deal, each has its own particularities that influence different aspects of behavior. As they have for psychopathy, psychologists have developed scales for measuring degrees of narcissism and Machiavellianism. Someone who possesses any of the three traits to a significant degree has the capacity for violence. An individual with a disturbing concentration of all three traits could be extremely dangerous.

Even though Paulhus and his fellow researchers have not applied the Dark Triad to murderers, having studied it only in general community populations, I believe that the concept provides the missing link needed to explain the complex and often contradictory psyche of eraser killers—whose actions at one moment may be expertly calculated and at the next astonishingly self-defeating. It would explain why these killers are described by friends, by police, and sometimes even by their victims as charming yet callous, generous yet self-centered, solicitous yet highly controlling. The use of the richer psychological vocabulary of the Dark Triad allows us to describe and make sense of behavior that has heretofore seemed incomprehensible.

—⁓—

Let's explore the three psychological traits in a little more depth, beginning with psychopathy.

Not all psychopaths are like the humorless killing machines depicted in an entire genre of true-crime books and movies. Many are likeable, charismatic charmers, but their charm is slick and insincere. They may be able to mesmerize and manipulate others with finely honed skills of persuasion and flattery, but beneath the glossy surface, their words are devoid of any real meaning or honest emotion.

Some psychopaths can fake normality better than others. We may occasionally pick up on the sense that something is not quite right, the vaguely queasy feeling one gets when a movie and its soundtrack are out of sync. But more often than not we are fooled, even dazzled by the show they put on for us.

They know how to draw us into their web because psychopaths are masters of studied communication. But nothing they say connects to anything genuine inside. The classic description of psychopaths is that they "know the words but not the music." They move through the world with the deceptive verisimilitude of computer animation, their emotions painted on, their words spoken as though by an actor reciting lines. It is all a performance, calculated for the effect it will have on a select audience, to get what they want by pretending to give us what we want.

Psychopaths are practiced liars and expert manipulators. "Some psychopaths get this huge joy out of duping people," says Paulhus.

"Being on the sly, having a secret life: that is the greatest part of what they are doing." As one man who topped out on Hare's psychopathy test said, "I lie like I breathe, one as much as the other." They lie when there is no reason to lie, even when they are certain to be caught.

In a nationally televised interview with *Good Morning America*'s Diane Sawyer, Peterson said he told police about his affair with Amber Frey the very night Laci went missing, a statement police immediately contradicted, and he had to retract before the second part of the interview had even aired.

"A psychopath will look you in the eye and lie when the truth would be easier because they get a kick out of lying to people like Diane Sawyer," said former FBI profiler Candice DeLong. "They feel superior." When caught, they just shamelessly roll over into another lie or, in the words of Robert Hare, "rework the facts so that they appear to be consistent with the lie."

Even veteran researchers are taken aback by the sheer emotional emptiness of psychopaths, and the remarkable ability many have to hide that fact from those around them.

"[W]e are dealing here not with a complete man at all but with something that suggests a subtly constructed reflex machine that can mimic the human personality perfectly," Hervey Cleckley wrote in *The Mask of Sanity*. ". . . So perfect is this reproduction of a whole and normal man that no one who examines the psychopath in a clinical setting can point out in scientific or objective terms why, or how, he is not real. And yet we eventually come to know or feel we know that reality, in the sense of full, healthy experiencing of life, is not here."

Now let's examine the second dimension of the Dark Triad: narcissism.

Narcissists have a grossly inflated sense of their own abilities and importance. They believe they are unique, special, blessed, touched, golden, and they want to be recognized for it—even without the achievement to back it up. Like the mythological Narcissus, who died of excessive pride because he could not stop gazing at his reflection, pathological narcissists have an insatiable need to be admired. They also have what forensic psychiatrist Martin Blinder calls "an overweening sense of entitlement" and are consumed with fantasies of unlimited success, power, sex, brilliance, and love. Yet they have little capacity for genuine love because they are only interested in being loved. Narcissists live life behind a mask, and many lead elaborate double lives, pretending to be something or someone they are not.

But the flip side of narcissism—what lies behind the mask, on the other side of the mirror—is insecurity. Any evidence that does not fit the grandiose view a narcissist holds of himself must be denied, devalued, avoided at all costs. A highly narcissistic person's need for constant external self-validation may be so great that if access to his "supply" is frustrated, he may act out violently.

Blinder, who has consulted on hundreds of domestic homicide cases over the last four decades, believes intimate partner killers are intensely narcissistic and somewhat psychopathic. They feel no remorse or guilt for their crimes because they don't believe they have done anything wrong. In fact, they often see themselves as the victim.

Psychopaths, narcissists, and Machiavellians are all manipulators, but narcissistic manipulation is the most emotionally insidious, the kind to which an unsuspecting woman is most vulnerable. When Scott was forced to admit to Amber that he lied about being married, he spun another more elaborate and self-serving lie about having recently "lost" his wife, something so difficult to talk about that he just pretended he was never married. It was a lie so emotionally loaded, told with Academy Award–caliber drama, that within seconds *she* was feeling sorry for *him*. *She* was holding *his* hand. *She* was comforting *him* and forgiving *him*. And she was no longer asking any questions.

The third aspect of the Dark Triad is Machiavellianism. Like the author of the sixteenth-century political treatise who advocated an end-justifies-the-means approach to wielding political power, people with a high degree of Machiavellianism have a strongly utilitarian view of the world. Other people are just pawns in their game, objects to be used for their own gratification.

A high degree of Machiavellianism is associated with sexual aggression and has been found in otherwise "normal" college students who commit date rape. "High Machs" are schemers who use every means at their disposal—flattery, manipulation, deceit—to gain advantage over others. Where the psychopath acts impulsively without any concern for the consequences, a Machiavellian is a more strategic manipulator.

"One can connect all three of these characteristics in someone like Scott Peterson," said Paulhus. "If indeed he is a major narcissist he feels like he is special, like laws don't apply to him. He's entitled to do things that other people are not supposed to do. That leads into

Machiavellianism. That sense of superiority means he can manipulate others because they are not as clever as he is. Then you work your way down into psychopathy: remorselessness, impulsiveness."

When I asked Dr. Paulhus why someone like Scott would continue to call and pursue Amber Frey even when it was so against his own interest, he explained by showing the relationship and differences between the closely linked Dark Triad concepts.

"A pure Machiavellian would not be that stupid," said Paulhus. "If you're driven purely by Machiavellian self-interest, the last thing you do is set yourself up in any way to get caught. But narcissists are driven by more than self-interest, or at least a different type of self-interest: a superiority, a grandiosity that needs to be nurtured."

Machiavellianism may account for the almost perfect plan Scott came up with to get away with murder. But his continued communication with Amber—against his attorney's strict orders, and when only a fool would not realize she was working with the police—seems to be a reflection of his narcissism. He needed her to fill up a vacuum inside him, to admire and adore him—to believe, as he begged her to believe in one of their calls, that he was "not a monster." Despite her nationally televised appearance at the police station, it was inconceivable to him that she would betray him, that he would not be able to keep her in his thrall.

Thomas Capano was so strongly narcissistic and Machiavellian that he insisted on controlling every aspect of his defense—a strategy that backfired horribly and certainly contributed to the jury's decision to recommend death over life in prison for the murder of his girlfriend. He then unsuccessfully used the mistakes caused by his own orchestration to claim ineffective assistance of counsel and demand either a new trial or a lighter sentence. In papers his lawyers filed in response to Capano's motion, the extraordinarily manipulative nature of his personality was revealed.

Capano hired four accomplished attorneys to represent him at trial, one of whom was the state's former attorney general, but refused to follow their advice and ordered them to do his bidding. He forced one to deliver an opening statement that stunned everyone in the courtroom, acknowledging for the first time that Anne Marie Fahey was dead but blaming her death on a "tragic accident"—while refusing to tell the attorney what might possibly back up such a claim. (He would ultimately claim that a second mistress found him and Fahey together and pulled a gun out in a jealous rage, which went off as she and Capano struggled over the gun—a woman who had nothing to do with the murder but whom Capano had manipulated into buying the gun he used to kill Anne Marie.)

He insisted on testifying in his own defense against his attorneys' better judgment and refused to allow them to prepare him for cross-examination. Grossly overestimating his abilities, he claimed he didn't need any preparation, but then became so belligerent on the stand that the judge at one point had him removed from the courtroom.

Just as he had carefully planned his crime and its cover-up (in addition to obtaining a gun that he believed could not be traced to him, he bought in advance the 40.5 gallon cooler he would use as a coffin), he told his attorneys what questions to ask and exactly what words to use in asking them.

Capano seemed to delight in the way he pulled the strings on his own advocates and parceled out information only when he felt like it. As counsel Joseph Oteri remarked in contemporaneous notes he took just thirteen days before trial, Capano admitted that "he was playing with our heads about his defense" and wouldn't tell them any facts about what happened. Even with his life on the line, and despite his intelligence and legal prowess, Capano could not overcome his darker instincts.

The trial judge, and subsequent appellate courts, rejected his argument of ineffective assistance of counsel. However, seven years after his conviction, the Delaware Supreme Court set aside Capano's death sentence because one juror had held out on the issue of premeditation and planning. The state could have retried the penalty phase before a new jury and sought another death penalty verdict, but that would have required remounting virtually the entire six-month case. Not wanting to put Anne Marie's family through that again, prosecutors agreed to a sentence of life in prison without the possibility of parole.

———

The cardinal feature of all three syndromes, which plays into all the individual characteristics of Dark Triad disorders, is the absence of empathy. The ability to empathize with others, to "feel their pain," is a core part of what makes us human. People with this ugly constellation of traits can lie, cheat, use, manipulate, hurt, and kill with impunity because they are completely indifferent to the suffering of others. The utter callousness displayed by eraser killers is all the more astonishing, considering that their victims are supposedly their "loved" ones.

When it came to disposing of his wife, Katherine, ironworker Joseph Romano exhibited no more compassion or remorse than the professional assassins in Brian de Palma's blood-soaked remake of *Scarface*. After beating his thirty-nine-year-old spouse to death, most likely with a baseball bat, in their Quincy, Massachusetts, home in 1998, he carved up her corpse with a power saw he had borrowed earlier that month from a neighbor. He placed her severed remains in fifteen plastic garbage bags, which he helped city trash collectors hoist into their truck the following day. He then set about cleaning up, repainting the basement where the dismemberment took place, and hosing down Oriental rugs in his yard—the latter act so strange that neighbors noticed and remembered it.

Their two-year-old son witnessed the dismemberment of his mother, acting out the scene with dolls when questioned later by pediatric trauma specialists.

"The last memory that Bruno talks about is seeing his mother's head in a bucket," said Mary Louise Fagan, Katherine's sister, confronting her brother-in-law at sentencing. "That's what you gave Bruno, Joe: nightmares, memories, and horror."

The Romano's marriage had been breaking down for years, and Katherine had given her husband a deadline to leave the home she owned by the first of the month. Three days before that deadline, she disappeared. Like many eraser killers, Romano was dead set against sharing anything with a soon-to-be ex-wife, even if it actually belonged to her. When police came to his door after her father reported her missing, Romano expressed a profound lack of empathy and indifference to her absence.

"Who the hell knows where she went?" he told the astonished officers.

Romano had once threatened to put his wife "where her family would never find her." In that, he succeeded. Her body was never found, the trash bags incinerated before police could ever search the dump. But bits of bone, cartilage, and deep-body tissue were detected on hidden parts of the saw after Romano returned it to the neighbor, and minute amounts of blood spatter were found in the bedroom and basement.

For months before the murder, Romano had been talking about how much he hated his wife and wanted to kill her. Only one juror at his 2002 trial, however, pushed for a first-degree murder conviction. A conviction for first-degree murder requires a finding of premeditation and intent, that the killer thought about and planned the murder in advance. Another juror actually wanted to vote for manslaughter, which would have meant Romano did not even intend to kill his wife—an option the jury was not allowed to consider. Instead, the panel found the forty-four-year-old guilty of second-degree murder, making him eligible for parole in fifteen years.

"I guess he did feel as though he was backed into a corner and acted out in a rage without any thought or plan," juror Jane Palermo said after the verdict. Under Massachusetts law, jurors could have convicted Romano for first-degree murder on the basis either of premeditation or that he acted with extreme cruelty. But the panel discounted the dismemberment as evidencing extreme cruelty because Katherine was already dead when her husband cut her up.

In another case demonstrating a killer's incredible lack of empathy, Gerald Miller offered nothing but shrugs and sarcasm in response to the "mysterious" disappearance of not just one but two different wives. First his childhood sweetheart and wife of twenty-nine years, Crystal, disappeared without a trace from the Oregon farm where they were living in 1984. Then, in 1989, his second wife, Carol, vanished from the ranch where he was employed. Miller was not investigated in the disappearance of his first wife until his second wife followed the first into the ether. Neither body has been found. No physical evidence was discovered indicating that a crime had occurred, and Miller denied having anything to do with their disappearances.

Unlike Scott Peterson, who at least attempted to appear to be a grieving husband in front of the police and media, Miller could not bring himself to act as though he cared that either of his wives went missing. Both before and after each disappearance, he was pursuing other women he met in local country-western bars, plying them with offers of marriage and money. He made no real effort to search for either wife, gave away some of their possessions soon after they went missing, and made contradictory and cavalier statements about what may have happened to them—claiming sarcastically that one had been abducted by aliens. Only because he had the nerve to erase a second wife was he ever charged with a crime. In 1993 he was convicted of murdering both women based wholly on circumstantial evidence.

Peterson was a better actor than Romano and Miller, but his publicly expressed concern for his missing wife—noticeably absent in his discussions with Amber or with the sister with whom he spent so much time after the crime, Anne Bird—was an act. As Robert Hare has noted, "Some psychopaths are more concerned with the inner workings of their cars than with the inner worlds of their 'loved' ones."

These are not merely theoretical observations. Numerous scientific studies have measured the actual autonomic response in individuals exposed to a series of distressing images, such as a photograph of a crying child, and watching others receive what the participants believed to be electric shocks. In all the studies, psychopaths showed markedly less distress about the suffering of other people than control subjects.

Physiological studies of skin conductance, startle response, and, before such studies were banned, actual electric shock have also shown that psychopaths experience fear and anxiety at far lower levels than the rest of us. This complete indifference to the feelings of others, coupled with a lack of fear, may account for how Scott Peterson could spend time dawdling on the Internet on Christmas Eve morning before embarking on the task of disposing of his wife's corpse. As Cleckley noted in *The Mask of Sanity*, psychopaths are almost as incapable of anxiety as they are of empathy and remorse.

—⁓—

Many men experience some ambivalence about having children, but for eraser killers these feelings seem to be particularly acute. A pregnancy, its impact on the relationship, and the impending or already strained responsibilities of fatherhood seem to have been a primary motivation for the murders committed by Peterson, Mark Hacking, and numerous other eraser killers profiled in this book.

These men felt nothing for their children, whose lives they took along with their mothers': no warmth, no empathy, no sense of responsibility. The kids were virtual nonentities to them. Perhaps a child is the biggest threat imaginable to narcissistic men because they don't want to share. They want to remain the center of attention. They want to be in control. They are like children themselves in their selfishness and grandiose sense of entitlement.

Green Beret doctor Jeffrey MacDonald, very much a narcissist in the Scott Peterson mold, seems to have been motivated by the same desire as Peterson for a free and unencumbered life when he killed his pregnant wife, Colette, and their two small children in their home on the Fort Bragg Army base in North Carolina in 1970.

To this day he maintains that a gang of "drug-crazed hippies" stabbed him and butchered and bludgeoned to death the rest of his family in a satanic rampage reminiscent of the Manson Family killings. Prosecutor Vincent Bugliosi believes that MacDonald staged the scene himself based on an *Esquire* magazine article on the Tate-LaBianca killings that was found inside the home—down to scrawling the word "pig" in Colette's blood on the headboard of their bed as the Manson Family members did with actress Sharon Tate's blood on the front door of her Los Angeles house.

Although Colette's family supported their son-in-law during a military inquest, at which charges were dropped, forensic findings convinced them of his guilt, and his wife's stepfather hounded the Department of Justice until MacDonald was tried and convicted in federal court.

During the dozen years between the crime and MacDonald's imprisonment for three life terms, the doctor completely transformed his lifestyle from dependable soldier and humble family man to swinging hedonist. Working in the private sector but free of medical school debts due to his military service, his income skyrocketed. He moved three thousand miles away to Southern California, bought a $350,000 beachfront condo, a Maserati, and a thirty-foot yacht, and dated a bevy of beautiful women—enjoying precisely the kind of lifestyle Scott Peterson probably imagined for himself after he got rid of his inconvenient wife and child.

As little feeling as Scott seemed to have about his "missing" wife, he had even less concern about his unborn son, whom he and his wife had decided to name Conner. I don't believe Peterson felt anything for his son except for the pressure of a ticking clock as his birth drew near. In every interview he gave to reporters after Laci's disappearance, he had to be prompted even to mention his unborn son. In his taped conversations with Amber, he never refers to Conner as his baby, only as "Laci's baby."

Even when Amber asks him directly if Conner is his child, he refuses to say. I believe he did not think of the baby as his, but not because he thought Laci was cheating on him or that anyone else could have been Conner's father. He simply felt no emotional attachment whatsoever to his child.

In reality, Scott Peterson was a fertilizer salesman with a glorified title who was running a failing start-up business that was not performing up to the expectations of the parent company. He was living in humble Modesto in a modest home, a married man with a baby on the way. With that baby would come a new set of responsibilities, new demands on his time, and an inevitable change in lifestyle, which was contrary to every fantasy he had of his life.

In his mind, he was someone very different. A star golfer. A successful entrepreneur with a collection of homes and condos. A footloose, irresistible ladies' man. A guy who could swan around Europe, partying with imaginary French friends, who could pick up his life at a moment's notice and do as he pleased, as he portrayed himself to Amber, and who could expect that woman to trust him implicitly even if he lied to her about everything that mattered.

He could carry on for years as though he weren't married—have his cake and eat it, too—but a baby was an altogether different proposition. The more he and Laci prepared for the baby, the more real it became. Ultrasound sessions and Lamaze classes. Baby showers and the nursery. The bigger Laci's belly grew, the more she turned from wife to mother, the more real it all became. His life was about to change forever. He couldn't deny it anymore. Anyone who stood between Scott Peterson and the fantasy he held so dear, the narcissistic fix he desperately craved, was in mortal danger.

The jury's decision to convict Scott of first-degree murder for the killing of his wife but just second-degree for Conner mystifies me, because I firmly believe that if Laci had not been pregnant, she would probably be alive today. I think Scott would have gone on having affairs and leading a double life, while pretending to be the perfect husband. In my opinion, it was the impending birth of Conner that triggered his murder plan, not his romance with Amber Frey. It was the idea of becoming a father, especially father to a son, that he could not abide.

"To use the baldest example of the Theodore Dreiser story," says Martin Blinder analogizing the Peterson case to the story depicted in *An American Tragedy*, "once the woman is pregnant the man is trapped, in his mind. There is no escaping the domestic responsibilities. And any purely sexual fantasies he had about the woman are now shattered by the onset of all the trappings—and I mean that in both senses of the word—of domesticity. If he's profoundly disturbed, disposing of both the mother and the child in a criminal fashion seems like a logical, reasonable way out of that trap. Rather than going the route of divorce, however painful, the sociopathic part of him chooses a darker solution—which in his mind is low cost. Being a narcissist, he has a heightened sense of his own capability. He believes he can get away with it. He believes he can commit the perfect crime."

James Alan Fox, a professor of criminal justice at Northeastern University and the author of numerous books and studies on the subject of homicide, says narcissistic partner-killers view love in purely instrumental terms—"by what their beloved does for them." When the role of husband or father no longer suits these men, wives and children become expendable.

Narcissists crave the admiration of others. Murder is more palatable than divorce for men like Scott Peterson because simply leaving or divorcing a pregnant wife would tarnish the image they have crafted of themselves, however false—that of the nice guy, perfect husband, loving father. Fox believes that they may even look forward to playing the role of grieving widower and enjoying the attention and sympathy that would involve.

"Never underestimate the overconfidence of a narcissist," Fox wrote in a 2006 op-ed piece for the *Boston Globe* on this very special breed of killers. "Sure Scott Peterson may have failed despite elaborate steps to cover up his wife's murder, but others smugly believe they can pull off the perfect crime. While we often hear about men who tried successfully to beat the spousal murder rap, how many unsolved killings involved men who fooled everyone—not just their slain spouses?"

CHAPTER THREE

The Real American Tragedy

N early one hundred years before Scott Peterson's "fishing" expedition on San Francisco Bay, a seemingly ordinary young man named Chester Gillette took the woman who loved him out for an afternoon excursion on Big Moose Lake in New York's Adirondack Mountains.

With a mixture of fear and excitement, Grace Brown stepped gingerly into the seventeen-foot rowboat her boyfriend had rented for the day. Not only did she not know how to swim, but she was four months pregnant. Yet a boat ride in beautiful surroundings on a warm July day seemed like such a romantic gesture that she felt a surge of hope that the day would end with what she wanted more than anything else in the world: for Chester to propose marriage.

Although few could have imagined it on that bright summer day, within a few months Chester Gillette would be known as the most famous murderer in America. Gillette's murder of Grace Brown was the first intensely documented eraser killing in American history.

Unfortunately, no one at the time was able to shed much insight on what would make an intelligent and well-connected man kill his pregnant lover and simultaneously attempt to wipe away all connection to her—a connection well known to many other people. Instead, our understanding of the crime was reshaped on a grand scale when the up-and-coming novelist Theodore Dreiser based his magnum opus, *An American Tragedy*, on the Gillette case. And in Dreiser's view, Chester Gillette was nothing like an eraser killer because he himself was just as much a "victim" of events and forces outside his control as was his dead girlfriend.

Just like Dreiser, many today still find it hard to believe that there are people among us who seem normal and upstanding but who are so devoid of any genuine human feeling that killing a loved one is no different than throwing away a worn out sweater.

The similarities between Scott Peterson and Chester Gillette are striking, beginning with the fact that both were such seemingly ordinary all-American boys. Like Peterson, Gillette did not look like what anyone imagined a killer should look like in 1906. He had never been arrested for any crime, nor had he had any encounter with the police.

Twenty-year-old Grace Brown believed that Chester was at his core a good man, but she had no illusions that the handsome coworker two years her senior would be the perfect husband. His endless philandering was the talk of their small industrial town, and the increasingly desperate letters she had written him from the city where she had taken refuge in order to hide her pregnancy were filled with pleading and despair.

It was not a casual or commonplace matter to be an obviously pregnant young woman without a husband in 1906, and in a very short time her pregnancy would become visible to everyone. Britain's Queen Victoria had died just five years earlier, and the widely shared standards of morality and propriety that bear her name had not been seriously challenged on either side of the Atlantic.

In the small towns and tightly knit rural communities of upstate New York, religious conservatism prevailed. There had been so many waves of revivalism and evangelism in the previous century that the region in which they lived was known as "the burned-over district"—viewed as a place where there were no more unsaved souls left to be saved.

Grace Brown's parents may have already felt a certain amount of shame that their farm was not prosperous enough to support their nine children, that their middle daughter had left home at eighteen to get a job in the new skirt factory owned by Chester's uncle some thirty miles away by muddy road in the growing town of Cortland, New York.

Grace's hard work earned her a promotion to inspector, examining the finished skirts to make sure they had no defects. Chester's job in the stock room was ostensibly not much grander than Grace's, but he was clearly being groomed for a position of authority. Although he lacked the fortitude to stick out college, he hoped his uncle's largesse would lead to a more prosperous life than the hobolike existence he had been living as a railroad brakeman. It had already provided him entrée into a social world whose trappings he coveted, which would never include a girl as unsophisticated as Grace Brown.

The trip that she and Chester had embarked on a few days before was a very special event for Grace. In all the months her suitor had been courting her, he had never taken her out in public—never brought her to the colorful parties and social events he himself loved to attend. Instead, he would spend time with her in the parlor of her rooming house—and eventually in a secret rendezvous spot where she had, after months of pressure, yielded to him sexually.

Not long after that, she discovered, much to her chagrin, that she was pregnant.

But when she stepped into the rowboat and sat down on the wooden seat at the stern, she hoped against hope that Chester Gillette, who had impressed everyone with tales of his adventures living and traveling to places far away, might finally be ready to settle down and accept the responsibility of rapidly approaching parenthood. The man who faced her in the boat that afternoon was the person with whom she wanted to share her life.

Tragically, the long boat ride of July 11, 1906, was not the beginning of a life together, but instead the last day in the life of young Grace Brown. It sparked one of the most sensational police investigations and, later, murder trials in American history.

Around six in the evening, Chester rowed the boat into the only secluded part of the lake—a little bay away from other boaters and out of view of any of the handful of lodges that dotted the lake. There, according to the theory advanced by the prosecution at trial, he struck her, probably with the tennis racket he had insisted on bringing along with him in the boat. Either before or between the barrage of blows—on autopsy, wounds were found on both sides of her head, including one that penetrated into her brain—Grace was able to emit a single piercing scream. Her cry was loud enough to be heard by a woman on another boat far across the lake, but she could not see the rowboat with the defenseless woman tucked into a cove. Gillette then tossed Grace, unconscious but still alive, into the lake to drown.

He had done it! He had solved the problem of this girl and her incessant pleas, her daily letters pouring out her anguished ruminations on the state of their relationship. Most important, he had solved once and for all the looming problem posed by her increasingly brazen threats to "go public" with the news of his callous disregard for her honor.

He tossed his own jaunty straw hat into the water, having already removed the sewn-in tag from the store from which he had purchased it, knowing that a straw hat would float on the calm surface of the lake. An experienced swimmer, he probably hopped into the water and intentionally overturned the otherwise quite stable boat. As a final touch, he placed atop its upturned keel the distinctive silk cape Grace had taken off earlier.

Then Chester swam to shore and fled the scene following a clever plan he'd charted out with maps and a railroad time schedule, after changing to dry clothes from the suitcase he had also conveniently, if suspiciously, brought along with him on their rowing outing. Within two days he joined a group of vacationing friends at another lake, betraying no sign that he had killed his pregnant girlfriend a short distance away.

What happened between Chester and Grace that fatal day on Big Moose Lake was no rash act, no sudden murderous impulse. Chester had crafted an elaborate scheme that included the creation of a make-believe persona, registering at the hotel at Big Moose Lake under the name Charles George of New York, New York, and as Carl Grahm of Albany, New York, when he rented the boat—both names that conveniently matched the initials on Chester's monogrammed luggage. However, he signed Grace into the hotel register under her true name and parents' hometown because he wanted her to be identified, wanted there to be an explanation for her sudden disappearance.

His doppelganger, Grace Brown's fictional boyfriend, did everything possible to leave a convenient trail of fabricated evidence that would lead anyone investigating Grace's disappearance to believe that the young woman had been traveling in the company of another man—a man no one else would know or be able to trace, and that the two seemed to be traveling as intimate partners, thus drawing any suspicion away from Chester.

He also attempted to orchestrate the murder scene to make it appear that Grace and her mysterious male companion both met their deaths in a tragic boating accident, using his discarded hat to make it seem that although Grace's body floated to the surface, the man's body might be lost at the bottom and irretrievable.

A boating accident, in an area with hundreds of lakes, where accidental drowning in the summertime was not an infrequent occurrence and where the local sheriff's department had scant resources, was not likely to be investigated very thoroughly. Two young people apparently dead, one just a factory girl, the other an unknown stranger—just the kind of unfortunate event Chester assumed the authorities would quickly accept as an accident even if a few details did not appear to fit.

With this too-clever-by-half ruse, Chester believed he would turn any suspicion away from himself and, in fact, never be associated with Grace's death. Both he and his pregnant lover would disappear—she to an unceremonious death by an apparently accidental drowning, and he back to his increasingly active life in the society circles of Cortland.

And who knew where he might go beyond that small factory town? He had other rich relations he could prevail on. There would be plenty of time to figure that out.

Or so he thought.

Sheriff's deputies became suspicious when they called the factory to find out more about the dead young woman they had quickly identified, and also about the mysterious Carl Grahm.

"But surely you mean Chester Gillette," the factory manager stammered, as Chester's fondness for Miss Brown was all too well known at the factory.

Then, in a strange twist of fate, another young man who also worked at the skirt factory happened to arrive at Big Moose Lake, which was about 150 miles away from Cortland by the roads of the day—and walked close enough to the precise spot where local lawmen were discussing the case to overhear their talk. Why, he himself knew Chester quite well, the man explained. When he gave the officers a detailed visual description, they immediately realized that the mystery man they thought they were tracing did not just share the same initials as Chester Gillette; he appeared, in all likelihood, to *be* Chester Gillette.

Their suspicions were mounting. A strange drowning on a calm, quiet lake. A missing body. A mysterious young man who seemed to have lied about his own identity, while encouraging his female companion to use her own name. Then they found out that the man raised eyebrows when he boarded the little rowboat carrying a suitcase and a tennis racket—something the boat rental agent had found even more peculiar than the usual silliness he observed in the city folk who came to the Finger Lakes in ever larger numbers thanks to the recent railroad expansion.

These incidental oddities were all that it took—then as now—to turn a routine investigation of an accidental death into an aggressive pursuit of someone who may have committed a heinous crime. In less than twenty-four hours of their arrival on the scene, local law enforcement officials believed they were probably investigating a murder. Chester Gillette's grand plan of deception was already crumbling, although he didn't yet know it.

—⁓—

Aided by a few more lucky breaks, the police quickly picked up Chester's trail and realized that he was just a few miles away at another Adirondack resort. Gillette was stunned when the local district attorney and undersheriff suddenly interrupted his "vacation" frivolity. Ironically, they found him dressed for tennis—but without the tennis racquet he had carefully hidden back at Big Moose Lake after killing his paramour and which was later found by the police. When they asked to question him, he tried to stave them off with the protest, "but I have to play tennis."

Chester initially denied being anywhere near the scene of Grace's death. But he soon changed his story when faced with rapidly mounting eyewitness identification and other evidence that made it clear that there was no "other man" who happened to share Chester's initials, only Chester trying to create an illusion by traveling under a pseudonym. He admitted he had brought Grace to Big Moose Lake and had taken her out for a long boat ride, but claimed that a tragic accident occurred.

Gillette changed his story about precisely what happened several times—at one point he claimed that he might have upturned the boat himself when he bent over to pluck a water lily for Grace.

But the story he settled on and the one he told on the witness stand at his trial was that Grace committed suicide.

For many weeks before she left Cortland, Grace had been distraught, bursting into tears at work, falling into deep depression as her worries over the future mounted. Although it was not unheard of for single girls from "good homes" in farm country to become pregnant, the only socially acceptable outcome was for the father of the child to take responsibility and marry the young woman as quickly as possible. There were a host of polite euphemisms available at that time for describing children born less than nine months following a marriage.

Chester claimed under oath that he had suggested to Grace toward the end of the day on the lake that the two of them go back to her parents' farm and tell them that she was pregnant and that he was the father. Gillette wavered on the witness stand as to whether he intended to marry Grace, stating yes, no, and "I can't answer that in that way" at various times in his testimony.

According to Gillette, Grace became hysterical at the thought of telling her parents, exclaimed "I will end it here," and threw herself into the lake. Chester said he tried to reach for her but was not quick enough and tumbled into the lake, too. In all the commotion, the boat flipped over.

As soon as he surfaced and shook the water from his eyes, Chester said, he grabbed hold of the boat—now floating bottom up—and looked around. Surprisingly, he didn't see any sign of Grace. By his own testimony he stayed in the water for only "a minute or two" and, not seeing Grace, simply gave up and swam to shore. He neither called out her name nor shouted for help, nor did he swim around trying to find her.

Even if she had jumped into the water, it is difficult to imagine how her body would have simply sunk or how she would have suppressed the instinct for self-preservation that causes even people who don't know how to swim to flail about. Strangely, Chester did not report seeing the telltale rising of bubbles that accompany a sinking person, or the slightest sign of turbulence in the water. When her body was found the following day along with the upturned boat, she was floating—as dead bodies will do shortly after a drowning—in calm lake water just eight feet deep.

The jury did not find Chester Gillette's version of events credible, even though he was the only living witness. Like all men who carefully plan the killing of an intimate partner, he had the chance to draw any picture he wanted. But strangely, Gillette, like so many other eraser killers, chose what seems to be the least credible of all possible explanations.

Why would Grace commit suicide right at the moment when Gillette is saying that he is willing to take the responsibility to face her parents and tell them the truth? Why did Gillette make no effort whatsoever to rescue the drowning girl? After all, death by jumping into a relatively shallow lake is no instantaneous matter. Why, following such a terrible tragedy, would he not run to the nearest cabin or lodge along the shore to call for assistance or at least to report the incident?

The truth is that Chester Gillette wanted to make Grace Brown disappear, to erase her existence and his connection to her. If the police had been less curious or less competent, and if the autopsy of Grace's body had been less accurate in identifying bruises, contusions, and a probable concussion that seemed to precede her immersion in the water, he might have gotten away with his plan.

But what clearly marks Chester Gillette as a psychopathic eraser killer is his total lack of any sense of guilt or remorse. During their intensive investigation, police discovered that Chester had been making plans for what he would do after erasing Grace from his life even as he was riding the train to their purported romantic idyll.

Although Grace was actually on the same train, Chester carefully avoided being seen with her, purposely boarding a different car where he spotted two female acquaintances he knew from Cortland. He struck up a long, friendly conversation, in the course of which he learned that the young ladies were going to be staying a few miles away from Big Moose Lake. Chester claimed that he was on his way to meet a friend whose uncle had a cabin on a nearby lake, but that he was planning to be very near the lodge where the women were staying later in the week, and would love to meet up with them. They agreed and invited him to join them.

After disposing of Grace in the lake, Chester calmly hid the wooden tennis racket under a log and found a trail he had picked out after having carefully studied maps of the region; and by catching a small train on its scheduled run, he was able to reach another lake miles away that evening and check into a lodge—using his own name for the first time during the trip. Traveling from lake to lake, by steamboat and canoe, he joined up with the two young women with whom he had chatted so engagingly on the train out of Cortland. At no time did he appear to his friends to be upset, distracted, depressed, or in any way emotionally unsettled. He never mentioned anything at all about Grace Brown, whose "tragic suicide" he had so recently witnessed—although he creepily mentioned to his friends during a card game at the second lake hearing "terrible" news of a woman drowning nearby.

—∿∿—

Much to his shock, Chester Gillette was arrested and charged with Grace's murder. His trial and subsequent execution became one of the most intensely covered murder cases in American history—reaching Peterson-like proportions in terms of public interest for its time.

What riveted the public about Chester Gillette was the same question that would draw millions to follow the Peterson case a century later: Could a seemingly upstanding young man, someone who had no previous history of any kind of violence at all, commit such a horrible crime?

Several factors made the murder of Grace Brown seem more of a mystery than an obvious homicide: a perceived lack of any clear motive (few at the time could actually imagine anyone wanting to purposely kill a baby); the fact that virtually all the evidence assembled in the case was circumstantial rather than direct; and the complex planning and deception that had to have gone into the crime, if it was indeed intentional.

Most confounding to those who followed the case was the inexplicable notion that a man who had been brought up in a strongly religious family (his parents were dedicated full-time workers in the strongly evangelistic Salvation Army and, later, members of another devoutly religious sect) and who seemed to have a promising life ahead of him could murder a defenseless pregnant woman in cold blood and abandon her body so casually.

Other aspects of the crime quickly became subjects of more salacious public interest, such as Grace Brown's affair with the attractive but incorrigible womanizer, her secret pregnancy, and the scores of painfully intimate letters the two had exchanged.

Grace's letters to Chester—large portions of which were published by newspapers that were competing with each other in search of every scandalous tidbit on the case—detailed her every emotion on an almost daily basis, revealing a sensitive and vulnerable soul. Chester's letters to Grace, sent with significantly less regularity, were far more perfunctory, exposing very little of the man behind the mask.

If nature abhors a vacuum, the media abhors a crime without a motive it can understand. The search for motive is natural enough: after learning who, what, when, and where, people want to know *why*. The crime occurred just when one of the greatest newspaper circulation wars in U.S. history was in full sway. William Randolph Hearst's *New York Journal* was competing ruthlessly with Joseph Pulitzer's *New York World* in an epic battle that involved, quite literally, war and peace and, of course, money. Just a year before the trial, Hearst had egged on his editors to crank out ever more sensationalistic stories so that the newspaper's headlines would "bite the public like a bulldog"—giving rise to the term "bulldog" journalism. Veracity was not merely low on the list of journalistic priorities but seen as an impediment to telling a good story.

What the mass circulation newspapers wanted was not simply a good murder mystery, but ideally one that contained other elements. Eventually, the idea that the real motivating factor behind the murder was a love triangle—and not just a love triangle but one that had a young man choosing between a "Miss Rich" and a "Miss Poor," as the tabloids put it at the time—was the kind of formula that editors of the day knew they could milk endlessly.

So a myth was born, a myth that rapidly took on a life of its own. At least part of the myth had a factual basis: Chester Gillette had been born to a poor family, though the poverty was to some extent self-imposed in a religious climate of strict self-denial. As evidence of his yearnings for upward mobility, he began to date a number of young women in Cortland from high-society circles, including one, Harriet Benedict, whose name became inextricably linked with his when some reporters picked up on the fact that Chester had taken Harriet herself out for a boat ride just one week before his deadly trip with the "factory girl."

In reality, there was no love triangle. Chester and Harriet were only acquaintances, and she did not even count him among her friends. But when the newspapers discovered that Chester's prized camera still had film in it containing pictures of Harriet Benedict, she quickly became known as "the other woman."

The insistence that Chester killed Grace Brown so that he could pursue "rich girl" Harriet Benedict was proclaimed as fact elaborately and with great imagination by many newspapers—especially the large-circulation New York papers that were each trying to outdo the other in sensational coverage.

One newspaper even invented out of thin air a second set of letters, which "Miss Rich" was supposed to have secretly sent to Chester while he was being held in jail.

———

Dreiser wanted his novel to center on a crime story, but also to evoke the social complexities he saw in the world around him and that he had experienced in his own life. When he settled on the Chester Gillette case as the raw material from which he would carve out his fictionalized story, he had his own recollections of the crime and the trial as newspapers in New York had reported it at the time. But he relied primarily on clippings from just one newspaper, the *New York World*, where Dreiser had briefly worked many years earlier. The *World* was one of the original "yellow journalism" newspapers, which had, for example, run stories stating how and when Chester Gillette had completely confessed his crime after his conviction—a confession the paper's "journalists" completely made up.

Armed with his clippings and a brief trip to the scene of the crime, Dreiser plowed onward to produce one of the longest novels ever published in America, two fat volumes when it first came out in 1925. Because almost nothing had been written about Chester Gillette's younger years, Dreiser filled the first half of the book with details from his own rigidly conservative upbringing in a first-generation German American household in Indiana, which included what for Dreiser were the intolerable strictures of a Catholic school education. He overlaid his experiences onto the framework of Chester's roughly parallel childhood and developed a growing empathy for him, feeling as though he had a deep understanding of the forces that were pushing and pulling young Gillette.

This artistic merging of elements from Dreiser's own childhood and formative youth with Chester's life and his very real act of murder

coalesced into one of the great American novels—but one that identified the "tragedy" as the inevitable collision of economic and social
forces, which Dreiser believed drove all human events. In his view,
Chester Gillette was not a cold and calculating killer but the piteous
victim of a battle far beyond his control, in which the unfortunate
death of a woman and her baby was really just collateral damage.

The actual tragedy of *An American Tragedy* is that the premeditated
murder of a pregnant woman—whom Gillette viewed as standing
in the way of the life he wanted and believed he deserved—comes
across more as an act of nature or fate than a consciously planned
erasure. Dreiser, trapped by his own constructs and his identification
with his protagonist, could not see the killing for what it really was:
a man's attempt to erase a "mistake," the baby he created and the
woman he saw as dragging him down.

Literary critic Mary Gordon, herself an accomplished novelist,
explains in her book *Good Boys and Dead Girls* that "Dreiser wants
us to believe that Clyde didn't mean to kill Roberta [the names
given to Chester and Grace in the novel].... He only meant to
push her away [so] that he could get on with life," unencumbered
by the pregnancy he didn't want. But, as Gordon points out, "the
problem is that Dreiser has just spent a hundred pages showing Clyde
plotting the perfect murder. Clyde goes to his death believing himself
innocent, and we are sympathetic to him because in the context of
the corruption around him everywhere, he is the most pure." In the
end, when Clyde is executed just as the real-life Chester was, "we
mourn his death as we don't mourn Roberta's. She was the heavy,
dull, clinging object."

Dreiser himself later reflected on the novel and the real-life murder
by saying that he had been noticing since the early 1890s, when he first
began working as a newspaper reporter, a pattern of "a certain type
of crime in the United States. It seemed to spring from the fact that
almost every young person was possessed of an ingrown ambition
to be somebody financially and socially. In short, the general mood
of America was directed toward escape from any form of poverty.
... Fortune-hunting became a disease." Dreiser believed that it was
a craven grasping for material wealth that lay at the heart of this
particular killing. Gillette's crime was caused fundamentally, Dreiser
argued, by his ambition.

Gillette had started out as "the young ambitious lover of some
poorer girl, who in the earlier state of affairs had been attractive

enough to satisfy him, both in the manner of love and her social station, [but] with the passing of time and the growth of experience on the part of the youth, a more attractive girl with money or position appeared and he quickly discovered that he could no longer care for his first love," he explained. "What produced this particular type of crime . . . was the fact that it was not always possible to drop the first girl. What usually stood in the way was pregnancy, plus the genuine affection of the first herself for her lover, plus also her determination to hold him."

What is disturbing here about Dreiser's reasoning and his novel is that the perpetrator of the crime is portrayed as an apparently helpless pawn tossed about by "ambition" and drawn inexorably from one woman to the next, always seeking the "more attractive girl with money or position." In fact, he comes close to blaming the victim for her own death because of her efforts to hold on to the man she loved.

In truth, the one character element entirely lacking from any reading of the facts about Chester Gillette is ambition—meaning a strong desire to achieve a particular end. Ambition is a quality we usually attribute to people who exhibit its associated outward manifestations: hard work, a drive to succeed, focused efforts to achieve a goal, a willingness to sacrifice short-term pleasures for long-term success.

When a man claims to want to better himself but isn't willing to put in the work and sacrifice necessary to achieve the lifestyle he wants, when he merely believes he should be granted all the benefits and trappings of success as some kind of divine right, he is exhibiting not ambition but a sense of entitlement. That kind of narcissistic entitlement, rather than true ambition, is characteristic of many eraser killers, including Scott Peterson.

As Gordon put it, Dreiser's protagonist is someone "who cannot master his fate. He is never on top of the rules of the world's game." However, both Dreiser's character and the real-life Gillette were never greater masters of their fate, more on top of the game, more creative and goal directed than when they were engaged in planning a "perfect murder." The same could be said of Scott Peterson.

Dreiser's blindness in this respect is difficult to understand or explain away. Before he settled on the Gillette case to use as the basis for his novel, he researched the case of a young medical student in New York named Carlyle Harris, who in the 1890s got a young woman pregnant, married her in total secrecy, forced her to have an abortion through a doctor he knew, then poisoned her with morphine, killing her after he had started an affair with another young woman.

He also researched the case of one Reverend Richeson, a young Baptist minister in Massachusetts and a graduate of the prestigious Newton Theological Seminary, who was involved in a scandalous crime just a few years after the Gillette case. Rev. Richeson had a lengthy relationship with a beautiful seventeen-year-old girl named Avis Linnell, the daughter of one of his parishioners.

The girl was attending a local teachers college, but as her feelings for Richeson deepened, she decided to apply to the New England Conservatory of Music to be closer to him and to advance her musical training as a talented young soprano. Richeson proposed marriage to her and gave her an engagement ring. But before the date of the planned marriage, Avis told the preacher that she was pregnant with his child. Richeson responded by telling her that he had found a new woman—a wealthy heiress—with whom he was in love and whom he planned to marry instead of her.

Shortly thereafter, Avis was found dead under circumstances that initially led investigators to believe she had killed herself. An autopsy, however, revealed that she had been poisoned with cyanide, and confirmed that she was pregnant. Richeson might still have gotten away with murder by claiming that the young woman had simply poisoned herself. It was only the intervention of a local crusading newspaper that assigned investigative reporters to the story—reporters who actually found the druggist who had sold a vial of potassium cyanide to the good reverend—that pushed the local police to turn a closed suicide case into an open homicide investigation and led eventually to Richeson's trial and execution for murder.

Each of the cases Dreiser studied were murders committed by men who meticulously planned their killings, men who were not driven by any immediate rage or argument, men who showed absolutely no signs of remorse or basic human compassion. From all we can learn about them at this distance, these murderers showed the same Dark Triad characteristics we see in today's eraser killers. Each of these men demonstrated Machiavellianism in their ability to plan and manipulate their way toward a goal; psychopathy in their inability to accept responsibility for the consequences of their actions and in their utter callousness toward their victims both before and after the crime; and narcissism in their relentless need to ensnare those who could feed their toxic self-love and to destroy those who would threaten their inevitably fragile self-image.

The love triangle Dreiser invented for *An American Tragedy* was even more pronounced in the Hollywood film version released in 1951. *A Place in the Sun* starred Montgomery Clift as the sympathetic but troubled Clyde/Chester and a highly unsympathetic Shelley Winters as a shrill, cloying Roberta/Grace. But it was Elizabeth Taylor, considered the world's most beautiful woman at that time, who played the pivotal role in the film as the rich girl–other woman—offering an easily understood motive that simply did not exist in the real murder case. Astonishingly, the movie was marketed as a modern romance: "A love story of today's youth ... filling the screen with ecstasy!" promised the promotional poster touting the film's release.

———

The trial of the real Chester Gillette drew a thousand spectators a day to the unusually large courtroom in which it was held. Essentially penniless, Gillette was appointed two very able defense lawyers, one of whom had been a state senator. Defense attorney Charles Thomas insisted that Gillette was guilty of nothing more than moral cowardice, of running away after a rash and tragic suicide because he was young and immature, just a "boy" at the time Grace died.

"If you strip this case of its sentimental features and the excessive imagination of the district attorney, you will find little in it that would lead any reasonable man to believe that the charge is true," said Thomas. Even an unwanted pregnancy was not motive for murder, the defense argued. Gillette could have simply left town, abandoning Grace and her baby.

George Ward, the district attorney, laid out all the evidence of premeditation and of cover-up and flight after the crime, and the efforts Chester took to disguise his identity while with Grace and to disassociate himself from her afterwards. The prosecutor argued that Gillette killed Grace Brown to "seal that girl's lips" before she could reveal her delicate condition, ruining any chance he had to pursue the more glamorous lifestyle he so coveted.

As in the Peterson case, an important piece of physical evidence was some of the victim's hair, which Ward argued became entangled in one of the boat's oarlocks as Chester threw her body overboard. In another parallel with the trial of Scott Peterson, the jurors were asked to asses the stability of the boat in question, as a key issue at hand in both cases was whether or not the boat was likely to remain upright in the water, as the prosecution claimed, or could be easily tipped over, as the defense claimed.

And like that of Scott Peterson, Gillette's demeanor—his apparent lack of empathy toward his victim's suffering—was an issue in the courtroom. Throughout the proceedings he showed little emotion, even when the letters Grace wrote to him, in which she poured her heart out over her anguished dilemma, were read into the record. The only dry eyes in the house during the reading of those letters, reporters noted, were Gillette's own.

The most damning testimony, however, was the medical finding that Grace suffered a blow to the head powerful enough to induce unconsciousness. The blow was so severe that if she had survived, she probably would have been rendered blind—evidence not consistent with Gillette's claim that Grace had voluntarily jumped into the lake. The defense was left to make the feeble argument that perhaps Grace hit her head on the boat as she leapt overboard, or that the wound was caused postmortem as her body was hauled from the lake down rutted roads.

The jury did not buy that or any other of the accused man's arguments. On December 4, 1906, after just five hours of deliberation, they found Chester Gillette guilty of first-degree murder. Just after Christmas, the judge sentenced him to be executed in the electric chair.

A key issue in the trial and the subsequent appeals in the Gillette case was the claim that the case against the defendant was almost entirely circumstantial, but the appeals court reiterated a legal precedent that was well established even then. They cited an appellate decision reached just a few years earlier in a different homicide case based on circumstantial evidence, in which the New York court ruled that "a defendant indicted for a homicide may be found guilty on evidence which is wholly circumstantial, and where it appears on a review of such evidence, that the uncontradicted and unexplained facts and circumstances proved on the trial . . . form so complete and strong a chain of evidence as to exclude, beyond a reasonable doubt, every hypothesis save that of a defendant's guilt."

Although the appellate court upheld the verdict and Gillette was executed, there are still many people today who rise to his defense, who insist he never planned to kill his pregnant paramour. Craig Brandon, the author of the most popular nonfiction book on the Gillette case, has stated his personal belief that Gillette really was just planning to take Grace Brown to some kind of home for unwed mothers in upstate New York, where he could leave her in the care of others, even though there is not a single piece of evidence that supports such a theory, including Gillette's own testimony.

PART TWO

Getting Away with Murder

CHAPTER FOUR

The Lady-Killer

E raser killers play the odds. They bank on the widely held belief that when there is no body, they cannot be held responsible for their crimes. To prove beyond a reasonable doubt that someone committed murder, there must be sufficient evidence to establish what is known as the corpus delicti of the crime. That has nothing to do with the corpse per se, but more figuratively means the body of the crime—in simplest terms proving that someone is dead and that the person died by criminal means at the hands of the accused.

Surmounting this burden can be exceedingly difficult in murder cases where there is no body at all, or, as in the Peterson case, when discovery of the body is so delayed that the cause of death cannot be determined, because all the important questions—the who, what, when, where, how, and why of the crime—can be answered only by inferences.

However, the Scott Peterson case was no milestone in the history of conviction purely by circumstantial evidence, no shocking aberration in the standard of proof required for finding someone guilty of murder—contrary to the way it was portrayed by many media and legal pundits. Clear and unequivocal legal precedent was established half a century earlier in a California case as sensational in its day as the Peterson case would become, a murder mystery full of shocking twists and turns that involved another scheming charmer who just happened to be named Scott, and a missing wife who to this day has never been found.

L. Ewing Scott traveled not among the rugged farm folk of California's Central Valley like Scott Peterson, but in the highest social circles of Bel Air, one of Los Angeles's most exclusive enclaves. He called himself an investment broker but earned no income of his own; he didn't need to, because he had his wife's money to spend. In 1949, at age fifty-three, Scott had married Evelyn Throsby, a wealthy widow four years his senior, who had accumulated close to a $1 million fortune through four previous marriages and her own savvy investment skills.

Ewing Scott's father was a failed wildcatter who drank away his misfortune. Worried how this might affect Ewing, his mother sent him away at a young age to live with a series of relatives. He would later tell police that he had gone to college, but the school he named had no record of his ever having attended. It was one of many aspects of his life that he would fabricate and mold to get what he wanted without having to earn it.

As a young man, he first found work as a bookkeeper at a brokerage, but worked his way up to salesman by carefully studying and copying the dress, manner, and speaking style of the firm's investment counselors. He practiced reading aloud to himself in front of a mirror and memorizing information on a wide variety of topics so as to sound cultivated, educated, and worldly—all things he was not.

Whereas Scott Peterson joked about putting the motto "Horny Bastard" on his business cards, Ewing Scott posted a quotation over his desk that served as an Iago-like credo for his Machiavellian view of the world: "Never be associated with failure. Never defend the weak, even when he is right."

Ewing Scott is a case study in narcissistic entitlement. He tried to use his contacts from the brokerage to go into business for himself, but failed to consummate a single transaction. Instead, he found another way to live well: marrying an heiress to a mining fortune. When that marriage ended, he lived for a while off his substantial divorce settlement, then worked briefly for the government during World War II. The job was nothing more than a clerk's position, but he told everyone he was actually a spy involved in negotiations with foreign allies. After the war, Ewing tried his hand at a series of ill-fated ventures—most of them out-and-out cons, such as selling a phony hair-growth tonic for men.

As would be true of so many future eraser killers, lying, conning others, and living a double life—the signatures of psychopathy, narcissism, and Machiavellianism—came easily to him.

He considered himself such a ladies' man that he self-published a book titled *How to Fascinate Men*—basically a manual outlining the same approach he used to snag wealthy women, recast for the opposite sex—but was sued when he failed to pay the cost of the ten thousand copies he had printed. By the time he set his sights on Evelyn Throsby, he was nearly broke, but no one in Evelyn's circle was aware of his dire straits. He was a handsome, attentive, well-mannered bon vivant, a seemingly successful man of the world. They married after a whirlwind courtship.

The new Mrs. Scott would have preferred to remain in her more modest Pasadena home, but Ewing insisted they move to a much more expensive house in Bel Air, which not only satisfied his craving for status but also served to isolate his wife from her friends. To pull off the plan he had in mind, to make it seem plausible that his wife would disappear of her own volition, he needed to isolate her from those who knew her best. He even made his wife fire her longtime live-in maid after she overheard a violent incident between the couple.

Ewing pressured his wife to relinquish control of her finances, claiming he knew more than her about handling investments because of his "illustrious" background. Evelyn resisted, but eventually gave in. She had lost two husbands to divorce, two to illness. Perhaps she was desperate to hang on to what she may have considered her final chance at love. She likely also feared displeasing a man with a temper.

Scott began priming the waters for his wife's soon-to-occur disappearance by telling their friends that he didn't trust the American stock market, that he feared a nuclear attack on the United States, and that after converting his wife's assets to cash they planned to relocate overseas. He also began planting rumors among their circle, hinting that his wife was unwell physically and mentally. Evelyn told her worried friends just the opposite. Although she had occasional bouts of diverticulitis, the doctor had given her a clean bill of health.

On May 15, 1955, one of Evelyn's friends hosted a dinner party in honor of her sixty-third birthday. She spoke excitedly of a European vacation she and Ewing had planned. The day after the birthday party, they went for a test drive in a new Mercedes-Benz, telling the salesman they were thinking of buying one to drive around on their European vacation.

"We'll only be gone for a few months," Evelyn told the salesman. "We love Spain, but I don't think I could stand to be away from Los Angeles for very long. We have so many friends here." The salesman was the last person, other than Ewing, to see Evelyn alive.

The following day, Ewing called to cancel his wife's weekly hair appointment.

"For this morning?" asked the salon manager.

"That's right," Scott responded coldly, "and all the future ones, too." Evelyn would never again need to have her hair done.

Only Ewing Scott knows what happened to his wife, how he managed to erase her so completely that no trace of her remains has ever been found. What is known is that he sure wasn't worried about her sudden disappearance, and was certainly convinced that she was never coming back.

He never reported Evelyn missing, never looked for her. He did immediately start converting her assets to his name. He also began giving away some of his wife's most intimate possessions, including bedclothes and furs.

He ignored letters and phone calls from Evelyn's worried friends, but when they showed up at his door, he gave a series of evolving and inexplicable reasons for her absence. He told some that Evelyn had suddenly fallen ill and gone East for treatment. He told others that she was suffering from a mental illness or alcoholism and that he had committed her to a sanitarium, again in some location in the East that he would not identify. Sometimes he claimed to have no idea where she was. Other times he said she was right there at home, but he never let any of them speak to her.

Her friends were mystified. They had never known Evelyn to behave strangely or impetuously, and she hardly drank liquor at all.

After a few months, Scott disconnected the telephone and booked passage on a round-the-world cruise. Just one ticket, he specified. His wife had already been around the world, he said, and had no interest in doing that again.

Authorities did not get involved until Evelyn had been missing for two and a half months, and only then after some of her influential friends personally visited the district attorney and laid out the strange and troubling facts surrounding her disappearance. Perhaps because of the Scotts' social standing, or due to the inherent difficulty of grasping that a crime has occurred when there is no body or crime scene to work from, the DA did not contact police, but he did launch his own quiet investigation.

The story Ewing Scott told the DA's investigator was as baffling and absurd as what he had told Evelyn's friends, and would become ever more salacious over time. He said his wife went out on May 16, the day after the test drive, to buy toothpowder and never returned. He claimed he found her car two days later near a cemetery, but without reporting anything to police, he subsequently disposed of the vehicle. He said he later discovered that she had withdrawn $15,000 from her bank account.

When asked why she would leave home without any word to anyone, Scott claimed that his wife had throat cancer, had resisted his efforts to help her, and might have gone off to seek treatment on her own. He also alleged that she had been drinking heavily and suggested she might have gone someplace to dry out. He would later throw in that he believed that his wife was a lesbian and had run off with another woman, that he had discovered pictures of nude women among her possessions.

By the time authorities began looking for his wife, Ewing Scott was already looking for a replacement.

He wooed one wealthy widow, claiming Evelyn had abandoned him, and tried unsuccessfully to convince the woman to join him on his cruise. He quickly moved on to another prospect. Marianne Beaman, an attractive forty-six-year-old divorcé, was not a wealthy woman—she worked as a receptionist at a dental office—but perhaps now that Ewing had his wife's money, he no longer felt that he needed a wealthy wife. Marianne claimed that he told her he still loved Evelyn and hoped she would return to him. Yet he gave Marianne a number of Evelyn's possessions, stating they were things his wife no longer used, including very expensive pieces of his wife's jewelry.

As the new year rolled around, he was ready to embark on a fresh, new life. He was so confident that he would never be held to account for his missing wife that he asked Marianne to marry him, and she happily accepted—even though they knew they'd have to wait seven years for Evelyn to be declared legally dead before they could wed.

Scott believed he was in the clear. He planned to cruise off into the sunset without a backward glance, but then the story of his missing wife hit the newspapers. Evelyn's brother, fed up with the slow pace of the DA's investigation, filed a petition in court asking to be appointed trustee of his sister's estate to prevent her husband from squandering the rest of her fortune. An embarrassed and irate police force jumped into the investigation, and a media storm ensued.

Scott hired an attorney and was now happy to "cooperate" with authorities. He attempted to cast Evelyn as the dangerous one in their relationship, pointing out that all her former husbands were dead. He even claimed that he suspected Evelyn was trying to kill him at one point early in their marriage, that he thought she was poisoning him and had taken a Coke bottle to a chemist to see if any residue could be detected.

The test results were negative. But curiously, at another point in the interrogation, he described that his wife was sick around the very time he ran those tests. Might he have actually been trying to poison her and running his own test to see if he could get away with it?

He allowed police to search his house. Officers even probed the backyard for buried remains, plunging six-foot-long steel rods into the earth, then sniffing the tips for any smell of decomposition, but found no sign of a body or that any murder at all had occurred. The DA knew that Evelyn's signature had been forged on several bank documents. But without her around to testify that a crime had been committed against her, it would be hard to charge her husband with fraud. Without a body or some other strong evidence that Ewing had killed her, it would be impossible to charge him with murder. They were about to give up the search when a cop's hunch broke the case wide open.

One of the detectives searching the yard recalled a case he had worked on in which a man buried his wife's body in his next-door neighbor's yard, thinking police would never look outside the suspect's own property. He hopped over the wall demarcating the

Scott's property from the canyon below it, near an incinerator, and began brushing through the dense foliage and dumped incinerator ashes.

First he found a dental bridge, then a few other small items, mostly women's toiletries, some pills Evelyn took for diverticulitis, and two pairs of glasses.

Evelyn's dentist positively identified the bridge as one he had made for Mrs. Scott and recalled her wearing it when he last saw her—just days before she went missing. Her eye doctor also confirmed that the frames and lenses matched what Evelyn had ordered and picked up two weeks before she disappeared. Would Evelyn have left home of her own volition without the very things she needed to be able to eat or read?

All the items, each of which was tied to Mrs. Scott, seemed to be things she might have kept in the bathroom medicine cabinet or atop a dressing table. They found no evidence that Evelyn herself had been cremated inside the incinerator. But they did find the charred remnants of women's undergarments—which Scott claimed he burned because they were soiled and had a foul smell. He may have been trying to simply hide and destroy bloody or otherwise incriminating evidence. But to burn or bury items of such a personal nature—dentures, undergarments, medicine, and toiletries—suggests something even more insidious. He had no problem living off his dead wife's wealth, but he seemed to have a great need to exorcise the most private and intimate reminders of her earthly existence.

A grand jury was convened, and Ewing Scott was subpoenaed to appear. Marianne was subpoenaed, too, after police learned she had been staying overnight at various clubs with him, even signing room service checks as Mrs. L. E. Scott. She initially denied that they had discussed marriage, but changed her testimony later in the day, acknowledging that they talked of a future after "Mr. Scott's affairs were straightened out."

Ewing took the Fifth when he was called to the stand. But he was placed under arrest after a car dealer testified that two days before the start of the grand jury proceedings, Scott purchased a car from him in cash under the name R. E. Scott—requesting the fastest car on the lot, one that could travel "at least eighty miles per hour," and that had a large trunk whose dimensions he carefully measured. It appeared that he was preparing to go on the run.

The grand jury returned an indictment on thirteen fraud charges regarding misappropriation of his wife's assets. Ewing Scott quickly made bail, despite the DA's pointing out that he likely "had done away with" his wife. The grand jury was supposed to reconvene to consider murder charges, but within days of making bail, the defendant vanished. His wife's car was found on the street—pierced with two bullet holes. If Scott was trying to set up a kidnapping scenario, to make himself look like a victim of foul play, he hadn't thought it out carefully enough. Both shots were fired from inside the car, and there was no blood indicating that anyone had been hurt.

Ewing Scott remained at large for eleven months. While hiding out in Canada, he was indicted for his wife's murder. Moving around under a variety of assumed names, he tried to woo yet another woman he met in a cafe, promising her he would have "plenty of money" as soon as his financial affairs were straightened out. She had no idea that he was a fugitive wanted for killing his wife, but was put off by his "overly smooth" come-ons.

During the time he was on the run, police learned of another disturbing relationship Ewing had before he married Evelyn. A man told police that his mother, heiress to a cannery fortune, dated Scott for several years, until she came to believe that he was trying to poison her. She had since died of natural causes, so they were unable to investigate that relationship further. Had he, in fact, already tried to kill another lover?

Ewing Scott was finally caught due to his smug overreaching. He had slipped back into the United States to buy a new car in Detroit and was nabbed by Canadian customs agents as he drove it into Canada. It was a foolish and reckless thing to do, evidence of the kind of narcissistic indulgences that seem to override an eraser killer's more hardened and criminally astute psychopathic instincts.

For the first time since Mrs. Scott went missing almost two years before, her husband publicly appealed for his wife's return—to "clear this thing up," he said, audaciously hosting a press conference right in the U.S. attorney's office in Detroit. Describing himself as "the goat" of a vast unnamed conspiracy, he went on the offensive, threatening to sue "certain individuals in authority in Los Angeles as well as other persons for defaming my character and causing me mental anguish by making unfounded and unprovable statements relating to my actions and the disappearance of my wife."

He insisted that he had not attempted to flee justice but had been waylaid as he left for a business trip by some thugs who forced him off the road and stole his car. Believing himself a marked man, he headed across the country and eventually to Canada.

He also began to point the finger toward an alternate suspect, Raymond Throsby, Evelyn's brother, who was fighting him for control of her estate. In reference to the denture and eyeglasses found near the incinerator, he claimed that Throsby had surreptitiously taken a key to his home and had been seen lurking around the property. (Throsby, however, had an alibi for the time Scott said his wife disappeared. He was working and had time cards to prove it.)

"It is my belief that my wife is alive," Scott insisted, in his first excursion into what would become a concerted effort to court the press and win over public opinion. "I fervently believe she would come forward if it is at all possible, unless she is held against her will by those who stand to profit from such actions, or else she may be suffering from amnesia." Like Scott Peterson a half century later, Ewing Scott seemed utterly confident that he would be exonerated—so confident that he vowed to "crucify" those "sons of bitches" who he said were out to persecute him.

On the day he entered a plea of not guilty, he mused about the suave British actor Ronald Colman playing him in the movie version of his life. He contracted with an agent to sell his story rights, demanding full script approval, and hoped to get as much as $200,000, with which he could "follow up a number of hot leads" on his wife's whereabouts.

Perhaps the defendant should not have been so confident. The deputy district attorney appointed to prosecute him was J. Miller Leavy, the man who sent the lovers' lane bandit-rapist Caryl Chessman to the gas chamber, as he had Barbara Graham, whose execution was memorialized in the film *I Want to Live!* But Scott had an ace up his sleeve, a card no one knew was even in the deck until after the trial was over.

—∿∿—

The nine-week trial of Ewing Scott was at its time one of the longest in state history. Prosecutors argued that Ewing carefully planned and premeditated his wife's murder. They theorized that Evelyn was killed after she had gone to bed on the night of May 16, 1955, after she had removed her dental plate. (The fact that the retainer she wore to keep her remaining teeth in place while she slept was not found supported this scenario.)

Marianne Beaman, who hadn't seen Ewing since he jumped bail, testified that he had actually proposed to her twice. A particularly damning piece of evidence was the discovery of a codicil Ewing added to his will after his wife's disappearance, bequeathing 50 percent of his estate to Marianne and just $1 to his wife "because she had ample financial provisions for her needs." Although Scott had argued that he had no motive to kill his wife because her brother was actually her primary beneficiary, in fact Evelyn's will stated that he and Throsby were to share her fortune equally.

The defense argued that Ewing's bizarre and frequently changing explanations for his wife's disappearance were simply a husband's foolish but understandable attempts to assuage his own bruised ego, to shield himself from the painful realization that his wife had abandoned him. Scott never took the stand—on the advice of his lawyers and against his own wishes, his attorney insisted. Instead, they put on a few witnesses who claimed to have seen a woman who looked like Mrs. Scott after she went missing.

Both at the beginning and end of the trial, the defense attempted to abort the whole proceeding, claiming that the court had no jurisdiction to try Scott because it had not been proved where (not to mention if) his wife died. At best, the court should have to wait seven years for Mrs. Scott to be declared legally dead. That "Hail Mary" attempt at a legal pass was denied.

In his closing argument, Leavy described how circumstantial evidence fits together like pieces of a jigsaw puzzle, forming a complete and compelling picture of the defendant's guilt.

"In no circumstantial case does one bit of evidence stand alone in establishing a corpus delicti of murder, establish the essential elements of murder, or the guilt of the defendant," Leavy began. "You have to take one circumstance that may be meaningless standing alone, then you take another circumstance that may be meaningless standing alone, and the two together may not give meaning. But maybe there's another circumstance, a fourth, a fifth. When you take all of the circumstances together, they are a mosaic, a picture, of the corpus delicti of murder. They establish together each link in the chain of circumstances that is inconsistent with any rational hypothesis of innocence.

"By your good reasoning, by your good judgment, you will come to the conclusion that Evelyn Scott is deceased . . . and that the defendant is the perpetrator," the deputy DA continued. "No, we can't say that she was suffocated, chloroformed, poisoned, or whatever, but that by some criminal agency she met foul play. And there is only one person, with the exclusion of all others, that the evidence points to, and that is L. Ewing Scott."

Defense attorney Tom Williams tried to use Scott's mistakes as proof of innocence, as Mark Geragos would a half century later for Scott Peterson—as if anyone is ever capable of pulling off a perfect murder.

"If Mr. Scott is clever enough to murder his wife and conceal her body so that it has not been found for two and one-half years, then that man is not stupid enough to leave anything on the surface of the ground," Williams said, referring to the eyeglasses and other items found in the cast-off incinerator ashes.

His cocounsel, Al Matthews, was left with the task of putting the fear of God in the jury—to scare the jurors into believing they could be executing a man whose "victim" might actually be alive. "Even if everything the prosecution has brought into this courtroom is absolutely true," said Matthews, in a Perry Mason–like moment, "it still doesn't stop Mrs. Scott from walking in that front courtroom door—and you know it."

Ewing Scott was so sure he would be acquitted that he told reporters he was looking forward to being home for the holidays. He was wrong. Four days before Christmas 1957, he was convicted of murder in the first degree, but the jury voted to spare his life. Perhaps they did feel some subliminal fear that Evelyn Scott might one day reappear.

—∿—

All was not lost, however, from Scott's point of view. He still had not played his ace. Unfortunately for Ewing Scott, he never got to play that card, as it was soon revealed how he attempted to rig the game.

Scott had devised a scheme he hoped would clear him of murder, a plot so macabre that it sounds like something from a horror movie.

But I believe it is emblematic of the extreme Machiavellianism and overweening narcissism of eraser killers, the psychopathic level of callousness that can be found only in the darkest of hearts.

After Scott was convicted, a small-time television actor told police that two men had asked him to say he saw Evelyn Scott living it up in Rio de Janeiro after she disappeared. When questioned by police, one of the men he identified, a private investigator who worked for Scott's defense, confessed to an even more sinister plot. The private eye said that at the direction of Ewing Scott, he and another investigator on the defense team had attempted to frame someone else for Evelyn Scott's murder.

The story he told was chilling: the two investigators attempted to obtain a severed arm from a cadaver, which they intended to plant on the property of William Brawner, the friend and former neighbor who hosted the sixty-third birthday party for Evelyn Scott the day before she disappeared and who had been the first to take his suspicions of Ewing Scott to the district attorney.

The conspirators hoped to pass scientific scrutiny by injecting the arm with blood matching Evelyn's type. (There was no DNA testing in those days.) To make it appear even more believable that the arm belonged to the late Mrs. Scott, they planned to place Evelyn's actual wedding band on the cadaver's ring finger. The private investigator claimed that Scott provided a sketch of Brawner's property and told them where he had hidden Evelyn's ring at the Bel Air house.

It is unclear whether the idea was actually to frame Brawner or Evelyn's brother, whom Brawner assisted in his fight for trusteeship of the estate. But there was plenty of evidence that such a plot existed. Two chiropractors testified that the investigators asked them a few weeks after Scott was found guilty if they could supply a body part and blood of a certain type. Two police officers testified that they had seen the investigators near the Brawner home. A third private investigator said that one of the conspirators approached him during the trial and offered him $150,000 to plant the incriminating evidence.

Scott appealed his conviction, contending that the evidence presented at trial was insufficient to establish the corpus delicti of murder—in other words, that it was not proven that his wife was indeed dead and that he killed her. There was ample precedent in

U.S. law that corpus delicti can be proved by circumstantial evidence. But in all cases reported up to that time there had been some proof of death in the form of a body or some part of the victim's body, direct evidence of how the person was killed (such as cases where a sailor was tossed overboard at sea in front of witnesses), or an admission or confession by the defendant to the crime.

In reviewing the conviction of Ewing Scott, the California District Court of Appeal acknowledged that the evidence against him was wholly circumstantial, reiterating the standard put forth in English law and previous U.S. cases that circumstantial evidence is sufficient to prove guilt if it is so convincing as to preclude every reasonable hypothesis of innocence. In its 1960 ruling, the court stated in the boldest possible terms that a killer is not entitled to a free pass because he is clever enough to erase evidence directly connecting him to his crime.

"Appellant contends that since no body was produced, no direct evidence of death was introduced and there was no confession, the people's case was based on mere suspicion and conjecture," the court stated in its published opinion on the Ewing Scott case. "If this contention is valid it would mean that a man could commit a secret murder and escape punishment if he was able to completely destroy the body of his victim, however complete and convincing the circumstantial evidence of guilt. No one would say that the law should be powerless to uncover such a crime and inflict punishment unless the accused had made a confession."

The test set forth so clearly in the Ewing Scott ruling is the same one jurors were instructed to follow in weighing circumstantial evidence in the Scott Peterson case: that the chain of circumstances must be so powerful as to preclude any reasonable explanation pointing toward innocence. Jurors are entitled and entrusted to draw inferences from the statements and actions of the defendant both prior to and after the crime as they shed light on character, motive, and state of mind.

"Every circumstance in evidence respecting the conduct of appellant tended in some degree to shed light upon the question [of] whether he believed his wife would return, or knew she could not return," Clement Shinn, the presiding justice, wrote in the Ewing Scott ruling. "There were many incidental questions to be answered. What did the evidence prove as to appellant's character? Would he have been capable of taking the life of the woman who had been his wife of six years? Why would he have wanted to be rid of her? What were the reasonable deductions from his conduct after May 16th with respect to his state of mind? Did it indicate that he knew his wife was dead? Presumably the jury gave answers to these questions that were unfavorable to appellant."

The circumstantial evidence so derided by some commentators in the Scott Peterson case helped answer similar questions. Peterson's lack of concern for his missing wife and child as captured on the Amber tapes, his efforts to sell Laci's car and home, his request for grief counseling for Laci's friends and family within hours of her disappearance, his statements to Amber that he did not want any biological children, and his talk of a future without responsibility were all telling indicators that he knew his wife was never coming home and that his baby was never going to be born.

The appellate court cited ample grounds to support the jury's verdict in the Ewing Scott case. They found it completely implausible that Evelyn would have left home voluntarily without her dentures and eyeglasses, without baggage or clothing, without drawing on her bank accounts or communicating with any of the friends she held so dear. There was no evidence that she was ill, mentally unstable, alcoholic, or unhappy with her life, no evidence that she had harmed any of her previous husbands or sought to harm Ewing, as he alleged.

Ewing, however, did have motive for killing Evelyn: to loot her estate. For years even before she disappeared, he had angled for control of her financial affairs, liquidating her assets and depositing large sums in bank accounts all over the country. He showed no sadness or loss at her disappearance, did not even report her missing. Instead, he acted in all ways as if he knew she would never return.

He forged her name and fraudulently accessed her accounts. He dated other women and even proposed marriage within six months of his wife's disappearance. He brought Marianne home to spend the night with him in the bed he had shared with his wife. Since Evelyn's disappearance, he had done nothing but disparage her character. When he finally faced possible punishment for his actions, he fled from justice.

"The jury could reasonably have found, and no doubt did find, that every statement of appellant, every act and failure to act, tended to prove that he was pleased to be rid of his wife," wrote Justice Shinn. "We can only conclude that appellant has felt immune from a conviction of murder in the belief that his wife's body lies where it cannot be found."

Shinn declared that the circumstantial evidence in the Ewing Scott case "was as strong and convincing as a confession would have been" and more convincing than testimony for which credibility could not be proven.

Scott "wove about himself a web of incriminating circumstances that was complete," Shinn wrote. "He has evolved from the evidence no theory of innocence; the jury could not find a theory, nor can we. [He] merely says, and others may say, 'But Mrs. Scott may still be alive.' They would have to rest their belief upon some mythical or miraculous hypothesis, since it could not find support in any reasonable deduction from the established facts. But the law is reason; it does not proceed upon fantasy or remote and unrealistic possibilities."

—⁓—

If there was any lingering doubt that Evelyn Scott was dead and that her husband had killed her—even after exposure of his failed plan to, almost literally, finger someone else with the cadaver arm—it was extinguished by Ewing Scott himself in the waning years of his life.

After he was sent to San Quentin, Scott became something of a jailhouse lawyer, peppering the courts and politicians and reporters with pleas to overturn his sentence. Cocksure to the end that he would eventually be exonerated, he even refused two offers of parole because, he claimed, that would be tantamount to admitting guilt. He finally was released outright in 1978.

Six years later—enfeebled and living in a tiny apartment, the luxury he had known while married to Evelyn gone forever—Scott confessed to Diane Wagner, a journalist who was writing a book on the case, that he had killed his wife. He stuck to part of his long-held story, claiming he did it because she had tried to poison him (although by his own time line, her alleged poisoning attempt was four years before he murdered her).

He said he struck her once on the top of the head with a rubber mallet in their bedroom on the night of May 16, 1955, then drove her body out to the desert near Las Vegas and buried her. He claimed he didn't care that he had gone to prison, but still seemed to relish one thing: that her body was never found, that he put one over on the police and everyone who cared about Evelyn Scott.

"I was smarter than they were, wasn't I?" he bragged.

CHAPTER FIVE

Disappearing Acts

Before the Ewing Scott case, some states actually forbade prosecution for murder without a body. The principle dates back to English common law and the influential jurist Sir Matthew Hale, who proclaimed in the eighteenth century that one should not be convicted of murder unless "at least the body be found dead." His logic was reasonable enough, as he was aware of a few instances in which men were convicted and executed in the absence of a body, only to have the "victim" turn up later very much alive.

Over time, however, Lord Hale's "rule" struck other jurists as dangerously one-sided, especially in cases of murder on the high seas, where bodies were almost never recovered. In the mid-nineteenth century, British barrister William Best, who authored a highly influential treatise on circumstantial evidence, noted that Hale's rule was unintentionally encouraging killers to dispose of their victims' bodies and cover up crime scenes by arson and other means to escape punishment.

Although the Hale rule has long since been interpreted by judges and legal scholars as more of a caution than a prohibition, the concept of "no body, no crime" has so permeated the public consciousness that it is not only criminals who still believe it to be true. For example, Joran van der Sloot's father, who was training to be a judge on the island of Aruba at the time his son and two friends were detained as suspects in the disappearance of a vacationing American teenager, Natalee Holloway, used those very words to assure the three that without a body they would never be prosecuted. He was right, at least so far. Within a few months all three were released. As this book goes to press more than two years after her disappearance, Natalee has still not been found despite extensive searches in and around the island with cadaver dogs and high-tech sonar equipment, and no one is facing any charges whatsoever in regards to her disappearance.

The erroneous but widespread belief that murder cannot be proved without a body is a problem not only at trial but at the investigative stage as well. Without a body or apparent crime scene, a missing persons investigation may be derailed before it ever becomes a homicide inquiry.

Don Weber and Lynda Singshinsuk each seemed destined for great things. The two had grown up in the same small town of Robinson, Illinois, about two hundred miles south of Chicago. Don was a high school track star and a member of one of the town's most well-to-do families; Lynda, a Thai immigrant whose physician father worked at the local hospital. They didn't begin dating until they were both undergraduates at the University of Illinois. For the next six years, on and off, they maintained a mostly long-distance relationship as Don went off to law school and Lynda into training to become a doctor.

In January 1990, Lynda decided to end the relationship for good. By that time, Weber, twenty-nine, was living in New York City, having graduated from Fordham Law School and taken a job with the accounting firm Peat Marwick, and was pursuing a master's in law at NYU with hopes of working in international business. Lynda, twenty-four, was in her third year of medical school at Northwestern University in Chicago, and had fallen for another man, a fellow med student.

Weber came to Chicago to win her back. When she refused to resume their relationship, he became enraged. According to what Lynda told friends, he threatened to kill her and her parents. Before he left her dormitory apartment, he poured his cologne over her bed sheets, as if marking territory with his scent. Lynda was so shaken by his threats that she considered seeking a protective order against him, but decided not to pursue it, perhaps afraid that to do so would only inflame the situation.

According to the attorney who would come to represent Weber, Kevin Smith, who supervises homicide and death penalty prosecutions in the Cook County public defender's office, Weber was fixated on Asian women, and Lynda in particular. Although she tried to move on with her life over the next four months, Don either quit or lost his job in New York, dropped out of school, and moved back to his parents' home in Robinson, where he bided his time performing manual labor and brooding about Lynda.

"He had this obsessive view that she was part of his perfect life, and he couldn't have this life without her," said Smith. "He was overcome with this idea that if he couldn't have Lynda, no one could."

According to his attorney, Don heard that Lynda was making plans to visit relatives in Thailand with her new boyfriend, as they once had, and interpreted this as meaning that the two were preparing to be married.

On the night of April 16, 1990, Weber secretly borrowed his stepmother's car and drove unannounced back to Lynda's dorm armed with a .22-caliber pistol. Along the way he stopped and bought soda pop, fashioning the container into a homemade silencer—which he told his lawyer he learned how to make from an article he read in *Field & Stream* magazine.

"I told her I was sorry but I couldn't live with what she had done," Weber said in an interview. He pulled the gun out of his backpack and shot her six times in the chest.

He claims he waited around for an hour after she died, fully expecting the police to burst in and arrest him. But if he wasn't planning and hoping to get away with murder, why did he use a silencer? Apparently the device worked. No one heard a thing. So he cleaned up the blood, zipped Lynda's body inside a sleeping bag, and carried her corpse, secreted inside a laundry hamper, nine stories down to his stepmother's car. He drove straight back to Robinson and hid her body beneath some auto parts in a dump.

Then he did something very strange, perhaps as symbolic as spraying his scent on Lynda's bed sheets. By his own account, he took a ring off her finger and buried it, along with some other personal items he had taken from her room, in a cemetery. Why did the ring deserve a more dignified resting place than Lynda herself, whom he literally threw out like trash? It seems as if he were mourning the death of an illusion—the relationship, as symbolized by the ring—but not the death of the woman. He was stripping her not only of her life but also of any object he considered meaningful.

Several months later, however, fearing that her remains might be discovered in the dump, he decided to move her to a more secure location. He retrieved her corpse and drove fifteen hundred miles across the country, finally pulling off the highway near Flagstaff, Arizona, where he buried her in a national forest. "He just drove until he saw what looked like a good place to bury a body," says Smith.

—◁◈▷—

After a friend reported Lynda missing, police found her dorm room locked, her keys and wallet inside, her car parked nearby. The only physical evidence possibly indicating foul play was two small spots of dried blood on the floor—too little to test for DNA or even to match to Lynda's blood type, thanks to Weber's diligent clean-up efforts. And if it was Lynda's blood, there could be an innocent explanation for how it happened to fall there, such as during one of the frequent nosebleeds Lynda was known to suffer.

"We don't have any proof that a crime has been committed," the lieutenant overseeing the missing persons investigation declared a few weeks later. "There isn't enough evidence to indicate anything."

It is a conundrum that makes cracking eraser crimes so challenging: without obvious evidence of a crime scene, police may not be persuaded that any crime at all has occurred. The investigation into the disappearance of Lynda Singshinsuk was assigned not to homicide detectives but to the Chicago Police Department's youth division because Lynda fell into an age group that led police to view her as likely to be a runaway. The homicide squad was assisting only in an advisory capacity.

Consequently, the investigation tilted toward the theory that Lynda had run off somewhere voluntarily or committed suicide rather than that she had been the victim of a crime—despite the fact that she was a dedicated medical student pursuing her lifelong dream of becoming a doctor like her father. It also didn't make sense that she would have run away without her car, credit cards, or checkbook. Authorities searched Lake Michigan for weeks, thinking that if she had taken her own life, she would most likely be found in the lake just outside her dorm.

There were reasons to suspect that Weber might have harmed her. Police quickly learned from Lynda's family and friends that Don had not taken their breakup well. Two months before she disappeared, Weber called Lynda's mother and threatened to damage Lynda's medical career by distributing sexually explicit pictures he had taken of her unless they paid him $20,000—recompense, he said, for all the money he claimed to have spent on Lynda over the years. When the family failed to accede to his blackmail demands, he mailed some of the photos to other students in her dorm.

Weber had no ironclad alibi for the day Lynda disappeared, but there was no evidence that he was anywhere near Chicago at the time, having driven there and back the same night without even his parents knowing that he had ever left Robinson. The fact that he was a lawyer himself from a respected family, who had also engaged a prominent defense attorney to represent him after he was questioned about sending the intimate photos, helped keep police at bay. They insisted he was not even a suspect.

At their wits' end, Lynda's parents offered a $30,000 reward for her safe return and took out ads in the newspaper promising not to press charges if anyone who might have kidnapped Lynda set her free. On Christmas Day, eight months after Lynda vanished, the Singshinsuks received a shocking call: Weber telephoned them asking for $50,000 in exchange for telling them where they could find their daughter. It was both astonishingly malevolent and foolish. Weber managed to be careful and clever enough in carrying out the murder that it appeared he would never be prosecuted. But he could not resist exploiting and tormenting Lynda's family with his knowledge of their daughter's fate, a clear example of narcissism and Machiavellianism trumping the savvier self-preservation aspects of psychopathy.

After receiving this call, the Singshinsuks hired a private detective to do what police had failed to do: find their daughter's body and bring her killer to justice. The family employed Jay J. Armes, who gained national attention in the early 1970s after he managed to find and rescue Marlon Brando's young son, who was kidnapped and slipped out of the country in the midst of a custody dispute. Armes traced phone calls by Weber to the Singshinsuks and some of his relatives and discovered that he was calling from Chiang Mai, an area in Northern Thailand known as a haven for sex tourism.

Armes flew there, following a slender trail of clues Weber had left behind. It was difficult detective work because many locals in Chiang Mai are protective of the semilegal and illegal sex industry, and do not welcome inquiries of any kind. Armes, of course, had no official status to help open doors. After visiting countless hotels, showing Weber's picture around, Armes tracked Weber to a room where he discovered that the American had already hooked up with a Thai girl who looked eerily similar to Lynda. He was eking out a living teaching English and seemed to have settled in with his Lynda substitute, beyond the arm of the law back home even if U.S. authorities could be persuaded of his involvement in Lynda's disappearance.

As if finding Weber weren't difficult enough, Armes now faced a monumental challenge. He needed not only to induce Weber to admit he killed Lynda and identify where he had hidden her body but also, ideally, to get him back to the United States so he could be held accountable. And, as merely a private investigator, he had to do all this without any real leverage—no money to offer Weber for his cooperation, no ability to cut a deal with prosecutors, no legal threats to hang over the killer's head, no police power in either the United States or Thailand to back him up. In fact, Weber was not even a wanted man. There were no charges pending against him. Indeed, he had gotten away with murder.

Weber admitted to the investigator that he had come to Thailand specifically to avoid prosecution, as Thailand had no extradition treaty with the United States at the time (although it is clear from Weber's fixation on young Southeast Asian women that the lack of extradition was not Thailand's only attraction). As a lawyer, Weber was beyond any empty threats a wily private investigator might attempt to use. Nevertheless, in what must be one of the most remarkable engagements between an investigator and an eraser killer on record, Armes managed to establish a rapport with Weber and gain his trust. By assuring him that Lynda's family was not interested in prosecuting him but only wanted to find their daughter's body, Armes got Weber to confess to him.

When psychopaths confess, there is no dam-burst of pent-up emotion—that mixture of pain, remorse, pity, and self-pity that constitutes contrition in other criminals. Weber wasn't tearful or remorseful when he described what he did to Lynda. In Armes's words, "When he was talking about killing her, you would have thought he was talking about killing a chicken."

The private eye also talked Weber into drawing a crude map of where he had buried Lynda. Armes flew home and searched the area Weber had indicated with both metal detectors and cadaver dogs, but found no body. Armes called Weber back and, with the same assurances, convinced a very reluctant Don to return to the United States and help him find the unmarked grave. He sent him an airline ticket to the United States, personally flew him on to Flagstaff in his own private plane, then drove him out to the national forest where they dug until they found a foot.

Weber had been so wary of a setup that he took Armes on a circuitous route to the grave to make sure they were not being followed. Little did he know that FBI agents were already hiding in the woods near the place Weber had mapped out. As soon as the body was uncovered, the agents swept in and arrested him.

———

Having literally led authorities to Lynda's grave, there was no way Weber could deny putting her there. He gave prosecutors a detailed confession and, after being assigned a public defender, shocked Smith, one of the most experienced capital case defenders in the country, by refusing to cooperate in preparing a defense. The state was seeking the death penalty, and Smith wanted to explore whether depression and the painkillers Weber was taking may have played a role in his actions—if not for a full-out insanity defense, then at least as mitigation in the penalty portion. But Weber told his attorney he wouldn't fight the charges. He wanted to die.

Of the hundreds of murders I've researched that I believe could be classified as eraser homicides, I can count on one hand the number of killers who ever took any measure of responsibility for their actions. In most if not all of those instances, it could be argued that their decision to plead guilty was more selfish than noble—they were caught dead to rights and had little choice but to cut a deal, often to eliminate the possibility of receiving the death penalty. Other than an insanity defense, there was no credible way for Weber to say he was not responsible for Lynda's death. But to actively lobby for execution is extraordinary and unprecedented among eraser killers. Still, even his own attorney wasn't sure if what his client felt was actual remorse or something more narcissistic.

His family could afford to hire private counsel for Weber, but they refused to help him. His father and brothers, self-reliant men to the core—one brother a doctor, another a fighter pilot, his father a successful businessman—wanted nothing more to do with him. Smith believes Weber's wish to be executed was really a desire to escape the untenable situation in which he found himself. He was grieving not so much what he had done to Lynda but what had become of his life.

"In terms of where the focus is, in genuine remorse there has to be a level of selflessness and concern and empathy for the victim, more so than for yourself," said Smith. "Here there was concern, but not for the victim. The overriding thing was 'Poor me, look at what she has done to me, I can't get on with my life, I've embarrassed my family.' In terms of what the motivating factor was I think it was more self-pity: 'If I'm dead I don't have to deal with this.' It was like, 'God, I've screwed things up, and I'm never going to have a productive life, so I might as well just take this way out.'"

As the time set for trial grew closer, Weber changed his mind. He began to buy into the idea that maybe something was mentally wrong with him. On the eve of jury selection, a deal was struck. Smith had made it clear that the defense planned to use the explicit photographs Don had taken of Lynda as part of its case, to show the extent of the relationship and Don's obsession with her. Lynda's parents did not want to be put through a trial that sullied their daughter's memory any further. If Weber agreed to plead guilty and admit responsibility for his crime, they were amenable to sparing his life.

The plea was entered in February 1992. In a barely audible voice, Weber apologized for killing his "best friend" and for the pain he caused her family and his own. He was sentenced to seventy years in prison. He will be eligible for parole in 2028, when he will be sixty-eight.

"At the very end, I think there was a component of sorrow for what he had done to her, wanting to do the right thing for her family if for nothing else," his attorney says. "In the end it came close to genuine remorse. But all the drama about the death penalty had nothing to do with remorse. That was self-centered: 'What's the best thing for me, poor pitiful me; I'll just take the death penalty.'"

—⁓—

Richard Crafts believed he could never be held responsible for his wife's murder if he was able to ensure that no trace of her would ever be found—and he very nearly succeeded.

In one of the most notorious, and literal, acts of erasure ever conceived, the forty-eight-year-old airline pilot killed his flight attendant wife one snowy night in Newtown, Connecticut, in 1986, then attempted to obliterate all trace of her by putting her body through a wood chipper.

At the time she disappeared, thirty-nine-year-old Helle, a Danish immigrant who spoke or understood six languages, was growing increasingly afraid of her husband. A few months earlier, she had begun making preparations to leave him, hiring a private investigator to find out if he was once again cheating on her, and a divorce lawyer.

"If anything happens to me," she told several friends, as well as her divorce attorney, "don't assume it was an accident."

Crafts had physically abused his wife and had affairs with numerous women throughout their eleven-year marriage. A month before she went missing, the private investigator showed Helle pictures of Crafts with a woman, a fellow flight attendant, he had been seeing on the side for at least a decade. (He also resumed an affair with an ex-girlfriend around the time of his wife's disappearance.)

Like so many eraser killers, Richard Crafts was well practiced at keeping secrets. He lied to Helle about his flight schedule to make time to see his girlfriends. He had the couple's phone bills sent to a secret post office box to hide evidence of his calls to paramours. He even lied about his medical situation.

Two years earlier he had been diagnosed with colon cancer and had surgery and chemotherapy. When Helle filed for divorce, Crafts told his wife he was dying and had chosen to abandon treatment. She found out by calling his doctor, however, that his treatment was complete and that his health was stable.

Even with his parents and siblings, Crafts was extremely guarded, refusing to answer any questions about his personal life. Friends characterized him as aloof, and Helle described him to her divorce attorney as "cold" and "detached." At home he spent much of his time alone in the basement, drank heavily, and showed little interest in their three children. He felt absolutely entitled to what he described to police as his "extracurricular activities" with other women.

"I'm away from home [many] nights every month and you run out of books to read," he said, as casually as one might describe an evening of channel surfing.

He also harbored a sadistic streak. During and after serving in the Marines, he flew flights for Air America, the CIA-run airline then involved in a clandestine operation in Vietnam and Laos. He bragged of leaving the hatch open and performing hotshot maneuvers when he was assigned to ferry prisoners, watching his terrified passengers scream for their lives as they rolled around the open plane. He also described how the pilots amused themselves by throwing monkeys attached to little parachutes out of their planes.

Helle had long believed she was unable to bear children. When she got pregnant, Crafts was enraged. He beat her and forced her to get an abortion. When she got pregnant again, he left her. Helle scheduled an abortion, but suddenly Crafts changed his mind, saying he wanted the child after all. They married a few days later, but soon Crafts was back to expressing his reluctance, questioning whether the child was actually his. He was no happier with her subsequent two pregnancies, not even coming to the hospital when she gave birth to their daughter, Kristina.

He once punched his wife in front of guests at a dinner party. At other times, friends saw her with black eyes and other injuries. Crafts was exceedingly tightfisted with money and made Helle foot most of the household expenses, even though she made about a third of what he did. He did splurge on a few things he enjoyed: expensive tools and machinery, such as a $20,000 backhoe, and a weapons collection that included fifty guns. A cop wannabe, he spent his spare time working as a $7-an-hour auxiliary officer for a neighboring town. He outfitted his personal auto, a Ford Crown Victoria, the same model as most police cars, with a siren and flashing red light on the dashboard. He even crafted his own ammunition.

After seeing the incriminating photos of her husband, Helle instructed her attorney on October 14, 1986, to begin divorce proceedings. She tried to keep things civil between them. They made an agreement that he could keep living in the house until the divorce went through as long as he didn't see his girlfriend (a deal that he promptly broke, she discovered). Helle arranged to have the divorce papers served on November 14 while the children were at school. Crafts told her he would accept service, but instead slipped out the back door when the sheriff arrived.

He had already put into motion a very different plan for his wife.

—∿∿—

The day before he was supposed to accept service of the divorce papers, Crafts went out and bought a large-capacity freezer, which he picked up the day before she disappeared. He paid cash, refusing to give his name even for the receipt. He also bought a shovel and heat-resistant gloves. On November 18, 1986, the last day she was seen alive, he rented a large wood chipper—powerful enough to chip logs a foot thick.

That evening, Helle returned from working a flight from Frankfurt. A huge snowstorm hit that night, knocking power out for hours. At six the next morning, Crafts ushered their three children and live-in nanny out of the house, telling them he was going to take them to his sister's house to wait out the power outage. He claimed his wife had already left and would meet them there, which would have meant she had driven by herself before dawn in a blinding snowstorm, but Helle never arrived.

In the days that followed, Crafts gave a number of different explanations for his wife's whereabouts. He told some friends she had gone to visit her sick mother in Denmark (who wasn't sick at all and hadn't seen or heard from her daughter), even claiming she had phoned him from there after November 19. He later claimed, at various times, that she went off to visit a friend in Florida, went to Club Med in the Canary Islands, and ran off with a lover.

Authorities believe he killed his wife the night of the storm and placed her body, wrapped in plastic like a side of meat, in the brand-new freezer until she was frozen solid. He then transported her corpse to a secluded piece of property he owned nearby, carved it up into manageable pieces with a chainsaw, and fed the remains through the wood chipper.

It was an almost foolproof scheme, uncovered only by exemplary forensic work, lucky breaks, and the ceaseless tree-rattling of the private eye who feared that Helle's sudden disappearance could mean only one thing and urged authorities to look at her husband.

The lucky break came from a snowplow operator, Joey Hine, who happened to come across Crafts and his U-Haul-pulled wood chipper on deserted River Road along the banks of the Housatonic in the early morning hours a few days after Helle disappeared. Apparently, Crafts pulled over there to try to clear out any bits of human remains inside the wood chipper by running branches and vegetation through it before he returned it, and to dump the detritus into the river.

A second stroke of luck occurred when the plowman led detectives to the location and a small pile of debris from the chipper was still there, more than a month after Helle went missing. They found remnants of shredded plastic and paper intermingled with the wood chips. On one of the scraps, apparently a piece of mail that had been in Helle's pocket when she died, they could make out the missing woman's name and address.

It was a stunning and almost unbelievably fortuitous discovery. Police searched the surrounding area extensively, even lowering the river to drag its bottom. They simultaneously tracked down the actual machine and truck Crafts had rented. All told, they recovered fragments of a finger, toe, bits of skull and other bone chips, and two dental crowns—about three-quarters of an ounce of Helle Crafts. Hair, bone, and tissue were also found in the U-Haul. A chainsaw was pulled from the river, human tissue and hair still attached to both the blade and the tool's housing.

During a search of the Crafts home, they found that carpeting had been pulled up and removed from the master bedroom, where the nanny had noticed a dark stain, and from several other rooms. Bloodstains were found on the mattress and on towels in the home. When police searched the home, the mattress was lying flat on the floor, the box spring missing. On November 19, the day Helle failed to show up at her sister-in-law's, Crafts purchased a new comforter and pillows. A few days later he purchased new carpeting.

"It's difficult to imagine a more sadistic and surreptitious disposal of remains," Walter Flanagan, the state's attorney, said. "Whoever did this would have to have nerves of steel, ice in their veins . . . [and be] totally free of emotion. Most of us couldn't even do that to a rat."

———

Crafts was indeed a cool customer, so cool that two weeks after his wife disappeared he took and passed a lie detector test; at the time that he took the test, the lieutenant in charge of the investigation for the Newtown police considered it to have cleared him. (The Connecticut State Police, who ended up taking over the investigation, were much more convinced of Crafts's guilt.) However, many people, especially psychopaths, are able to pass polygraphs because the test does not really measure lies. It measures the fear of getting caught in a lie, the physical signs of psychological stress.

A person without conscience, who feels no guilt about lying, who feels supremely self-confident and immune from the consequences of his behavior, who experiences no sense of fear whatsoever, may very well pass a lie detector test. It's amazing to me how many eraser killers resist taking a polygraph, which could allay the suspicions of police if they pass it. Even if they fail, the results cannot be used against them in court.

Above and beyond any psychological predisposition, Crafts had no fear of getting caught because he believed he had made it impossible for his wife ever to be found.

However, Crafts had failed to completely obliterate his wife's corpse. The tissue and bone matched Helle's blood type, as did the bloodstains on the couple's mattress. The more than two thousand hairs found were blond and treated, like Helle's. Forensic odontologists matched the crowns to Helle's dental X rays. The serial number on the chainsaw pulled from the river was filed down in an attempt to make it untraceable. But the state crime lab, under the direction of the renowned forensic scientist Henry Lee, was able to restore it. It matched a number on a warranty found among Richard Crafts's records.

While in jail awaiting trial, Crafts talked his brother-in-law, David Rodgers, into getting rid of some potential evidence—including clothing and other personal items belonging to Helle that Crafts had burned in backyard barrels, presumably while wearing the fireproof gloves. Rodgers also paid two strangers to say they had seen Helle at a drug-filled party after the date she disappeared. By the time of trial, however, Rodgers no longer supported his brother-in-law, and the two "eyewitnesses" never appeared.

Surprising most courtroom observers, Crafts testified on his own behalf. He admitted his wife was serious, at last, about divorcing him. "My continuous playing around was a sore point," he remarked dryly. But he insisted he never hurt her.

"I never raised a finger in anger at Helle in my life," Crafts said. He claimed that their last night together was unremarkable: he made dinner for her when she returned from her flight, and they watched TV. He said he assumed when she left the next morning that she was going to his sister's, but she didn't actually say where she was going.

Everything else, according to the defendant, was a coincidence or misunderstanding. When he said Helle called him a day or so after she disappeared, he meant a different Helle, one of his wife's friends (but she hadn't called either, the woman testified in rebuttal). Yes, he rented a wood chipper, but merely to clear brush on his property. True, he bought a new freezer, but only to store the frozen food his wife bought in bulk. (Crafts also had his brother-in-law dispose of the freezer while he was in jail.) He said the stain his nanny noticed on the rug was kerosene he spilled while refilling a portable heater during the blackout (a claim Dr. Lee refuted in experiments with various types of kerosene, showing that none left a dark stain behind).

Crafts claimed that he believed his wife was still alive.

"I certainly hope she is," he told the jury. "I hope she's coming home soon."

The trial of Richard Crafts was the first murder prosecution in Connecticut history without a body. Despite overwhelming evidence against him, the case ended in mistrial after seventeen days of deliberation—a state record—after a lone holdout refused to continue deliberating with the rest of the panel.

The holdout, forty-seven-year-old Warren Maskell, so infuriated his fellow jurors that they asked if he could be prosecuted for misconduct. They claimed he violated the judge's instructions, discussing the case with his wife and reading newspaper coverage; repeatedly forgot testimony; and behaved irrationally. An Army veteran who told jurors he had killed in Vietnam, Maskell strongly identified with the defendant. He was not convinced that Helle was dead, a belief based at least in part on the erroneous idea that Helle's mother had smiled at her son-in-law from the witness stand.

Crafts had dodged the bullet, at least temporarily. While in jail awaiting retrial, he vowed, like Ewing Scott, that he'd rather die in custody than admit that he had anything to do with his wife's disappearance.

At the second trial, his brother-in-law testified against him, revealing how Crafts had bragged that divers searching the Housatonic River would never find Helle's body because "it's gone." He was equally unconcerned when police tracked down the wood chipper. He had seen to it that no one could ever prove his wife was even dead, much less that he murdered her—or so he thought.

The defense conceded nothing the second time around, but asked that the jury be given the option of manslaughter in addition to murder, arguing that even if Crafts did kill his wife, there was no convincing evidence that the crime was planned.

The jury rejected that argument, convicting Crafts of first-degree murder. In early 1990 he was sentenced to fifty years in prison. He could, however, be released after as little as twenty years.

Some eraser killers are willing to do anything to get away with murder, including eliminating those who threaten to bring them to justice.

When Nashville attorney Perry March was finally arrested for killing his wife, Janet, he hired a fellow inmate to kill his wife's parents, believing that without their efforts to bring him to justice, the case against him would fall apart. His in-laws, Lawrence and Carolyn Levine, had loved March as they would their own son, paying his way through prestigious Vanderbilt law school and hiring him to work in Lawrence's own practice. But he paid them back by stealing from the firm, murdering their daughter, refusing to let them see their grandchildren after the murder, and trying to kill them on several occasions as well.

Through his legal skills and sheer chutzpah, March had managed to elude justice for a decade, eventually moving to Mexico, where he believed he was beyond the arm of the law. He was so confident that he would never be held accountable that a year after the murder he penned a manuscript for a ghoulish police-procedural novel called "@murder.com," trumpeting his knowledge of forensics and other investigatory techniques.

At the time police arrested March and extradited him back to the United States in 2005, the case against him was not appreciably stronger than it had been in 1996, when March claimed that his wife left on an impromptu solo vacation and never returned—offering as proof a twenty-three-item to-do list of tasks he said his wife had typed up and forced him to sign promising to complete before she returned, including tasks as routine as changing light bulbs and balancing their checkbook. He may very well have been able to beat the system at trial, but his narcissistic need to stack the deck and bend the world to his will gave the state of Tennessee the smoking gun it needed to put him away.

March was so Machiavellian that he had enlisted his own father after the murder to help him dispose of his wife's body and to coordinate the logistics with the hit man he hired to kill the Levines. But the second murder plot was foiled when the would-be assassin got cold feet, contacted authorities, and agreed to record conversations with March and his father. Janet's body was never found, but based in part on his father's own statements against him, he was convicted in 2006 of murder and conspiracy to commit murder and was sentenced to fifty-six years in prison.

Probably no one has gone to greater lengths to cover up the murder of a spouse, and been more successful at eluding justice, than Robert Durst. The heir to a billion-dollar Manhattan real estate fortune, Durst is suspected of three separate killings over a quarter century, all stemming from the mysterious disappearance of his wife Kathleen in 1982. He has been charged with only one of the murders, a case that ended in acquittal even after Durst took the stand and admitted killing and dismembering his victim and submerging the body parts in Galveston Bay.

Kathie Durst, twenty-nine, was just three months away from graduating from New York's Albert Einstein School of Medicine when she vanished after spending a tumultuous weekend with her husband in a cottage they owned in Westchester County outside New York City. At the end of the weekend, Durst claimed he stayed on in Westchester and put his wife on a commuter train back to their Manhattan apartment, as she had classes to attend in the city the following morning.

They had first met when Kathie, then a nineteen-year-old tenant in a building his family owned, came to his office to pay her rent. Durst swept her off her feet, jetting her around the world and taking her to star-studded events. On their second date he asked her to move in with him, and two years later they tied the knot. It seemed like a fairy tale, but it was too good to be true. Durst had a dark side, an anger that perhaps stemmed from witnessing his mother jump to her death from the roof of their home when he was seven years old.

The marriage turned abusive when Kathie began pursuing a career. Durst had millions of dollars at his fingertips, but he wouldn't pay for his wife's medical school tuition. He cheated on her and forced her to get an abortion. Once while visiting her mother, Durst grabbed Kathie by the hair and yanked her off the couch when he wanted to leave and she didn't. A few weeks before she disappeared, she was treated in the ER for contusions to her head and face. She told several of her friends that she feared for her life and wanted out of the marriage.

"If something happens to me, check it out; I'm afraid of what Bobby will do," Kathie said in her last conversation with girlfriend Gilberte Najamy on the same day that Durst claimed he last saw her. It wasn't the first time Kathie had made such an ominous statement to her friends, but it would be the last. She had gone alone to a party Najamy was throwing that Sunday, but left abruptly to return to her husband at the Westchester house after he angrily called and demanded she come home.

Kathie never showed up at school that Monday morning, and no one ever saw her again. But someone claiming to be her called the dean's office at Albert Einstein College and said she was sick and would not be coming in that day (a strange thing to do because students did not report absences to the dean's office). Police believe Kathie never lived to see Monday, that Durst killed her that Sunday and somehow disposed of her body. That call, however, was tantamount to an alibi for Durst because it made it seem that Kathie had made it back to the city alive after her weekend with Robert.

Jeanine Pirro, former Westchester County district attorney, who believed Durst killed his wife and who reopened the cold case eighteen years after Kathie's disappearance, suspected that the person who made that call was actually Susan Berman, a college friend of Durst's who acted as his spokesperson after Kathie's disappearance. The two were so close that Berman, a writer, dedicated some of her books to Durst, and he gave her away at her wedding. One of the bonds Berman and Durst shared was that both of their mothers had committed suicide. At one point, she had even considered asking Durst to father the child she so desperately wanted.

When Pirro reopened the investigation into Kathie's murder, investigators from the district attorney's office planned to interview Berman, but they never got a chance. On Christmas Eve 2000, she was found dead in her Los Angeles home, shot once execution style in the back of the head. There was no sign of struggle or forced entry. In fact, both the front and back doors were found unlocked—a strange fact, considering that Berman was notorious for her paranoia about security, always keeping her doors locked—leading police to conclude that she must have known and trusted her killer very well to have let him in.

Police believe Durst killed Berman to eliminate the one witness who could potentially do him harm. Shortly before she died, Durst sent Berman two checks totaling $50,000, leading authorities to wonder if he had been attempting to buy her silence.

Five days before she was killed, Berman told a close friend, "I have information that is going to blow the top off things." After Susan's death, one of her friends told *New York* magazine that Berman had made the "false alibi" call but believed Durst was innocent. Police say they have documentation proving that Durst was in Los Angeles at the time of Berman's killing, but he has never been charged with that murder either.

—~~~—

After Pirro reopened the investigation into Kathie Durst's disappearance and again after the murder of Susan Berman, Robert Durst went on the lam, crisscrossing the country using a series of stolen identities, both male and female. He eventually ended up at a seedy Texas boardinghouse, where he dressed in drag and posed as a mute woman who communicated only in writing and paid her rent in unsigned money orders.

There in 2001 at the age of sixty, Durst killed a seventy-one-year-old neighbor named Morris Black. He claimed Black was shot in the face accidentally when he found Black in his room and they struggled over a gun. Prosecutors believe he planned to kill Black, who looked somewhat like Durst, in order to assume his identity.

One fact is unassailable. Robert Durst knows how to get rid of a body. By his own admission he dismembered Morris Black with a bow saw and paring knife, placed the body parts in plastic garbage bags, and dumped them in Galveston Bay. He believed that the tide would take the remains out to sea, but instead it caused them to wash up near the shore—all except for the head, which Durst disposed of somewhere else because he feared it was most identifiable. Hack marks indicated that he also tried unsuccessfully to cut off Black's fingertips, presumably to prevent fingerprint identification should the remains be discovered.

A few days after the body was identified, Durst was arrested when he was pulled over in a traffic stop and the patrolman noticed a bow saw on the floor of the car. The license number on the car had been tied to the mysterious woman who had lived down the hall from Black and in whose room police found a blood trail that connected to Black's room.

Facing ninety-nine years in prison if convicted of Black's murder, Durst jumped his $300,000 bail and once again went on the lam, posing as his murdered neighbor, shaving his head and eyebrows to look even more like Morris Black. He was apparently hoping to stay hidden for a good long time. While at large he had his second wife attempt to withdraw $1.8 million from one of his accounts, only to discover that authorities had frozen it. (Kathie had not been declared legally dead, but Durst had legally divorced her in 1990 claiming "abandonment," and remarried in 2000. This was yet another shock to Kathie's friends and family, none of whom knew Robert had ever remarried until after he was arrested for the Black murder.)

He was caught not by crack detectives but by supermarket security guards in Pennsylvania for shoplifting a sandwich, even though he was found to have $37,000 in the trunk of the car he had rented under Black's name. Also inside the car were two guns and a notebook that contained a list of aliases Durst was using, and the workplace address of Kathie's friend Gilberte Najamy, who had lobbied tirelessly for Durst to be prosecuted for his wife's murder. Was she next on his hit list?

After failing to win motions seeking to suppress the saw found in his car, and a paring knife and other bloody evidence found in his rooming house trash, Durst admitted that he killed Black, but claimed he did so only in self-defense.

In his opening statement, Durst's lawyer said that his client suffered from Asperger's syndrome, a mild form of autism that he claimed dulled Durst's emotions so much that he could not become angry enough to commit murder. The syndrome also, conveniently, caused him to go into a fugue state after the killing and remember nothing about his attempts to conceal Morris Black's body, the lawyer said.

But the defense never put on the psychiatric expert hired to back up that assertion. Instead, Durst took the stand, testifying that he got rid of Black's body in a panic because he feared no one would believe the killing was an accident.

Security camera footage of Durst calmly paying Black's rent a few hours after the murder so that no one would know he was missing, however, belies his assertion that he was in a panicked or dissociative state. A witness also identified Durst as a man who asked her one day shortly before the killing whether the place he later dumped the body parts was a good place for night fishing, which seemed to indicate that he had scouted out a dumping spot in advance and thus had premeditated the crime.

Astonishingly, in his closing argument, one of Durst's defense lawyers blamed Black's death on the Westchester DA's "hounding" of his client for his wife's murder, insisting that if "Ms. Pirro had kept her mouth shut, none of this would have happened."

That statement sounded eerily like words Durst himself wrote in the notebook police found when they apprehended him six weeks after jumping bail, in which he seemed to blame the whole tragic course of his life on his dead wife, railing about "what Kathy did to me." He couldn't even bother to spell her name the way Kathie preferred it spelled.

Durst eluded justice one more time. In a verdict that seemed to stun even the defendant, who stood with his mouth agape, the Texas jury acquitted Durst, concluding there was not enough evidence to prove that he intentionally murdered Morris Black. Local authorities found a way to keep him in custody a while longer by charging him with tampering with evidence—for hiding and dismembering Morris's dead body—and bond jumping.

While Durst was in custody on those charges, one of the trial jurors actually visited Durst several times and even referred him to a realtor so that he could find a new place to live in Galveston. That raised a suspicion in the minds of some fellow jurors as well as the trial judge that Durst may have paid off the juror. An investigation was launched, and some of the visits between the two were tape-recorded by sheriff's deputies, but no evidence of jury tampering was found.

Another five years have passed since the Black trial, and it seems more and more likely that no one will ever be held accountable for the disappearance of Kathie Durst. No body, no crime. The Durst case is another example reinforcing the widespread belief that a killer clever enough to erase his victim will never be punished.

Today Durst is a free man. In 2006, while serving out his parole in Texas after being released from jail on the cutting-up-the-corpse charge, he had one more brush with the law, running into the trial judge at a mall beyond the jurisdiction he was allowed to travel. After she reported the violation to the parole board, she found something very disturbing outside her home: the severed head of a cat.

—⁓—

Men who kill their wives or girlfriends are hardly ever given the harshest punishment, even when their crime involves multiple victims or some other "special circumstance"—such as lying in wait, murder for financial gain, or murder by solicitation—that would make them eligible for capital punishment. From the judges and juries who decide cases to the prosecutors who determine how to charge them, people largely still view domestic homicide as a rash, unplanned act committed in the heat of the moment. Very often when a conviction is obtained it is for second-degree murder—meaning that the killing was intentional but not premeditated.

University of New Mexico law professor Elizabeth Rapaport refers to this phenomenon as the domestic discount, a tendency in the law and in sentencing policy to view domestic homicide as mitigated by some emotional suffering from which the killer was seeking relief—in essence, the belief that killing an intimate partner is by its very nature a "hot-blooded" crime of passion, not cold-blooded premeditated murder. In a study she conducted of all men sentenced to death in six states from 1976 to 1991, Rapaport found that less than 12 percent of those who received the ultimate sanction had killed an intimate partner or other family member.

However, the discount appears to apply only to men. Half of all the women in the United States who are on Death Row are there for committing domestic homicide.

At the very least, the killing of an intimate partner is viewed as a crime not likely to be repeated. The most emotionally compelling argument Scott Peterson's attorneys made for sparing his life was that he was not the "worst of the worst," no Adolf Hitler or even Charles Manson, not someone who would kill again. However, that argument overlooks the fact that Peterson had already taken two lives, and perhaps was considering eliminating the woman who was working with police to bring him down.

A surprising number of eraser killers do kill again, or attempt to. Some, like Barton Corbin and John Smith, murder a subsequent wife or girlfriend and are only caught after a second or third murder. Others kill someone they fear may expose them, as Steven Poaches said he was prepared to do to the man he asked to help him move his victim's body. Still others, such as Perry March and Bryce Thomas, turn their aggression against those who may be attempting to hold them accountable for their original crime.

John David Smith erased at least two women from his life—maybe more.

Fran Gladden Smith, forty-nine, was still practically a newlywed when she vanished from their New Jersey home in 1991. Her husband of sixteen months claimed that he came home from work one day to find his wife gone, and a note reading simply "Going away for a few days. Don't forget to feed the fish." He wasn't concerned. He said he just assumed she had gone to visit relatives.

Fran's relatives have never believed that she took off on her own or left behind such a cryptic note (which Smith said he threw away). Fran was barely mobile at the time she disappeared, still recovering from a broken hip she had suffered a month before on their belated honeymoon, and could not even walk without the assistance of crutches.

Thanks largely to the efforts of Fran's sister and daughter, who pursued their own dogged investigation and discovered that Smith had a previous wife who had also mysteriously disappeared, John Smith is in prison today—but not for Fran's murder.

John told Fran when they first met that he had never been married before. But Smith, as Fran's horrified relatives later discovered, was a master of deceit. He lied about having a college degree; he was actually a dropout. He convinced employers that he was an aeronautical engineer when he was really just a computer programmer. He lied about his upbringing. He used altered names and the Social Security number of an exotic dancer.

While he was married to Fran he was leading a full-blown double life—spending weekdays with Fran in New Jersey, and weekends in

Connecticut with his "fiancé," Sheila Sautter, a woman he had been seeing for eight years. Neither had any idea the other existed. Smith's girlfriend believed his job required him to live away from "home" during the week. His wife believed that he spent weekends renovating a beach house he was "renting out."

Three months after Fran went missing, as he got dressed one morning at the beach house, Smith turned to Sautter and as casually as if commenting on the weather said, "By the way, I'm married. And she's missing."

Smith had also lied to Fran when he claimed never to have been married. In fact, in 1970, when he was nineteen years old, John had eloped with his high school sweetheart, Janice Hartman. Four years later, just three days after Janice's divorce from Smith was finalized, John reported Janice missing (claiming that he believed she, too, had gone to visit relatives).

But like so many erased women, Janice was never lost. John knew where she was all the time: in a plywood box he had built for her in his grandparents' Ohio garage. To make her corpse fit into the too-small box, about the size of a set of golf clubs, he sawed off her legs below the knees. For five years, she remained in the garage in her makeshift coffin, until Smith's curious younger brother, Michael, pried open the box one day and recognized his sister-in-law's mummified face.

Smith's grandfather made a family decision not to call Janice's relatives or report John to the police. Instead, he called John and ordered him to remove the box. Smith immediately drove the three hundred miles to collect it, put it in his car, and drove away. When he got to Indiana he tossed the box, with Janice's remains still inside, into a ditch alongside of the highway.

—~~~—

For a decade after she was found by a highway work crew, Janice was known as the "Lady in the Box," more formally as Jane Doe, the name under which she was buried in Indiana. She wasn't identified by DNA until 2000, some twenty-six years after she had gone missing. After years of pressure from authorities, John's brother eventually revealed the story of the box to the FBI. He recalled that when John built the strange contraption, he told him that Janice was a narc and had gone into the witness protection program. He asked Michael to help him clear all Janice's possessions out of their house, and he remembered seeing his brother rolling up some of her clothes and placing them around the edge of the box.

Agents began looking for Jane Does in Ohio but found no one who matched the "Lady in the Box." Eventually they started checking neighboring states and got around to Indiana.

In 2001, John Smith was sentenced to fifteen years to life for the killing of Janice Hartman. He will be eligible for parole after serving just ten. The trial judge did not allow the jury to hear evidence about Smith's second wife going missing as well.

"There are certainly some similar circumstances surrounding the disappearance of the defendant's first two wives," he wrote. "But the court finds lacking the substantial proof required before it can admit this evidence."

Fran Gladden Smith remains missing, and her family keeps searching. In a chilling postscript, during a search of a storage unit rented by Smith, police found pictures of some women they have not been able to identify, one wearing a wedding ring, and several fragments of bone identified as being from the skull of an unknown woman. That discovery raised a horrifying new specter. Could John Smith have still other missing wives out there?

CHAPTER SIX

Hiding in Plain Sight

Some killers erase not their victim but the crime they have committed. They make it appear that their wife or girlfriend died not in a domestic homicide but as the result of a tragic accident, a suicide, or a crime perpetrated by someone other than her intimate partner—such as a robbery turned homicide, a carjacking, or a rape-murder.

One might say that in this variation, the killer is hiding in plain sight. He does not disappear his victim's body. In fact, he wants her to be found, wants there to be an explanation for her death that clears him of any involvement. What he erases is the true nature of the crime, the actual motive, and his responsibility for her death. He may destroy and alter evidence at the true crime scene, or he may stage a completely phony scenario to account for the victim's death.

In some ways, this type of killing is easier to pull off than a more classic erasure. The man doesn't have to get rid of a body and account in any way for his partner's absence, doesn't have to pretend to search for her, doesn't have to keep the ruse of an open-ended mystery going over a long period of time. The crime is done and over with in one fell swoop. He can move on with his life without a shadow or question hanging over him; he may even be viewed with sympathy as the victim of a horrible tragedy. If he can distance himself from any appearance of involvement in the killing, he can get away with murder.

In other ways, however, the staging and deception involved in these disguised partner homicides are more difficult and risky than simply vanishing the victim. They require erasing all evidence of the actual crime and fabricating a scenario that is logically consistent with the story he is trying to tell.

Like that of a stage director, his goal is to create an alternate "reality" over which he is in complete control: setting the scene, dressing the set, directing the action, choreographing the movements of the players. Unlike an ordinary director, whose passive theater audience is willing to suspend disbelief, the director of this illusion must be able to pass the scrutiny of police, forensic, and medical investigators wandering through his set, picking up the props, checking behind the false fronts. One must be truly Machiavellian to be able to fool so many trained skeptics, or even to believe one could do so.

In constructing these elaborate illusions, they draw from their environment, their background, something that seems plausible in their view of the world. For an eraser killer from the inner city, that might mean staging a murder that appears to be a random street crime. Someone with training in science might draw on his specialized knowledge, killing by stealth with poison. Chester Gillette, for example, knew that boating accidents were fairly common in the lakes of the Adirondacks where he committed his crime and that most of them were not subjected to lengthy investigation.

An added thrill for this type of eraser killer is getting away with murder right under the nose of the law. One of the reasons we have no good statistics for how often murder by erasure occurs is that the true nature of many of these crimes is never detected. Instead, they are written off as accidental deaths, suicides, or other types of murders committed by unknown suspects or, worse yet, by innocent men wrongfully convicted.

—∿—

Perhaps the most nefarious of this breed of eraser killer are those who attempt to make a murder look like a suicide—in essence, making the victim out to be her own killer. These murderers inflict not only the trauma of sudden loss on the victim's friends and family but also the stigma of feeling complicit in the death, for not recognizing the victim's emotional pain and doing something to prevent the tragedy.

Atlanta dentist Barton Corbin may be one of the most audacious eraser killers ever. In 1990, he staged the killing of his girlfriend to look like a suicide and managed to fool authorities into believing she had taken her own life. Fourteen years later, he tried it again in the exact same way, this time with his wife.

He was ultimately caught and held accountable for both crimes, not because of lack of planning or care in execution, but only because his narcissism and Machiavellian arrogance blinded him to the danger of sticking so scrupulously to the same plan.

Neuroscientists have been studying this aspect of the psychopathic mind for years, but recent research indicates that psychopaths may have considerable difficulty processing "bottom-up" information. That is, they may be able to conceive a plan at the abstract level and carry it out in detail, but they have difficulty learning from or adapting to changes in the complex world outside themselves—the things they did not plan or create themselves.

Getting away with murder gives the eraser killer reinforcement that his plan was brilliant and that he was able to manipulate people and prove himself smarter than and superior to everyone around him—a veritable Nietzschean Superman. But he remains unable to take the long view, unable to understand that when another woman close to him dies in precisely the same way, or three or four wives seemingly walk off the face of the earth, he is dangerously pushing the odds. And because psychopaths have a greatly dampened fear response, he is unable cognitively to read signs of danger even to himself.

—〰—

Barton Corbin was a bright, football-loving Georgia dental student the first time he erased a woman. On June 6, 1990, three days before his graduation, his recently estranged girlfriend, classmate Dorothy "Dolly" Hearn, was found dead on her couch in her Augusta apartment from a single gunshot wound to the head, a pistol lying in her lap. Corbin was called a "person of interest," but neither the medical examiner nor an independent pathologist hired by Hearn's family could rule out suicide. The means of death was ruled undetermined, and Corbin was not charged.

Even though Corbin had made very visible his anger over the fact that Dolly had refused to reconcile with him, he was not thoroughly investigated. Six months before Hearn's death, when she first broke off with him, Corbin engaged in disturbing stalking behavior about which she had filed several police reports: breaking into her home, stealing her mail, vandalizing her car, stealing expensive dental tools and equipment she needed for school, pouring hair spray in her contact lens solution. He even kidnapped her cat.

Dolly had told several friends and neighbors that Corbin was harassing her, and was so fearful for her life that she asked to stay at a friend's house when her roommate was out of town. Her dad was so concerned for her safety that he lent her a gun for her protection—the gun that was used to kill her. Corbin admitted to a friend that he staked out her apartment one night with a gun. Another friend was so worried about Corbin's mental state that she begged his mother to hospitalize him so that he could get psychiatric treatment.

A few days before Dolly's death, Corbin told a friend that he had come up with a plan for the perfect murder.

One of the reasons that Corbin got a pass on his first killing was his skill in stage management. After Hearn's roommate came home and found Dolly, it was a deputy sheriff who first arrived on the scene and managed the investigation. What he saw was a young woman seated almost comfortably on a sofa, a .38-caliber handgun in her lap, dead from bullet wound to the right temple. With the help of others from the county sheriff's office (there were no forensically trained crime scene investigators at that time as there are today), he found no sign of forced entry, no signs of burglary or other crime, and no indication at all that any struggle had taken place. He wrote his judgment in his report—suicide.

When the coroner arrived, he made a brief examination of the victim and scene, and soon thereafter medics arrived to put Dolly in a body bag and take her away. There was no effort to secure a crime scene or check for fibers, fingerprints, or footprints, because the first impression of suicide was not questioned, and therefore the room was not considered a crime scene per se. Although Dolly's family and friends were extremely distressed at the cursory investigation her death received, the almost self-fulfilling nature of such quick labeling (no physical evidence of a crime was found in part because none was sought) is typical of many deaths labeled suicide. Although her family made attempts to investigate the case on their own after the fact, the handling—or mishandling—of the investigation in the first twenty-four hours gave this eraser killer all the extra advantage he needed to get away with murder.

—⁓—

Fourteen years later, on December 4, 2004, Jennifer Corbin, the woman Bart Corbin married in 1996, was found dead under almost identical circumstances: sitting up in her bed, a single shot to the head, a gun resting under her hand. Their seven-year-old son, Dalton, found his mother when he got up in the morning and ran next door screaming, "My daddy shot my mommy." He hadn't actually seen or heard anything, but he assumed that's what happened based on a frightening incident he'd witnessed the week before. In the car on the way home from Thanksgiving dinner with Jennifer's family, Corbin punched his wife in the face in front of their two children.

Corbin had discovered that his wife had fallen for someone she had met in an Internet game room—someone Jennifer initially believed to be a man named Christopher, but who eventually revealed herself to be a woman named Anita Hearn (no relation to Dolly Hearn). The woman lived in Missouri, and she and Jennifer had never even met. But after discovering explicit e-mails the two had exchanged, Bart was enraged—despite the fact that he had been having an affair of his own throughout his entire marriage, a relationship he continued after Jennifer died.

He was determined to prevent his wife from enjoying any of the fruits of their marital union. So extreme was his narcissistic rage that on the Monday after Thanksgiving, he filed for divorce, asking the court to grant him their house, custody of their two children, and child support, even though he was the primary wage earner in the family. A few days later, Jennifer called 911 after she caught her husband taking several items from her purse, including her cell phone and journal.

Neither Jennifer nor Dolly had gunshot residue on their hands, although the test for the presence of soot and particles expelled when the person fires a gun is not always accurate. More suspiciously, there were no fingerprints at all on the gun next to Jennifer.

Bart tested negative for gunshot residue as well, but he didn't take the test until a full day after the shooting. The reason for the delay was that on the day they found Jennifer, Corbin refused to come to the police department, to take a telephone call, or even to collect his two traumatized children. He hid out at his twin brother's home in Auburn, Georgia, and refused to give any statement to investigators.

His brother would try to provide him an alibi, claiming that Bart was at his house the night Jennifer died. But Bart's cell phone records would show that he was, in fact, near the murder scene at the time the medical examiner estimated that his wife died.

As investigators began looking into this second mysterious death, ugly facts and hidden truths emerged about his relationship with each of the dead women. After the second killing, several people finally came forward who had withheld potentially damning information about the Hearn case for fourteen years. Corbin had begged a dental school classmate not to tell police that he knew Dolly's father had given her the gun that was found in her lap. Corbin had admitted to another friend that he had been at Dolly's apartment and argued with her the day she died. Dental school classmates recalled his explosive temper. He had seemed to be most angry about the fact that Dolly was not as aggrieved by their breakup as he was.

A few weeks after Jennifer died, authorities in both jurisdictions brought murder charges against Corbin. Forensic experts who reexamined photos of Dolly Hearn believed that the pattern of blood spatter showed that her body was repositioned after she was shot. (At the time of the killing, no one on the force had expertise in spatter analysis.) Investigators came up with eyewitnesses who were able to place Bart Corbin at Hearn's apartment the day she died.

"The motive is clear," said Danny Craig, Gwinnett County district attorney. "You don't break up with Barton Corbin. If you do, you pay with your life."

Corbin was scheduled to stand trial first for his wife's murder in Gwinnett County, Georgia, then in Richmond County for the killing of Dolly. The Gwinnett DA asked the court for permission to introduce information about the previous killing in his case under the rarely invoked but well-established legal principle known as "similar transaction evidence." Information on a separate offense is usually inadmissible, but the prosecution argued that the staged suicides of Jennifer and Dolly were so similar that they revealed an unassailable pattern pointing solely to Corbin.

The defense launched a full-court press of motions, first and foremost to try to prevent the jury from learning about the other case. Corbin's lawyers argued that introducing evidence that he had previously killed another intimate partner would be "highly prejudicial." They attacked the search warrants served on his home and the wiretap placed on his phone—which picked up Corbin coldly referring to Dolly Hearn as "that Augusta bitch." They charged that Jennifer committed suicide because she feared losing her kids in a custody fight because of her romantic relationship with a woman. They filed a motion arguing that charges should be dropped in the Hearn case because too much time had passed and witnesses had changed their statements, evidence had been lost, and the defense could not examine the crime scene. In one motion, dripping with sarcasm that verged on contempt, they asked that the trial be delayed another fourteen years so that the recollections of witnesses could complete an "evolutionary epoch" and evolve back into the "truth."

Corbin had done everything he could to avoid ever being charged with murder, and now he was complaining that the delay in prosecution was preventing him from getting a fair trial.

As the first trial drew near, the prosecution had built a fairly strong circumstantial case. The Georgia Supreme Court refused to block the trial judge's decision to allow the similar transaction evidence, meaning that the jury would hear evidence about both deaths. According to the state's forensic experts, Jennifer's injury was inconsistent with suicide. Judging by the angle of the wound, they stated that it would have been difficult if not impossible for Jennifer to have shot herself. The medical examiner also determined that Mrs. Corbin would have died instantly, dropping the weapon. Yet both Jennifer's hand and the gun were tucked partially under the covers. How could that have happened if she had killed herself? More likely, Corbin killed Jennifer while she was asleep, then propped her up in a sitting position and rearranged the covers.

Interestingly, the divorce papers Corbin filed were on the bed next to her. The defense claimed that this fact supported the suicide theory, that Jennifer was so distraught at the thought of potentially losing her children that she decided to end it all right then and there. However, Jennifer had never been served with those papers. If Corbin placed them there, one could interpret that as further staging of his suicide scenario or as a coup de grace: Madam, you have been served!

The most damning piece of evidence against Corbin, the fact that clinched the case, did not fall into place until jury selection had already commenced.

For two years, authorities had been attempting to link Corbin to the gun that killed his wife. Police had long suspected that Richard Wilson, a good friend of Corbin's, had given him the gun, but Wilson denied it and refused to testify before the grand jury. They were unable to compel him to testify because he lived out of state, in Troy, Alabama, and police did not have strong enough evidence to exercise jurisdiction over him. Investigators leaned on Wilson time and time again, but the answer was always the same. He did not see Corbin any time around the murder and did not give him a gun. On the eve of trial, after an exhaustive search by multiple police agencies, they finally managed to trace the gun— to Troy, Alabama, where several years before police had run a check on the gun at the request of none other than Richard Wilson.

Once again, Corbin was betrayed by his cell phone records, which showed that he was in Troy the day after he filed for divorce and just five days before Jennifer died. On the second day of jury selection, the DA asked Troy's police chief to take a run at Wilson. At long last, Wilson broke and admitted that Corbin had come to see him that day and asked for the gun, saying that his wife was having an affair and that he needed a weapon for protection.

Of course, if Corbin had simply wanted "protection," he could have bought a gun in Georgia, which is one of the easiest states in the country when it comes to purchasing firearms. Unless Corbin was planning something illegal, there was no reason for him to spend eight hours on the road driving to Alabama and back to acquire something that was available right where he lived.

Wilson's begrudging admission was, in the words of prosecutors, "the straw that broke the camel's back." They had managed to put the gun in Barton Corbin's hand. The defense made a last-ditch effort to try to keep the friend out of court, filing a motion to quash an order allowing prosecutors to call Wilson as a material witness. But an Alabama judge ruled that Wilson would have to testify.

Corbin knew that if he was convicted of killing Jennifer, he could face the death penalty in the Hearn case. (The murder conviction could then be used as an aggravating factor in arguing for execution in the second case.) He agreed to a deal, taking death off the table in exchange for life in prison for both murders, with the possibility for parole in fourteen years.

In entering his formal plea in court on September 15, 2006, Corbin simply answered yes when asked by the judge if he committed murder. He offered neither an explanation nor an apology, in classic eraser-killer fashion expressing no remorse even when pleading guilty. His lawyer said on the record that Corbin made the decision "for many reasons, the most important one being not to have his children relive all of these things"—children he clearly cared so little about that he had allowed them to find their mother's body and then refused to comfort and console them after the life-shattering experience.

—‌ᴧᴧᴧ—

In committing his eraser crimes, Barton Corbin relied on the perception that women are likely to become despondent and suicidal when a relationship breaks up, regardless of whether those women have promising careers, new love, or children to live for. By sheer force of Machiavellian will he believed that he could commit cold-blooded murder, not once but twice, without anyone ever noticing. It seems hard to believe that anybody could be so presumptuous, so confident in his ability to manipulate everyone around him like characters on a stage. Yet his plan worked perfectly . . . once. Every time an eraser killer wields such godlike power over others it reinforces his belief that he can do anything he wants, that he is immune to the laws of man and nature.

Justin Barber was so convinced of his ability to defy nature that he was confident he could control the path of a bullet. On August 17, 2002, the thirty-year-old business analyst shot his twenty-seven-year-old wife, April, in the face and also shot himself in the hand, both shoulders, and right chest—telling police that a mugger had attacked them as they took a romantic moonlight walk along a deserted beach near Jacksonville, Florida, after going out to dinner to celebrate their third wedding anniversary. Whereas April's single wound was fatal, none of those to Justin was life threatening. The chest wound was a glancing one that did not even require surgery.

The beach was in an extremely secluded location, behind sand dunes in a state park that was closed to visitors at night. It was a place, according to Barber, they came to on special occasions, reminiscent of their beachfront wedding in the Bahamas.

Barber claimed he struggled with the gunman, blacked out after the first shot, and woke up to find his wife floating in the surf. He said that he tried nine different ways to carry her to their car, from throwing her over his shoulder like a sack of potatoes to dragging her by the waist of her pants, but was unable to get very far in his weakened state, and abandoned her at the foot of a boardwalk a hundred yards from the water's edge.

He did manage to make it to the car on his own and then drive ten miles before flagging down a passing motorist. His wife's cell phone was in the car, but he claimed he couldn't find it. He also passed countless homes and businesses, and presumably other motorists, in those ten miles, but did not stop to ask for help. He claimed to detectives that he hadn't wanted to wake people if their lights were out, but there were gas stations and fast-food restaurants and other twenty-four-hour businesses open along the route. Did he drive a good distance to give his wife time to die, and give himself time to get rid of the gun?

Barber's story never made much sense. Although he claimed that the phantom stranger had demanded money, he admitted that nothing was taken from either himself or his wife, even though both were allegedly unconscious and unable to resist after the attack. And if three of his wounds were incurred after he passed out, as he claimed, why were they so superficial?

More disturbingly, the pattern of blood flow from his wife's injuries, which ran directly down the side of her face in one direction, and the absence of blood anywhere else on the beach belied his description of having transported his wife in so many different positions. The medical examiner determined that April was shot where she lay on the walkway, not where Barber claimed the attack had occurred. Prosecutors theorized at his 2006 trial that he first incapacitated his wife by holding her under the water until she lost consciousness, then carried her to the walkway and shot her. White foam, from inhaling salt water, was pooled below her nose and mouth.

—∿—

Justin Barber was having an affair with Shannon Kennedy, his "tennis partner" at the time of the murder, a woman he met at a local hotel's car rental desk. Like Scott Peterson and Amber Frey, Barber and Kennedy had been seeing each other for only a few weeks at the time Barber's wife was murdered. He initially hid from her the fact that he was married. When she did find out and wanted to stop seeing him, he told her he loved her and couldn't live without her.

In testimony to a grand jury convened to investigate his wife's killing, Barber admitted to four other affairs, two with coworkers and two with women he met in bars. For the last year of his marriage, he and his wife weren't even living together, as he had taken a job out of state and only saw April on weekends.

As Chris Francis, the assistant state's prosecutor, put it at Barber's 2006 trial, "He was living the life of a single man."

He had also run up more than $50,000 in debt through day trading, recklessly buying and selling stocks. He financed his trading by getting cash advances on his credit cards.

According to her best friend, April had confronted her husband with suspicions that he and Kennedy were having an affair. Although he denied it, the friend said April told him on the actual date of their anniversary—two weeks before the murder—that she wanted a divorce. Barber later admitted that his wife asked him if he was having an affair, but denied that she said she would end the marriage. He claimed that their relationship was still loving and amicable the night of their belated anniversary dinner and shoreline stroll.

However, Barber's plan to kill his wife seems to have been in the works long before April found out about his cheating and threatened to leave him. A little less than a year before his wife died, Barber took out a $2 million life insurance policy on himself and April. It was an extraordinarily high amount of insurance to carry on a spouse who earned a relatively modest income as a radiation therapist.

Then, six months before she died, Barber did something that appeared even more suspicious, in light of what happened that day on the beach. Forensic analysis of his computer unearthed the fact that on Valentine's Day, no less, Barber did a Google search on his computer using the search terms "trauma cases gunshot right chest"—the exact part of the body where, six months later, he received his most potentially dangerous wound. Six days after that search, he searched again, Googling "medical trauma gunshot chest."

Police also discovered that he had purchased a bulletproof vest on eBay a few months before the killing, which he claimed he had done simply out of curiosity.

"What are the odds of somebody researching gunshot wounds to the right chest and getting a gunshot wound to the right chest six months later?" fellow prosecutor Matthew Fox said in his closing argument. "Those odds don't exist."

Police interpreted other activity found on his computer as indicating he was considering faking his own death. But it could just as easily be research he conducted to plan an eraser killing. He researched no-body murders and cases of missing persons being declared dead. He looked into how to get a death certificate in Mexico and the ability to collect on life insurance in the event of a homicide. He entered such specific queries as "How much blood is in the human body?" and "How much blood loss is required to be declared dead?"

He also researched bail bonds and moving to Brazil, apparently intent on doing whatever it took to get away with his crime. He never got the chance to flee, however. His mother and grandparents had put all their resources together, including title to the family farm, in hopes of securing his release, but bail was denied. He admitted in grand jury testimony that he knew Brazil did not have an extradition treaty with the United States.

Justin Barber was such a cool customer, so detached from normal human emotions, that on the day he carried out his grand plan, he took time out to play around on the Internet. In the hours before the murder, Barber downloaded sixteen songs to his computer, including a 1988 Guns N' Roses tune with the lyric "I used to love her but I had to kill her. . . . And now I'm happier this way."

—◌◌◌—

As soon as he was released from the hospital, Barber seemed ready to move on with his relationship with Shannon Kennedy, not returning to his home, but instead going to stay at the hotel where Kennedy worked and continuing to pursue her even though she refused to see him. At the same time, he denied having a relationship with Kennedy to police until detectives informed him that she was there at the station giving her own statement. One particularly disturbing thing Kennedy had told authorities was that right around the time of the murder, Barber started putting up pictures of his wife in his Jacksonville condo. He told her that relatives would be coming to town, and he needed to keep up appearances.

He filed to collect on the $2 million insurance policy within weeks of April's death, yet asked April's aunt to pay for his wife's burial, claiming he was broke. At her funeral, he avoided making eye contact with April's family and friends.

A few months after the murder, he transferred to a job all the way across the country, in Oregon, and quickly took up with a new woman. Two years passed before he was charged with killing April, as it took prosecutors a long time to feel that they had amassed a strong enough case. The fact that Justin was shot four times was one of the things that worried prosecutors. It seemed hard to believe someone would actually do that to himself.

The defense initially planned to point the finger at a convicted rapist who was arrested a year after the murder for assaulting women near the beach where April died. Barber's attorney filed court papers saying that his client saw a newspaper picture of the rapist and identified him as looking similar to the man he claimed attacked him and his wife. But cell phone and credit card records proved that this man was in Connecticut, a thousand miles away from Florida, on the night of the murder.

The jury was initially split, but after four days of deliberations found Barber guilty of first-degree murder. Barber declined to testify on his own behalf in both the guilt and penalty phases of his trial. After their guilty verdict, Barber's attorney announced to the stunned jurors that "on principle" Barber had refused to let any other relatives plead for his life.

"He will not . . . seek mercy for a crime that he did not commit," defense counsel Robert Willis explained. Willis simply entered into the record that his client had no criminal record and spoke for three minutes expressing incredulity at their verdict.

By a vote of eight to four, the jurors recommended a sentence of death over life in prison. Unlike most states, Florida only requires that a simple majority of jurors agree on the ultimate penalty. Three aggravating factors made Barber eligible for execution: "cold, calculated premeditation," financial motive, and that the murder was committed in an especially "heinous, atrocious and cruel fashion." Although judges usually follow a jury's recommendation, the trial judge opted instead for life in prison, saying that the murder "was not the most aggravated and unmitigated of crimes."

In an interview with the CBS news magazine *48 Hours* after his trial, Barber defended the verdict even while planning to appeal it.

"I would have never asked for mercy for the person who killed her," he said, still proclaiming his innocence. "If the jury believes that I'm that person, then they should send me to Death Row." Like L. Ewing Scott and so many other eraser killers, he was not about to admit his crime and ask for mercy, even if his silence meant receiving greater punishment.

Of all the methods used to conceal a murder and erase any connection to that death, poisoning is certainly the most time honored. Poisons and their detection have presented problems for the legal system for centuries. Today there are thousands of easily obtainable substances that in theory can be used to kill someone, ranging from prescription medicines, such as the benzodiazepine family of tranquilizers, to household chemicals like antifreeze, to toxic elements like mercury.

Most poisons can be detected in the body—that is, if someone takes the initiative to look for them. A killer with a working knowledge of human biology, chemistry, and the medical aspects of death, and, ideally, familiarity with how death is usually investigated, may be able to poison someone and get away with murder without raising any suspicions.

Robert Girts happened to have all those skills. The thirty-nine-year-old resident of Parma, Ohio, a suburb of Cleveland, was a licensed funeral director and embalmer. His job was to disguise the ugly aspects of death, to make the dead appear lifelike, serene, accepting of their fate. He had also worked earlier in his career for the county coroner's office, where he was able to learn quite a bit about "real-world" death investigation.

In September 1992, Girts's third wife, Diane, forty-two, was looking forward to moving into the home she and her husband had just purchased in a nearby town. Since shortly after their marriage two years before, the couple had been living in a rental unit on the grounds of one of the funeral homes where her husband worked.

"All Diane wanted to do since she was five years old was to get married and have the little white house with the picket fence," said her best friend since childhood, Barbara Madden, who was planning to fly in from her home in California in mid-September so that Diane could show her the new home.

Two days before Madden was to depart for her visit, when she called to confirm her plans, Diane's husband told her matter-of-factly that his wife had died two weeks earlier.

"Do you have any questions?" he asked abruptly, after providing just the most cursory of facts.

On the afternoon of September 2, Diane's boss called to see why she hadn't shown up that day; an employee from the funeral home went to look for her and found Diane's body floating in her bathtub. Mrs. Girts, a bookkeeper and office manager, appeared to have been getting ready for work when she died. Her dress was laid out on the bed, her curling iron turned on and ready for use.

Police who responded to the scene found no signs of foul play and no obvious cause for the woman's death.

Robert Girts had gone to Chicago the day before to help his brother move. When he heard the news, he rushed back, arriving before his wife's body was taken away. Robert tried to talk the paramedics into taking his wife to a local hospital instead of the coroner's office. They found the request odd, as Mrs. Girts was clearly dead and beyond hope of resuscitation.

Perhaps Girts was banking on his knowledge that in the case of an apparently natural death the decedent's spouse could request an in-hospital autopsy, and that those autopsies were typically not conducted by people specially trained to look for death by homicide. However, hospital autopsies are for those who die in the hospital. People who die mysteriously elsewhere go to the coroner. Girts had actually asked the ambulance crew to take her to a specific hospital, a small community facility that does not perform autopsies. Maybe he thought he could finagle things so that no autopsy would be conducted at all. He had done that once before, it would later be discovered.

The autopsy revealed no explanation for Diane's death. The coroner did note reddening of the skin that might indicate carbon monoxide poisoning, but tests revealed no significant levels of the gas in her bloodstream. Knowing that the police had found nothing indicative of a crime, accident, or suicide at the home, the coroner listed the cause of death as undetermined. Although key fluids from the body were retained for possible future examination,

Diane's grieving family and friends were forced to bury her without having any idea why she died.

—✺—

For the next few weeks very little happened in the case, and it might easily have slipped into the netherworld of successful eraser killings without resolution. Unfortunately for Robert Girts, the woman with whom he had been secretly having an on-again, off-again affair for more than a decade began talking to the police.

Elizabeth Bethea said she was stunned when she heard about the sudden death of Girts's wife because just a couple of weeks prior, he had promised her that he was finally going to be getting a divorce. In fact, he told Bethea he would be free when he returned from his brief trip to Chicago.

Girts told Bethea that Diane died of an aneurysm, but by mid-September he began telling the authorities that he believed she had committed suicide. On September 20, he gave police a handwritten note he claimed to have found tucked in his briefcase. The undated note in his wife's handwriting read, "I hate Cleveland. I hate my job. I hate myself." He said his wife had suffered three miscarriages and was despondent over the thought that she might not be able to have children. He said she was also depressed over her weight and her inability to find a satisfying job. No one else who knew her had seen any signs that Diane was depressed or suicidal, including a friend who spoke with her on the phone for forty minutes on the morning that she died.

Around this time, the coroner's office decided to run a screening for the most widely used poisons, including cyanide. Unlike in the flawless world of *CSI*, the test for cyanide came back negative. But it was discovered that the reagents used for testing had been somehow compromised. Another test was run, and as a backup, a sample of fluid was sent to another laboratory, which ran an independent screening using a different methodology. Both tests came back positive. Diane Girts was found to have twice the minimum lethal threshold of cyanide in her system.

At last the cause of death was determined to be acute cyanide poisoning, a particularly hellish way to die. The chemical prevents the cells of the body from getting the oxygen they need to survive. The victim basically suffocates even while gulping for air, like a fish out of water, sometimes going into convulsions before the heart stops. Reddening of the skin is one of the possible symptoms of cyanide poisoning.

The coroner had not found any of the other classic signs of cyanide poisoning, such as the bitter almond smell that often fills the room during the autopsy of a cyanide victim, nor the distinctive organ damage that typically occurs. Yet the results of two separate, independently conducted tests provided unassailable proof that a massive, fatal amount of the chemical was present in Diane Girts's body.

What the police and the coroner still needed to figure out was the manner of death—that is, how did the cyanide get into Diane Girts's system? Was it possible that she purposely ingested the chemical as a means of suicide? Not a single person who knew her thought that, other than her husband. The homicide detectives investigating the case thought it unlikely in the extreme that a woman would prepare for the day ahead—laying out her dress, heating up her curling iron—just before committing suicide. It also seemed highly unlikely that she would use one of the least pleasant of all ways to achieve that result. Besides, cyanide is not available through any retail means. It is not impossible to obtain, but its sale is restricted.

Diane's brother, Barry Jones, and his wife, Bettianne, are largely responsible for tracking the source of that deadly chemical directly to Robert Girts. The couple got hold of Girts's phone bill and spent months calling numbers, trying to find anyone who might know how Robert could have obtained cyanide. They discovered that Girts was enrolled in the Ohio National Guard, and spoke to the commander of his unit. He knew nothing about Girts and cyanide but happened to mention the conversation to Girts's superior officer, Susan Misconish, who blanched at the news. Shortly thereafter she went to police with a very disturbing story.

In her civilian day job, Misconish worked as a chemist for a company that supplied chemicals for industrial and commercial use. Five months before the death of Diane Girts, Robert asked her if she could supply him with a small amount of potassium cyanide, which he said he needed to rid his property of groundhogs.

The chemist would testify at trial that she told Girts that cyanide was a "terrible" way to kill pests and suggested he try something he could find at his local garden supply store. But Girts was adamant, claiming that he had an infestation of groundhogs so nasty that they were terrifying his St. Bernard—though, interestingly, no one else on the funeral home property had noticed a problem with groundhogs.

Misconish was still hesitant to disseminate such a dangerous chemical. A few days later, she received one of Girts's business cards in the mail. On the back he had written the words "Thank you for your help!" and the letters KCN, the chemical symbol for potassium cyanide. He seemed to Misconish like a solid citizen. After all, he was a fellow National Guardsman, and someone who had enough training in chemicals to know how to handle a toxin. So she relented, sending him a few grams of cyanide in care of the funeral home, as he requested.

—⁓—

Three days after the chemist turned Girts's business card over to police, Girts was arrested and charged with aggravated murder. Although when first confronted by police he told them he used the cyanide on the groundhogs, he would later claim that he never received it—would go so far as to assert that his wife intercepted the package and used it to commit suicide. He told a coworker yet another story. He said his wife probably obtained the chemical where she worked because she came in contact "with a lot of lowlifes." Would someone at a barber college or trade school, Diane's two part-time employers, have access to cyanide?

Barry Jones uncovered more unsettling information about his brother-in-law. He knew that Girts had a previous wife who died during their marriage, a young woman named Mary Theresa Morris, whom everyone called Terrie. He and Bettianne researched family names from the woman's obituary, but they were reluctant to reach out with such a terrible suspicion to people they had never met. Four months after Diane's death, they finally made contact with Morris's family.

Terrie was just twenty-five when she fell suddenly and precipitously ill in 1977. Three days after being admitted to the hospital, she lapsed into a coma from which she never awakened. According to her brother, Thomas Morris, Girts visited his wife only a handful of times while she was hospitalized, and went out shopping for a cemetery plot before she died.

Terrie's mother had requested an autopsy. But Girts as next of kin was able to block the procedure, as the death did not appear to be connected to any criminal act. Instead, he had her embalmed and buried. A heart condition was listed as the cause of death on the death certificate, even though she had no history of heart trouble.

Two wives, each of whom died under mysterious circumstances. For fifteen years the Morris family harbored suspicions that Robert Girts may have had a hand in Terrie's death. Now they were convinced that he had poisoned her, too. The symptoms immediately preceding her death closely matched those brought on by cyanide poisoning. But those symptoms, and the rapid collapse that follows cyanide ingestion, can be mistaken for other diseases—especially if neither doctors nor other potential investigators have thorough clinical experience in differentiating this particular kind of asphyxiation from other types of death, such as heart failure.

Terrie's body had been embalmed, then buried for a decade and a half before it was exhumed and tested to determine whether or not she had been poisoned. No trace of cyanide was found, but the coroner said that cyanide, unlike other poisons, such as arsenic, would have been destroyed not just by embalming but also by decomposition and the body's natural metabolism.

Terrie had been hospitalized for a full month leading up to her death, enough time to have purged all trace of the poison from her system. The coroner concluded that Terrie probably died from endocarditis, an inflammation of the lining of the heart. But she based that determination primarily on the treatment records during her hospitalization, as physical changes to the heart indicative of that disorder could no longer be determined due to decomposition. Although the findings were by no means conclusive that she had not been poisoned, Robert Girts would not be charged with his first wife's death.

There was yet another wife of Robert Girts who might easily have become his victim, but she managed to escape with a divorce. His second wife told police that he beat her and once threatened to kill her with a gun. On another occasion, following a fight, he left a trail of shotgun shells down the stairs of their home and into the kitchen, where he had propped open the Bible to the Twenty-Third Psalm. Was it a warning that she was walking in the "shadow of death," that he was godlike in his power over her? Even after their divorce, she was so fearful of him that she wanted nothing to do with the criminal case against him.

Robert Girts presented one face to the world—conscientious, serious, and dependable. But the three Mrs. Girts and their families had seen through the mask, into his ice-cold interior. The real Robert was a man who could refuse to let a mother discover how and why her daughter had died even though he was supposedly a man of practical science who dealt with physical facts of human death every day, someone whose profession was dedicated to giving comfort to those who grieved a loss.

He was an eraser killer, a hollow man living a secret existence, plotting and planning, scheming to acquire poisons, triangulating a path to avoid detection using all the science he had learned. He failed a polygraph, although that information would never be presented to a jury because lie detector tests are inadmissible in U.S. courts. His first wife's family said he shed no tears at Terrie's funeral. He never paid for Diane's funeral, sticking her brother with the bill. Within weeks of Diane's death, he seemed to be crafting a swinging new persona. He changed his hairstyle and started sporting an earring.

At trial the prosecution argued that Girts sprinkled the granulated poison in a bowl of pasta salad in the couple's refrigerator. Diane had eaten from the bowl shortly before she died, as undigested pasta was found in her stomach during autopsy. However, because the coroner had not suspected foul play at the time she died, the stomach contents were not saved for testing.

Girts was convicted, but the verdict was overturned. A state appeals court ruled that the prosecution had erred by referring to an incriminating statement it said Girts made to another inmate while in custody, then failing to put that witness on the stand to back up the contention. In the second trial, the defense changed tack dramatically. Girts's counsel no longer claimed that Diane had taken her own life. Instead, they argued that the cyanide was the natural result of the breakdown of blood in the body. Prosecution experts disputed that argument, running further tests that controlled for that phenomenon and still found fatal amounts of cyanide in her system. Girts was convicted again and sentenced in 1995 to twenty years to life in prison.

However, in September 2007 that conviction, too, was overturned. A federal appeals court ruled that the prosecutor had committed misconduct by commenting before the jury on Girts's refusal to speak to police during the investigation and to testify on his own behalf at trial. The court ordered Cuyahoga County to either retry him or set him free. His third trial was scheduled to begin in early 2009. Girts, however, is apparently so confident that he will soon be free that even before the U.S. District Court made its ruling he applied to have his funeral director's license reinstated.

———

Staging a murder to appear to be nothing but a tragic accident, often a fatal fall in the home, is one of the most common ploys eraser killers use to disguise a domestic homicide.

On December 9, 2001, Michael Peterson—novelist, editorial writer, and former Durham, North Carolina, mayoral candidate—claimed that his forty-eight-year-old wife, Kathleen, fell down a flight of stairs in their home after consuming alcohol and Valium. Her autopsy revealed something more sinister: seven severe lacerations to the top of the head indicating a vicious bludgeoning.

The fifty-nine-year-old novelist was a practiced deceiver who lied about everything from war medals he claimed to have earned to his secret sexual interest in men. Prosecutors believe that his wife's discovery of e-mails arranging a tryst with a male escort led to her murder.

After he was charged with murdering Kathleen, prosecutors exhumed the body of another woman to whom Peterson had become very close while living in Germany in 1985, a woman who also died in a seemingly accidental fall and whose children he had adopted after her death. Like Kathleen Peterson, Elizabeth Ratliff was also found at the bottom of a staircase with injuries to the head. Michael Peterson had been the last person to see Ratliff alive, driving her home after dinner at his house.

Authorities in Germany had accepted her death as an accident, believing she had suffered a cerebral hemorrhage and then fallen to her death, but their counterparts in North Carolina wondered if she too might have been the victim of a disguised homicide. A second autopsy revealed numerous deep lacerations in Elizabeth's scalp consistent with blunt-force trauma—eerily the same number of wounds in the exact same area of the head as Kathleen had suffered. The medical examiner concluded that she too had been bludgeoned to death.

Although North Carolina prosecutors had no jurisdiction to bring charges for the Ratliff murder, they were allowed to introduce evidence of the similarities of the crimes, over the strenuous objections of the defense at his trial for his wife's murder. He was convicted in 2006 and sentenced to life in prison without the possibility of parole.

———∿———

Accidental falls are very commonplace, and because they appear far more innocent than, say, a bullet to the temple, they may draw the least amount of scrutiny of any of the types of staged eraser killings. At least that is what David Mead was counting on when he came up with what he considered to be a foolproof plan for explaining his wife's sudden death.

On the night of August 15, 1994, the twenty-seven-year-old Utah man said he found his wife, Pamela, a twenty-nine-year-old flight attendant, floating facedown in a homemade fishpond in the backyard of their Salt Lake City home. His wails were so loud that a neighbor called 911. When the first officers arrived, they found Pamela lying on the ground next to the pond, unresponsive. David was inside the pond, yanking and pounding at the rocks and bricks that surrounded it.

His demonstration of grief was so exaggerated, so hysterical, that one of the officers had to threaten to mace Mead to get him to calm down enough to allow them to pull him out of the water. Outside the pond he continued to thrash about so violently that the officers were forced to handcuff him and set him in their police car. Even then they couldn't calm him down enough to get much information out of him.

Paramedics confirmed that Pamela was dead. A bag of fish food was near the pond. When authorities were able to elicit a statement from Mead, he told them that when he left to go to work that night at the Salt Lake City airport, where he cleaned out the inside of planes after they returned from flights, he told his wife not to forget to feed the fish.

Mead had completed the crudely constructed pond just four days before his wife's death. It was basically a six-foot-wide plastic-lined hole surrounded by piled-up brick and rocks, three feet deep and contained only a couple of goldfish. The day after Pam died, Mead and his brother completely dismantled the pond and filled it in with dirt. Mead said he didn't want anyone else to be hurt. In reality he was erasing crucial evidence.

The medical examiner concluded that the cause of death was drowning, although a small wound typical of blunt-force trauma was found on the back of Pam's head. It appeared to him that her head had come in contact with some hard object with considerable force—but not enough to kill her—just before she was immersed in water. She could simply have fallen as she went to feed the fish, hit her head on one of the surrounding bricks or rocks with enough force to make her lose consciousness, then drowned. After all, Pam was still recovering from foot surgery at the time of her death, and her gait was unsteady.

Of course, a brick or rock or some other blunt object could have been swung into the back of Pamela Mead's head, but there was no evidence at the time to explain how that might have happened or who might have done it. There are many deaths in which a forensic pathologist can determine that, indeed, someone's skull was beaten in with a bat or some other object with a force that could not be caused accidentally. But Pam's case appeared to be precisely in the indeterminate middle—she'd been struck hard, but only about as hard as one might expect from a sudden backwards fall. Forensics alone cannot resolve such cases.

The Mead case is not an example of shoddy police work. A homicide detective was called out to the scene immediately, and she looked extensively for signs of suspicious or criminal activity. Det. Jill Candland had previously investigated a case of apparent drowning, about which questions of possible staging were later raised. So she was not about to accept things on face value without a thorough investigation.

Candland used a high-intensity lamp to examine the footprints in the dirt surrounding the pond, looking for any sign of a struggle or of a body being dragged, and to check the bricks and rocks making up the retaining wall of the pond for blood and hair. She even checked the bathtub inside the home, as sometimes a drowning in one location is restaged at a different location that appears less criminal. She found nothing that drew into question the story Mead was telling.

In the days that followed, the detective continued to gather evidence, talking to people who knew the couple, and following up on the time line Mead provided of his activities on the day his wife died. A series of unsettling facts about David Mead quickly emerged. The man who had appeared so grief stricken that he had to be restrained from hurting himself had another woman on the side. His involvement with Winnetka "Winnie" Walls was not just a casual sexual affair but a serious ongoing relationship. Winnie was pretty and African American like his wife. (Mead was Caucasian.) When his wife was out of town working flights, Mead, like so many eraser killers, pretended to be a bachelor. Winnie was shocked when she eventually found out that he was married.

Mead was an attentive and ardent boyfriend. He paid her rent in a nice apartment and took her on exotic trips with him, using free airline tickets his wife received as an airline employee. He told Winnie that he didn't love his wife and that he was planning to divorce her. He seemed to have serious intentions toward his girlfriend, even asking to meet her parents. Winnie certainly had serious intentions toward him.

For the most part, Mead was thoroughly charming. But there were a few things that disturbed Winnie. He kept some mighty strange items under lock and key in Winnie's apartment, such as dresses, wigs, and explosives. He also videotaped their lovemaking.

In their talk of a future together, Mead would vaguely refer to "taking care of everything." A month before Pam's death, an impatient Winnie threatened to send one of the videotapes to his wife if he kept stalling and did not leave her. Mead told her not to worry. His wife, he said, was going to suffer a "nasty spill." Over time he got more specific, talking about killing his wife and staging it to look like a robbery, giving himself an alibi by either being at work or at one of his brothers' houses.

He even blurted out something menacing in front of Winnie's parents over Sunday dinner shortly before Pam died. When they pressed Mead to make things right with their daughter, he said he was going to murder his wife. He even claimed to have run over her feet and caused her to need surgery.

Mead also spoke of collecting insurance money he had on his wife. He told Winnie that he had several policies and that he had specifically purchased ones that paid double indemnity—meaning they would pay out twice the face value of the policy in the event of an accidental death. He claimed he couldn't simply divorce Pam because his business was in his wife's name and was largely kept afloat by loans from her parents. Although all this talk was disturbing, Winnie believed it was just talk. She didn't believe that a man who was so good to her could be capable of that kind of violence.

Winnie's ultimatum was not the only thing impinging on Mead's half-married, half-bachelor life around the time of the murder. The airline his wife worked for discontinued service to Salt Lake City. Unwilling to move, Pam was out of a job. She was home all the time now, interfering with Mead's extracurricular activity, and she wasn't bringing in any income either. In his mind, Pam was now nothing but dead weight. The plan for her that he had long fantasized about kicked into high gear.

Two weeks after that Sunday dinner, Winnie got a call from Mead's brother, who informed her that Pam had died in a tragic fall and that David would not be able to contact her until after the funeral had been held. Suddenly her world came crashing down around her. The man she thought she knew—charming, generous, loving—had a diabolical side she never let herself believe was really there.

Continuing her investigation, Detective Candland had gathered other bits of information pointing to some shady business activities in which David Mead may have been involved—a side business, using his unsupervised access to airplanes, as part of a drug-smuggling ring. His secret life was deeper and darker than anyone had suspected.

Candland contacted the medical examiner to go over her findings with him. The doctor did something he had every right and reason to do—but something too few medical examiners are willing to do: he took a fresh look at the case. The physical findings had not changed; they were still ambiguous. But based on the new allegations and information presented to him, he changed the manner of death in his report from accidental to pending.

It was a critical turning point in the case, as an erroneous determination of cause or manner of death can become not only an impenetrable roadblock to further investigation but also an albatross that a defense attorney can hang around the state's neck. The change sent a positive signal to the police, an assurance that their work would not be stymied by a supposedly definitive finding that Pam Mead died in a simple household accident.

By this time it wasn't just the Salt Lake City police who were looking into David Mead. His dead wife's family did not believe the fishpond story for a minute. Their daughter did not like water and did not like the dark. They did not believe that in her hobbled state she would have ventured out at night to feed the fish. In a face-to-face confrontation with her son-in-law, Pam Mead's mother questioned what looked like scratches and bruises on David's upper chest. He explained that they must be the result of all the flailing around he had done in the pond after finding his wife dead. The family hired an aggressive private investigator to do some digging.

On a third front, the insurance company from which David had purchased the unusually high double indemnity policies began its own investigation. As the colorful district attorney who ultimately prosecuted Mead, Howard Lemcke, puts it in a 2005 book he wrote about the case, "When someone makes eight $137 monthly payments, then files a claim for half a million dollars, most folks would have a few questions they'd like to ask."

David Mead hoped to throw suspicion off himself by agreeing to take a polygraph. The test was administered not by the Salt Lake City police but by two very competent polygraphers, both of whom were former cops. Mead passed the test with flying colors—his score far above the "questionable" range. Although the mere fact of being a fearless psychopath could explain how he was able to pass a polygraph, it was also revealed later that he bragged to his cousin Jack how he had obtained every book he could find on lie detector tests and studied every possible way of cheating.

With a seemingly solid alibi and a squeaky-clean polygraph result, David Mead believed he had gotten away with murder. But Candland discovered that his alibi was not really airtight. Mead claimed he was at work at the time of his wife's "accident" and came home at 11:00 P.M. to find her dead. Although the time he arrived at the Salt Lake City airport that night was recorded as 8:50 P.M.—suspiciously at an airport gate he had never before used, as if he were purposely attempting to construct an alibi—he was only seen briefly cleaning one plane. No one else saw him for the rest of the night. That gave him ample time to return home and commit the murder.

The investigation got one lucky break. Mead's cousin Jack was picked up on a burglary charge. Jack Hendrix had never really held down gainful employment; he was always in and out of prison on some robbery or burglary charge. He was also a drug addict. Jack made a deal with the police to get some charges cleared up in return for telling the detectives everything he knew about his cousin's involvement in the death of Pam Mead.

The story he told was a stunner. David had first tried to hire him to help stage a crime—the burglary-gone-bad scenario he had mused about with Winnie. While Mead was safely away at work, Jack was supposed to kill Pam, ransack the home, and take off with some valuables.

Mead promised to pay his cousin $30,000, and gave him $1,000 and sixty grams of coke as down payment. It was a fatal error on Mead's part because Jack went on a bender and failed to show up at the agreed-on time to commit the contract killing.

Presented with all this new and even more incriminating information, the medical examiner amended his report once again to read: "Pamela Mead died as a result of drowning. Contributory to death is blunt-force injury of the head. Investigation indicates the decedent's death was the result of action(s) by another person."

If this conclusion by the chief medical examiner sounds easy or obvious, it is only because few people understand how difficult, time-consuming, and possibly career-damaging it is for medical examiners to completely rethink cases on which they have already made assessments. The fact that the medical examiner amended his findings would be challenged both at trial and on appeal, but the manner in which the medical examiner made his changes and explained them in court was upheld as completely proper by the Utah Supreme Court.

As police uncovered more evidence from interviewing Pam Mead's family and friends and additional mistresses of David Mead, the story became even more ghoulish. Pam's distraught parents revealed that about a year prior to her death, Pam was at home and happened to pick up the phone to make a hair appointment. As soon as she put the receiver to her ear she heard her husband on the line talking apparently to someone with whom he was on intimate terms.

But it wasn't the intimacy that was so upsetting to Pam. She could clearly make out the steady voice of her husband telling his lover that he was thinking about murdering his wife. Pam heard David say that he wanted out of his marriage but would not divorce Pam because she held the strings to his business. Instead, he said he wanted to kill Pam and collect the insurance money.

Horrified, Pam packed up and left, heading for the safety of her parents' home in Colorado, confessing the details of the frightening phone call to her sister. But as a smooth-talking con man, David somehow reassured her that he never really intended to hurt her, that he loved her and only her.

Because of the difficulties encountered in rounding up uncooperative witnesses, and delays caused by civil litigation over the fat insurance policy David Mead had planned to collect, it took four years, until 1998, to bring the case to trial. Just as it was fortunate to have an aggressive and skeptical investigator, it was a happy accident that the case was assigned to a veteran prosecutor who did not flinch at the prospect of circumstantial evidence. The passion Howard Lemcke brought to the case, however, was not a relentless drive to convict David Mead so much as a determination to ensure that Pamela Mead received some form of justice. As he says, "She is the person I'm really working for. In a case like this, I'm the only voice she has left."

Despite the fact that at least three people testified independently that they had heard David Mead talk about killing his wife, there was no direct evidence that Mead had committed the murder—no witness who saw him or heard him do it. Lemcke had to present a "total tapestry of evidence" in which any one small piece may seem insignificant, but when woven together as a whole makes the sum total of evidence overwhelming. The jury was convinced, finding David Mead guilty of first-degree murder.

After the 1998 trial, most jurors said they did not believe that Mead conceived of the fishpond as a home improvement, as he claimed, but solely as a means of murder—the set on which he would stage the death of his wife, disappearing his involvement in that death right before our eyes. As one juror said, "He's just playing us. He's played everybody." Although he came very close to getting away with his crime, the audience was not taken in by his smoke and mirrors.

As the jurors looked even closer at the evidence in Mead's backyard "stage," they found something that was a clear and direct indication of premeditation. Mead had actually unscrewed the bulbs in the backyard floodlights, making it nearly pitch dark the night of Pamela's "accident." The jurors did not believe that Pam, who was fearful of the dark and could barely get around due to her recent foot surgery, would have ventured out on her own in a yard that dark.

"This was, in my estimation, a heinous crime in that you took advantage of someone who trusted and apparently loved you," the judge said in sentencing Mead to five years to life for murder and an additional one to fifteen years for solicitation of murder. "She was indeed a vulnerable victim and in a calculated fashion you planned her demise and carried out this murder knowingly and intentionally and you have shown, since the first day of trial, a total lack of remorse and . . . acceptance of responsibility."

With those impassioned words he captured the essence of an eraser killing: the utter vulnerability of the victim, the unconscionable betrayal of her trust, the remorselessness and deviousness of carrying out a personal execution.

CHAPTER SEVEN

Pregnant and Vulnerable

When a Child Is Seen
as a Threat

A large percentage of eraser killings are motivated, in whole or in part, by the fact that the victim is pregnant with her killer's child—a child he does not want and has no intention of raising or supporting.

According to Robert Hare, "psychopaths see children as an inconvenience," an inconvenience some are not willing to tolerate. Because they lack empathy and compassion, psychopaths cannot become caregivers in any real sense or sublimate their needs and desires to those of a child—who by its very helplessness and dependency must come first in the family hierarchy.

However, it is the added presence of the other personality traits of the Dark Triad that really puts the lives of these men's partners and children at risk. For the pathological narcissist, who is used to and relishes being the center of his world, and the high Mach, who needs to feel in control of everyone around him, a child may be seen as a direct threat to his dominion. In the same vein, he sees the woman attempting to bring that child into the world as betraying him, usurping his power and control, and irrevocably altering the balance of their relationship.

A woman's emotional center of gravity shifts dramatically with the discovery that she is pregnant, and continues to change and develop through term as the physical and psychological reality of the child grows inside her. As the woman becomes more preoccupied with the baby and less emotionally available to her partner, the unborn baby may be perceived as a direct threat and as a rival, according to British forensic psychiatrist Gillian Mezey. For men who feel no sense of attachment to their child and, at best, a fragile and purely narcissistic bond to their intimate partner, erasing both mother and child seems like the ideal way out of an untenable situation.

The emotional and economic demands of child rearing are especially disconcerting to Machiavellians, narcissists, and even lower-level psychopaths whose entire focus is on their own grossly inflated sense of self. Although many of these men are able to continue their bachelor lifestyle of affairs and irresponsibility after marriage, pregnancy and children make it much more difficult to live out their fantasies.

The threat of prematurely ended bachelorhood was clearly a major factor in Chester Gillette's decision to murder his lover instead of facing the responsibility of fatherhood. Theodore Dreiser, a progressive free thinker, believed that the reason there were so many murders like the Gillette case in the late 1800s and early 1900s was society's strict social and sexual mores, and the extreme difficulty and costliness of divorce at the time. (Dreiser wrote for the journal of Margaret Sanger, the early birth control advocate, and argued for the widespread availability of contraceptives and sex education.) He also believed that the social stigma against unwed mothers added to the tendency of young men to eliminate the women they had made pregnant.

Yet a century later—with birth control, divorce, and even abortion available on demand, and single motherhood ubiquitous and socially acceptable—men like Chester Gillette are still turning to murder to avoid the responsibilities of parenthood. Even in 1906, Gillette could have merely left town and abandoned his pregnant girlfriend without any severe repercussions, or he could have married her and stayed on at his uncle's factory, as his relatives had no objection to the pairing. But for Gillette, like so many other men over the last century, erasing his pregnant partner not only seemed simpler but also enhanced his sense of control over his destiny.

Recent research indicates that between 20 and 35 percent of men who kill their pregnant partners had no previous history of violence. They attack when their victims are most vulnerable, most in need of caring, and least physically able to fight back. Their youngest victims have no ability whatsoever to defend themselves.

———

On July 19, 2004, nineteen months after the disappearance of Laci Peterson made national news, twenty-eight-year-old Mark Hacking called police to report that his twenty-seven-year-old wife, Lori, had not returned from her regular morning run in a Salt Lake City park. Like Scott and Laci Peterson, the Utah couple had seemed to be embarking on an exciting future. They were days away from moving to North Carolina, where Mark was supposed to be starting medical school. They also found out that week that Lori was pregnant, news they were supposed to share with their parents over the coming weekend.

It wasn't a planned pregnancy, but Lori was thrilled nonetheless. Evidently Mark was not so happy. Fatherhood may not have been part of the life he envisioned for himself. For beneath the surface, little if anything about Mark Hacking was as it appeared to be.

Three days before she disappeared—the day after her positive home pregnancy test—Lori called the University of North Carolina at Chapel Hill to inquire about financial aid, an issue she was even more concerned about now that she knew she was pregnant. A puzzled administrator told her that her husband had not even applied to the medical school, much less been admitted. Mark had actually never graduated from college, although it is doubtful that Lori ever knew that fact. He had secretly dropped out of the University of Utah two years before, but had all the while pretended to go to class, bringing books home and even appearing to work on papers, while his wife largely supported them as an assistant securities trader.

Hacking claimed to have graduated with honors with a degree in psychology, dummied up a diploma, even went as far as to send out commencement invitations to his family, but at the last minute feigned illness and told relatives he would be unable to attend the ceremony. His wife helped him fill out applications for eleven different medical schools, which he apparently had no intention of mailing. He flew around the country pretending to interview at several top schools and insisted on his "first choice," North Carolina, over his wife's wish to relocate to Washington, D.C. She put her own plans to get an MBA on hold so that Mark could pursue his purported dream.

Lori was at work when she was blindsided by the news from Chapel Hill. It was a Friday, and she was so upset that she went home early. At some point over the ensuing weekend Hacking managed to convince her that it was all some kind of misunderstanding. On Monday morning, the UNC administrator retrieved a voice mail message from Lori stating that her husband explained to her that there had been a computer snafu and that he had worked everything out. It was the last time anyone would hear from Lori.

Hacking may have been able temporarily to appease his wife, but he knew he could not keep up the charade much longer. The clock was ticking, and the house of cards he had delicately built around himself was about to come down.

At ten on Monday morning, Hacking called his wife's office. When told she had never showed up he expressed panic, claiming his wife had not returned home from her regular predawn run. He said he had assumed that she had gone to straight to work, but now he noticed that her work clothes were still at home.

"You need to call police immediately," her supervisor told Hacking. "Get off the phone and call right now."

But Hacking didn't, and he may not even have been at home when he claimed to be looking in his wife's closet. A few minutes later, a good twenty minutes before calling police, he visited a store and purchased a new mattress for their bed. By the time he called 911, Lori's coworkers had already reported her missing.

Several of her office mates also beat Hacking to the site where he claimed his wife had gone to run. Her car was there, but no Lori.

—⁓—

Just as bank robbers and other types of criminals learn from the mistakes and successes of others, I believe that Mark Hacking used Scott Peterson's basic template for how to get away with murder, but tweaked it in an effort to avoid mistakes that Scott had made.

An entire branch of research into what is called the social learning theory of crime has demonstrated the many ways in which people learn and perfect their practical knowledge of how to commit crimes and minimize their chances of getting caught. I believe that the striking similarities between the Peterson and Hacking cases illustrate this kind of social learning. Even relatively isolated criminals like eraser killers become aware of the modus operandi in cases that offer a solution to their needs, such as the elimination of a problem wife or girlfriend. Either by living in the same community where these crimes occur or by hearing about them through the media, eraser killers consciously or unconsciously absorb the relevant details and strategies that fit their own Machiavellian needs.

As was well known at the time Lori Hacking disappeared, Scott Peterson had tried to convince the police that his wife had been abducted while walking their golden retriever, McKenzie, in the park at the end of their block. To make this scenario credible, he left the backyard gate open and let their dog out on his leash; he told police that Laci planned to walk McKenzie that morning and gave them the usual route she took through the park. (This scenario was drawn into question after friends and relatives reported that Laci had stopped walking on doctor's orders after she became sick and nearly fainted on two recent occasions while walking in the park.)

Another problem with Scott's cover story was the size and proximity of the park. It was small enough to be thoroughly searched within twenty-four hours by officers on foot and horseback, by divers in the river running through the park, and by helicopters equipped with body heat sensors. Search dogs also indicated that Laci did not go for a walk in the park. Instead, they detected her scent trail leaving home in a vehicle in the opposite direction of the park—a scenario that fit with the theory that Peterson had driven her corpse away with him on his trip to the bay.

Mark Hacking was clever enough to move the search location well away from his home by "placing" Lori, via the presence of her car, in a slice of urban wilderness with trails and roads leading up into remote canyons, where it was far more believable that something bad but undetectable could have happened to her.

However, Hacking was not as smart, tough, or meticulous as Peterson when it came to the actual killing or its aftermath. He tried to take advantage of the hysteria surrounding the disappearance of Laci Peterson, exploit the perception that women, like children, can be snatched by strangers in public parks and never be seen again. As in the Peterson case, there were false sightings by people who believed they saw Lori that morning in the park, and two who claimed to have seen a woman being abducted near the couple's apartment.

Hacking apparently overlooked the glaring fact that by the time he tried to stage Lori's disappearance, his "mentor" had been arrested and was on trial for his wife's murder. Perhaps he thought he would be luckier than Peterson, that he had been clever enough in disposing of Lori's body that she would never be found, unlike Laci.

What he was planning to do after getting away with murder remains unclear. Did he think that he could just move on, wifeless and childless, to North Carolina, perhaps keeping the rest of his family believing that he was a doctor in training? Or was he hoping that the "tragedy" of losing his wife would give him an excuse to walk away from his purported dream and fashion a new life more in accord with his fantasies, not to mention his true abilities?

Like Peterson, Hacking grossly underestimated public compassion—especially in this tight-knit community of Latter-day Saints, the church to which Mark and his wife both belonged. As thousands of volunteers working out of a makeshift command post at an LDS meetinghouse assisted police in the search for Lori, Hacking's story began to unravel with the discovery that he had been out purchasing a new mattress when he claimed to be frantically looking for his missing wife. He would try to claim that he had to throw away their old mattress because his wife had bled on it when she got her period—which sounded even more ludicrous when police found out from friends that Lori was pregnant.

On the morning Lori went missing, surveillance cameras at the University of Utah's Neuropsychiatric Institute, where Mark worked as a night-shift orderly, captured footage of a man who looked like Hacking throwing something into a dumpster. During a search of the couple's apartment, a knife with traces of Lori's blood and hair was found in a bedside drawer; Hacking had used the knife to cut the blood-soaked upper layer off the mattress. Lori's blood was also found in her car, which Mark had left at the entrance to the park. If Lori had been attacked or kidnapped while she was running, there was no reason for blood to be in her car. He also made silly mistakes, such as leaving Lori's car keys at home and forgetting to readjust the driver's seat and mirrors to the position his much smaller wife would have had them in if she had been the last person to drive the car.

As the weight of suspicion grew, Mark suddenly began to behave bizarrely. He checked into a motel four blocks from his home, where police, responding to a call of a disturbance at two in the morning, found him running around outside wearing nothing but a pair of sandals. Seeking refuge from questions he could not answer, he committed himself into the psychiatric ward.

After five days passed with no sign of Lori but more and more doubt being cast on Hacking's story, his own brothers—one a doctor, the other an electronics engineer—took the course that precious few families of eraser killers are willing to take. They applied as much pressure as they could to pry the truth from their brother and got Mark to confess to them that he had killed his wife. Hacking told his brothers that he shot Lori in the head with a .22-caliber rifle early that Monday morning as she slept, disposed of her body, the gun, and bloody mattress in three separate trash bins, then drove her car to the park to set up an abduction scenario.

Rather than keep his secret or cover up for him, as the family and friends of many an eraser killer have done, Hacking's family passed that information on to police. Now there was a good chance, in theory at least, of finding Lori's body and allowing her the dignity of burial in a marked grave. By the time authorities learned the truth, however, Lori's body was buried under thousands of tons of rotting compacted trash in the county landfill. When police, working with teams of cadaver dogs, finally found her remains seventy-five days later, they were so mangled and decomposed that all they could give her parents to bury were fifteen pounds of bone fragments and teeth.

It was impossible at that point to confirm that Lori was pregnant, so Hacking was never charged with a second killing and spared the death penalty. But after pleading guilty to avoid a trial, he admitted in open court that his wife was indeed pregnant.

"She was the greatest thing that ever happened to me," Hacking said in a halting voice, just before a Utah judge imposed a sentence of six years to life in prison. "But I killed her and took the life of my unborn child and put them in the garbage, and I can't explain why I did it."

Third District Judge Denise Lindberg said she would urge the state Board of Pardons to keep Hacking imprisoned for a "very, very long time," calling him "the poster child for dishonesty in its most extreme form."

Like Laci, Lori Hacking never shared her marital problems with friends or family. She did know something was seriously wrong with the relationship, but I doubt she had any idea that she and her baby were in mortal danger. After she was killed, police found a note Lori had written to her husband threatening to end the marriage unless "things changed," although when she wrote the note and exactly what those problems were remain a mystery.

"I want to grow old with you," she wrote, "but I can't do it under these conditions."

Mark Hacking long seemed to be at odds with himself, his professed feelings contradicted by his actions. He and Lori were high school sweethearts, and he told friends he planned to marry her, yet he cheated on her while away in Canada on the mission to spread the faith that all young Mormon men are expected to undertake for two years after high school graduation. Mark was sent home less than a year into his mission for having an inappropriate relationship with a recent convert he was supposed to be counseling. He lied to Lori about that, claiming he was wrongfully blamed for the misbehavior of others. He aspired to be a doctor like his father and older brother, yet would not do what it takes to become one. He defied the tenets of his faith by drinking, smoking, lying, and cheating, yet attended Sunday services with his wife the afternoon before he killed her.

Most of his friends and coworkers saw Hacking as warm and generous. But after the murder, his mother acknowledged that it "seemed easy for him to establish a pattern of not explaining himself or revealing where he was." He volunteered in the church nursery and appeared to enjoy kids, yet was capable of murdering his unborn child just days after learning his wife was pregnant.

In the years he claimed to be finishing his bachelor's degree and preparing for medical school, he retreated into adolescent fantasy: playing endless hours of Nintendo, hanging out at a convenience store near his apartment eating hot dogs and candy when he was supposed to be in class, shaving his head and growing a goatee to look hipper. He even began calling himself "Franz" at work, after a narcissistic bodybuilder in a *Saturday Night Live* skit. While Lori was ready to embrace the responsibilities of their life together, Mark was running from them.

One of the last places Lori Hacking was seen alive was at her husband's favorite mini-mart. As with his other recalcitrant behaviors, Hacking hid his smoking habit from his wife like a naughty child. At 9:19 that Sunday night when Mark and Lori came in to buy sodas,

Mark motioned to the clerk (to whom he had claimed to be a therapist) not to reveal to his wife that he normally bought cigarettes there.

The images captured on the store's surveillance tape provide a telling look at the real Mark Hacking. Four hours later at 1:18 A.M., Mark returned to the store alone. By that point, according to the time line he gave his brothers, he had already killed his wife and was on his way to dispose of her corpse. Showing no signs of stress or despair, Hacking walked up to the clerk and ordered a pack of smokes. While waiting, he casually studies his fingers as if looking for any blood he might have missed. This was no haunted Macbeth, begging "all great Neptune's ocean" to wash the guilt from his hands. It was just a cursory examination. The cigarettes were his reward, his declaration of independence. He could smoke all he wanted now. He no longer had to hide his true nature.

Was it some vestige of his religious faith, or pressure from his family, that caused Mark Hacking to admit his crime? And was his willingness to plead guilty a sign of true remorse? It is interesting that two of the very few eraser killers to plead guilty, Mark Hacking and Don Weber, did not have families that bought into their lies after their crimes, but instead expected them to take responsibility and do the right thing. Although Hacking did ultimately admit his crime, it took him a while to get there. Three months after he confessed the crime in private to his brothers, he had stood in court and entered a "not guilty" plea despite the anguished lament of Lori's brother, who begged Hacking not to put his wife's family through the painful experience of a trial.

His actions since going to prison may belie his claims of remorse. Hacking has gotten a jailhouse tattoo of a bulldozer on his chest. Is that the image he has of himself, powerful and strong, or as someone capable of "bulldozing" everyone around him with his special prowess? Or was he mocking the effort it took authorities to find his wife amid all that garbage?

Many eraser killings of pregnant women are brutally enforced abortions, with the added plus, from the killer's point of view, of excising from his life the baby's mother, who wants something from him that he is not willing to give.

Football star Rae Carruth staged a drive-by shooting to kill his twenty-four-year-old girlfriend, Cherica Adams, who was seven months pregnant with his baby. He believed that a young black woman dying in a hail of gunfire, whether she was viewed by police to be an innocent casualty or the apparent target, would raise neither eyebrows nor much inquiry. Sadly for our society, that might have been true; in this case, however, the victim survived long enough to expose her boyfriend's involvement.

Carruth was already supporting a child he fathered in college, after losing a paternity suit, and evidently had no intention of supporting another—even though he was earning more than half a million dollars a year as a first-round draft pick for the Carolina Panthers.

After he failed to convince Cherica to get an abortion, Carruth hired a career criminal who had performed odd jobs for him to kill her. To Cherica, however, Rae suddenly seemed to have changed his tune about the baby, claiming he wanted to do the right thing and even attending a Lamaze class with her. On November 15, 1999, Carruth invited Cherica to a late movie in south Charlotte (eerily, a movie about the hunt for a killer). They each had their own cars with them, and after the movie he told her to follow him back to her place, which surprised Cherica, as he rarely came over. En route, he abruptly stopped his car in front of hers, boxing her in as the hit man he had hired pulled up alongside Cherica and shot her four times. Carruth and his coconspirators then sped away from the scene, assuming she was dead and that police would believe she had been the victim of a street crime.

—◠◠—

Unfortunately for Rae Carruth, Cherica Adams was severely wounded but not dead. Despite her injuries, Adams managed to call 911 on her cell phone and describe what had happened to her. She was rushed to a nearby hospital, where the son she had already named Chancellor was delivered ten weeks premature. He survived, but due to oxygen deprivation suffered severe brain damage. Cherica lived for thirty days before succumbing to multiple organ failure. Before her death, she was able to scrawl down a few notes describing the attack and how Carruth prevented her escape.

As prosecutor Gentry Caudill put it so memorably at trial, "Cherica Adams was not supposed to be an eyewitness to what the defendant had done to her and her son."

—–⁓–—

A week after the shooting, Carruth was charged with attempted murder and released on bail with the agreement that he was to turn himself in if either Cherica or the baby died. Within an hour of learning of Cherica's death, however, he attempted to flee. He was captured the next day five hundred miles away in Tennessee, hiding in the trunk of a friend's car with a cache of candy bars to sustain him and two bottles holding his urine.

Carruth was charged with first-degree murder. At trial, the defense argued that the shooting was vengeance for Carruth's reneging on a drug deal. But two of Carruth's coconspirators testified against him, as did an ex-girlfriend who said he admitted his involvement in the murder—telling her that he didn't believe he would get in any trouble "because I didn't actually pull the trigger." Phone records also showed that Carruth and the wheelman of the other car called each other right around the time of the shooting.

The triggerman, Van Brett Watkins, said that Carruth initially hired him to beat Adams so severely that she would suffer a miscarriage, but then changed his mind, asking him to kill both Cherica and her baby. Carruth suggested shooting her outside a restaurant—a nearly identical plan to the one conceived by Robert Blake, according to prosecutors in that case. When Watkins balked at that idea, Carruth settled on a drive-by.

In fact, it was not the first time Rae Carruth wanted to erase a woman or child from his life. Amber Turner, another former girlfriend who had become pregnant by Carruth, testified that he had threatened to kill her if she did not abort their child. Turner, just eighteen years old at the time, complied.

"Don't make me send somebody out there to kill you," she recalled him telling her, stating that he had no intention of having a child with someone he didn't plan to be with long term. "You know I'll do it."

She also testified that he had "joked" about killing the woman he got pregnant while in college and the son she named Rae Jr.

Carruth could have received the death penalty if convicted of first-degree murder under either of two legal rationales: that the murder was committed with premeditation and deliberation (which it certainly was, according to the testimony of his coconspirators) or that it was committed during the commission of another serious crime, the latter known as the felony murder rule. Applying the felony murder rule was questionable, as the underlying felony charged, shooting into an occupied car, was the action that caused her death, not really an underlying crime.

Nevertheless, the jury spared him the death penalty, convicting him only of the lesser charges of conspiracy to commit murder, shooting into an occupied vehicle, and using an instrument to destroy an unborn child. He was sentenced to nineteen to twenty-four years in prison.

Even Carruth's defense attorney admitted that the verdict was logically inconsistent, as the jurors had found Carruth guilty of the underlying felonies leading to Cherica Adams's death, yet acquitted him of murder. One juror, acknowledging that the verdict was "illogical," described it as a compromise. The jurors all believed Carruth was involved in the crime, but because he didn't commit every element of it himself, they didn't see it as first-degree murder—an erroneous view of the law. Like the jury in the Robert Blake case, they were troubled because they couldn't put the gun in the killer's hand.

—⁓—

As Rae Carruth learned, an eraser killer's best-laid plans can go awry in unanticipated ways. Stephen Poaches might well have gotten away with killing his pregnant girlfriend if he hadn't enlisted the help of someone after the fact to help him cover his tracks.

LaToyia Figueroa, a twenty-four-year-old Philadelphia waitress, was five months pregnant with her second child when she disappeared on July 8, 2005. She never made it home from a prenatal appointment she attended that day with her unborn baby's father, twenty-five-year-old Poaches. She didn't show up for her shift that night at a local T.G.I. Friday's and never picked up her seven-year-old daughter from day care.

An aunt, who helped raise Figueroa after the girl's mother was murdered as the result of a love triangle when LaToyia was just four years old, immediately suspected that Poaches had harmed her

A crime as old as time: In 1906, nearly a century before the murder of Laci Peterson, Chester Gillette killed his pregnant girlfriend and dumped her body into a secluded lake. This photo of Gillette, at the helm of a boat similar to the one from which he would later claim Grace Brown committed suicide by jumping overboard, was snapped on a date with another woman just one week before Grace's murder.
CREDIT: Police files

As in the Peterson case, the small boat that carried Grace Brown to her death and a single lock of the victim's hair found inside of it were important pieces of evidence at Gillette's murder trial. A boat of the same make and model was brought right into the courtroom for jurors and spectators to examine.
CREDIT: *Utica Saturday Globe*, 1906

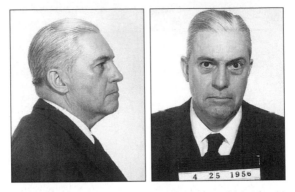

Ewing Scott played a cat-and-mouse game with authorities for years after his wife, Evelyn, disappeared, claiming at various times that she had checked herself into a sanitarium, gone off to seek cancer treatment, and left him for another woman. His 1957 murder conviction established legal precedent for prosecuting "no-body" homicides, yet the odds of getting away with murder by "erasing" the victim remain astonishingly good a half-century later.

CREDIT: Los Angeles Police Department mug shot

A shocked Richard Crafts at the moment of his arrest in 1987 for the murder of his wife, Helle. After completely obliterating his wife's remains by feeding her body through a wood chipper, he believed he would never be held to account for killing her.

CREDIT: AP/Wide World Photos

Considered paragons of their respective communities until they schemed to erase women who loved them from their lives: football star Rae Carruth, lawyer Perry March, author Michael Peterson, surgeon and Green Beret officer Jeffrey MacDonald, peace and environmental activist Ira Einhorn.

After crushing her skull one day in 1977, Ira Einhorn locked girlfriend Holly Maddux inside this steamer trunk, which he kept locked inside a closet in the apartment they shared. When police finally managed to obtain a search warrant eighteen months later and discovered her body, Einhorn claimed he had been set up by a vast conspiracy.

CREDIT: *Philadelphia Daily*/Corbis, 1979

Means of disposal: A massive plastic fish cooler, the makeshift coffin Thomas Capano used to dump the body of girlfriend Anne Marie Fahey in shark-infested waters sixty miles out into the Atlantic Ocean in 1996, was brought into the courtroom and placed before him when he took the stand at his 1999 murder trial. Capano's brother Gerry, who ferried him out to sea that day in his boat, eventually admitted to helping Capano toss the ice chest overboard and shooting into it with a shotgun when it failed to sink. Although Fahey's remains were never found, the cooler was recovered by a fisherman and its purchase traced to the prominent Delaware attorney.

CREDIT: Sketches copyright © by courtroom artist Susan Schary

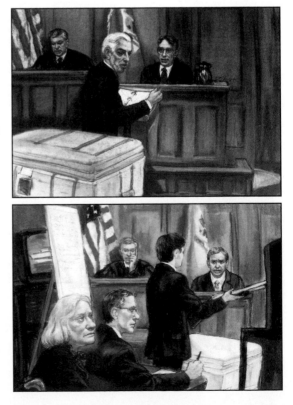

Kristin Smart in 1995, one of three young women who went missing in the small town of San Luis Obispo while Scott Peterson was a college student there. Years later, Peterson would base the plan he hatched to "disappear" his wife on lessons he learned from news coverage of those missing persons investigations.
CREDIT: Courtesy of the Smart family

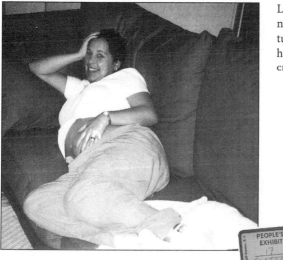

Laci Peterson was so happy to be pregnant; she loved to show off her growing tummy. Her husband told one relative he had been "hoping for infertility."
CREDIT: Trial exhibit

PEOPLE'S
EXHIBIT
17
SC-55500 A

Scott Peterson, on a date with Amber Frey nine days before his wife's Christmas Eve 2002 disappearance. Claiming he had already "lost" his wife, Peterson told Frey that he did not want to have any biological children and planned to get a vasectomy.
CREDIT: Trial exhibit

PEOPLE'S EXHIBIT

In one of the eeriest and most controversial pieces of evidence introduced at Peterson's 2004 trial, a pregnant staffer from the district attorney's office demonstrated that a body the same size and weight as Laci's could have been secreted from view on the boat Peterson took out on San Francisco Bay the day he reported his wife went missing.
CREDIT: Trial exhibit

Inspired by Scott Peterson's elaborate ruse, Mark Hacking staged a scene to make it appear that his pregnant wife, Lori, had been abducted while jogging in a Utah park in the summer of 2004. In fact, he had shot her in her sleep, then disposed of her body and the bloodied mattress in separate dumpsters.

CREDIT: Family photo distributed to media during search

It took authorities 75 days of sifting through rotting compacted trash to find Lori Hacking's remains in the county landfill.

CREDIT: AP/World Wide Photos/ Douglas C. Pizac, 2004

Missing or Murdered?
A Memorial to the Disappeared
CREDIT: Mark Powelson

Missing
Isabel Rodriguez

MISSING
Lisa Tu

MISSING
HAVE YOU SEEN
LATOYIA?

ISSING P
Janet Ma

She is 5'2", p
been mis
Philadelph
7/18/2005. I
details of he

MISSING
Kathleen Durst

issing
i Sherer

MISSING

Missing/M

MISSING PERSON
Helen (Holly) Maddux

Kristine Kupka
5 months pregnant
Red hair, blue eyes

Lori Hacking

niece. Poaches told her that LaToyia left on foot from his apartment after the prenatal appointment, but he changed his story several times. He also lived with a woman whom LaToyia thought was an ex-girlfriend—a woman who had just given birth to Poaches's baby and who had attacked LaToyia outside her home shortly before she disappeared.

The case received national attention largely through the efforts of a distant relative, who happened to be a Philadelphia city councilman, and Net bloggers who wrote an open letter to talk-show host Nancy Grace challenging her to devote airtime to a missing woman who wasn't white. (LaToyia was of mixed race, black and Latina.)

Friends, family, and hundreds of strangers aided police in an exhaustive search, but Poaches declined to participate, saying he preferred sticking to his regular routine—going to his job at an oil company and spending time with his other "babymomma."

Poaches hired an attorney, Michael Coard, who went on national TV insisting that his client was innocent and fully cooperating with police. Poaches did some of his own public relations work as well, repeatedly calling in to a late-night sex and relationship talk show on a Philadelphia hip-hop radio station where the case was being discussed incessantly. He didn't aid his cause, however, by showing no concern for LaToyia, repeatedly referring to her not by her name but as "the female." The radio host, who was so disturbed by Poaches demeanor that she turned all the tapes of their conversations over to police, asked Poaches to at least call LaToyia "Babymomma," a quasi-affectionate term in hip-hop circles, but he refused to show his missing girlfriend even that much respect.

"When I see her I am going to make sure she is OK, then I don't want to see her anymore," Poaches said dismissively of LaToyia during one of the on-air calls.

Without a body, without a crime scene to work from, police admitted that their investigation was floundering. Then they got lucky. Poaches had buried LaToyia in a grassy lot near the railroad tracks thirteen miles outside the city. Worried that her body might be discovered, he decided to move it. Because the police had already impounded his car, he asked a buddy to help him. The friend, however, quickly called police, who provided him with the van and body-size bag Poaches requested he bring. Then they followed the pair to LaToyia's makeshift grave.

Caught red-handed, Poaches confessed to strangling LaToyia at his apartment because she refused to get an abortion. He also admitted that he was considering killing the friend whom he had asked to help rebury the corpse, apparently planning to further cover his tracks by eliminating someone who could implicate him in LaToyia's death. (Poaches had a .45-caliber gun on him and was wearing a bulletproof vest when he was arrested.) Although Poaches led police directly to his victim, that didn't stop his lawyer from continuing to proclaim his innocence to the media.

"He was allegedly near the body," said Coard of his client's arrest. "That is not proof of murder and kidnapping."

Despite the fact that he had confessed to police, Poaches pleaded not guilty. He opted for a nonjury trial, however, a rare strategy sometimes employed when the defense feels that the available evidence may inflame the passions of ordinary citizens. The trial was held before a three-judge panel that heard evidence much the way a jury would.

The defense argued for voluntary manslaughter, claiming that Poaches acted out of "sudden and intense passion," not "malice, ill will or hardness of heart." The prosecution maintained that LaToyia's pregnancy was the reason for the killing and that Poaches planned and premeditated the killing after she refused his demands to get an abortion.

"He did not want this child to be born," said Carlos Vega, the assistant district attorney. "He planned it. He did it. And he almost got away with it."

The panel of judges found Poaches guilty on two counts of first-degree murder—Pennsylvania being one of thirty-four states at that time that allowed the death of a fetus to be charged as a separate murder. However, because Poaches agreed in advance that he would not appeal the verdict, prosecutors agreed not to seek the death penalty. Instead, he was given an automatic sentence of life without parole.

—⁓—

Whereas those close to LaToyia Figueroa had to fight to draw attention to her disappearance, the case of a purported attack on Charles Stuart and his pregnant wife on an autumn night in 1989 made headlines at every turn—for all the wrong reasons. Stuart famously, and fictitiously, claimed that a black mugger accosted the couple as they drove home from a birthing class in a crime-ridden section of Boston.

Stuart, twenty-nine, an Irish American bartender's son who raised himself up to become a highly successful fur salesman, claimed that the man forced his way into their car when they stopped at an intersection, ordered them to drive to a deserted area near the Roxbury projects, robbed them at gunpoint of money and jewelry, then shot them. Stuart's thirty-year-old wife, Carol, mortally wounded from a shot to the head administered at point-blank range, was taken off life support the following day. Their son, Christopher, who was delivered by cesarean section eight weeks premature, weighed just three pounds, thirteen ounces. Deprived too long of oxygen, he suffered extensive damage to his brain and other organs and lived just seventeen days.

Charles, or Chuck as most people knew him, was shot in the stomach and seriously wounded, but survived. The severity of his own wounds—which required two surgeries and a six-week hospital stay, and caused him to have to use a colostomy bag temporarily—made his story seem credible. Even when the truth came out, it seemed hard to imagine that anyone would take such a risk to get away with murder. Apparently, however, Stuart had never intended to put his own life in actual jeopardy. Like the plans of many other eraser killers, the one he carried out that night was riskier and more difficult to pull off than he had initially envisioned.

The media took up the story as a cause célèbre decrying the senselessness of random urban violence (when, in fact, it was an example of a quite purposeful act of marital violence). Stuart played his role to the hilt. Still hospitalized at the time of Carol's funeral, he asked the best man from their wedding to read a touching farewell letter he penned to his wife.

"Goodnight, sweet wife, my love," the letter read. "God has called you to his hands, not to take you away from me and all the happiness that God has brought but to bring you away from the cruelty and violence that fill this world. . . . Now you sleep away from me. I will never again know the feeling of your hand in mine, but I will always feel you." As his son died, Stuart begged the hospital staff to let him hold the boy "one last time."

In the racially charged atmosphere of Boston at the time, the heavy-handed search by police for men who fit the generic description

Chuck related—black male, running suit, baseball cap—caused enormous tension and anger in the African American community. Stuart stuck to his story for three months, as hundreds of black men were randomly stopped on the street, frisked, questioned, and sometimes strip-searched in public. He even went so far as to pick an innocent man out of a lineup.

As the man was about to be indicted, Stuart's twenty-three-year-old brother, Matthew, went to police and told them that Chuck had shot himself and his wife and cooked up the story of the mugging as cover. Shortly after learning from his family that Matthew had gone to the police, Charles Stuart jumped to his death into the Mystic River.

"I am sorry for all of the trouble," he said simply in a note left in his car.

—⁓—

The media then pounced on the idea that Stuart had killed his wife for financial gain. Some said he hoped to collect on her life insurance and use the proceeds to open his own restaurant. However, a widely cited *Boston Globe* article claiming that Stuart had cashed a half-million-dollar life insurance check on his wife before he died turned out to be untrue.

Eliminating an unwanted pregnancy and a wife he could no longer control seems to have been the primary motive, with financial considerations interrelated but secondary, much as in the Peterson case. A crucial fact that went unreported at the time of the crime and that is still largely unknown today was that Stuart had wanted his wife to get an abortion.

The killer took many of his secrets with him into the Mystic. But we do know some of the things that were on his mind in the months leading up to the murder. Like Scott Peterson at the time of his crime, Stuart was turning thirty and was unhappy about the direction his life was heading. Not only was his wife pregnant with a child he did not want, but she had told him that after the baby was born she wanted to be a full-time mom and not return to work.

He had also learned that previous summer that the owners of the fur store had no intention of ever making him a partner in their business, something he had convinced himself would happen because of his stellar sales record and their fondness for him. He wanted to find a job where he would be appreciated as much as he felt he deserved, be his own boss, maybe open that restaurant he had long dreamed of running. He didn't want a stay-at-home wife and a baby cutting into the lifestyle to which he had rapidly grown accustomed.

He was also obsessed with another woman, Debby Allen, a pretty twenty-one-year-old college student who worked summers at the fur store and whom he began pursuing while still convalescing from his self-inflicted wound. Although the woman apparently did not return his feelings, Stuart bought a gold brooch and a pair of $1,000 diamond earrings for her shortly after he was released from the hospital, but had not given them to her before committing suicide.

Attributing a purely monetary motive is too simplistic a way to look at the murder of Carol Stuart and her unborn son, or any other eraser killing. Carol was deviating from the script Stuart had written in his own mind of how he imagined their life would be. Like so many eraser killers, Charles Stuart felt entitled to all the things he had dreamed of and fantasized about and had no problem lying or killing to get what he wanted.

———

A poor student, Chuck had gone to the non-college-track vocational school, where he took an interest in two things: sports, despite his lack of any particular talent, and classes that helped prepare students for work in the restaurant industry. His high school yearbook photo depicts him wearing a chef's hat.

After several years spent cooking in restaurants, however, he tired of hot and greasy work and wanted to move closer to where Boston's money and status are centered. He answered an ad for a management trainee position at one of the city's oldest and most luxurious emporiums—Edward Kakas and Son's Fine Furs on Newbury Street, a boulevard sometimes called the Rodeo Drive of the East. He had no experience whatsoever in sales or management, and had grown up on the wrong side of the tracks in status-conscious Boston, so he decided to manufacture at least a partial blueblood pedigree.

He claimed to have attended Brown University, the prestigious Ivy League school in Rhode Island, on a football scholarship. In truth, he had never attended a day at Brown, had bailed on college altogether after less than one term at a state school. Unbeknownst to Stuart, Brown doesn't even offer football scholarships, but as the school of choice for many of New England's wealthiest and most illustrious families (John F. Kennedy Jr. spent his undergraduate years at Brown), Stuart knew what entrée a gold-plated degree would provide. Like many eraser killers, however, Stuart modulated his fabrications depending on the gullibility of his audience. If someone knew him well enough to know that he hadn't left Boston for any considerable length of time, he would say that he had to drop out of Brown after blowing out his knee on the gridiron.

The brothers who ran Kakas Furs were taken in not only by the lies Stuart spun but also by his extraordinary smoothness. Stuart quickly worked his way up to become their number one producer and the store's general manager, a trusted position, earning $100,000 a year in salary and commissions. Unlike Scott Peterson, Charles Stuart was an outstanding salesman who could seemingly talk anyone into anything. What the owners of the store did not know was that they had put their trust in one of the breed of charming and persuasive creatures known as white-collar psychopaths.

He obsessed over his appearance, wearing $1,000 suits and monogrammed shirts and getting expensive salon haircuts to cover his receding hairline. He worked hard to eliminate anything that gave away his humble roots, listening to vocabulary tapes during his daily commute and recording and playing back his speaking voice to work on losing his lower-class accent.

It was an impressive climb for a blue-collar kid from vocational school. He capped it off with his marriage, four years before the murder, to a hard-working and genuinely well-educated Italian American woman, an honor student all the way through undergrad and law school, whom he had met while still working in a restaurant. They had a beautiful house with a heated pool (a rarity in New England) and hosted many a party for Carol's lawyer friends and other high-level professionals. To everyone who knew him, Chuck seemed like a good man with a charmed life. But none of it was enough for Stuart.

He spent as much money as they earned, something that became an issue with his wife as the birth of their child drew near and she wanted to start saving for the future. Stuart controlled all their finances, forcing his wife to turn over her paychecks to him, and had taken out numerous insurance policies on his wife. He also made all the important decisions in their relationship, even choosing the china pattern for their wedding gifts.

However, there was one crucial decision that his wife made without his consent: getting pregnant and insisting on keeping the baby. He was furious when she told him the news, and he demanded she get an abortion. She refused. For a child, the thing she wanted more than anything in the world, she was willing to defy him.

Despite his controlling nature and sometimes frightening temper, Stuart had always lavished attention and gifts on his wife. He had wooed her with the same kind of romantic overstatement Scott Peterson was known for, surprising her with flowers for no particular reason and giving her a $4,500 engagement ring. After she got pregnant he seemed disgusted by her, referring to her behind her back as "the fat wop."

"Just when things are looking great, the sky's the limit, she wants to screw it up," he complained that summer to a friend about his wife's pregnancy. When the friend suggested divorce, he moaned about what it would cost him.

"A wife you can divorce," he said. "A wife and a baby gets a lot more complicated."

He was looking for a simpler solution. He said he wished his wife would get hit by a truck, then made a startling request: "You want to drive the truck?" The friend laughed it off, chalking the conversation up to a sick joke, and Stuart let the subject drop.

A short time later he asked his twenty-seven-year-old brother, Michael, to help him get rid of his pregnant wife. When his brother said no, Stuart acted as though he were kidding. He then approached a casual friend, David MacLean, whom he knew from the culinary arts program in high school and who happened to be a truck driver. Like a salesman baiting the hook with an irresistible pitch, he started off talking about the desire both men shared for opening up a restaurant. Then he segued into how he felt that his wife was standing in the way of his dream, admitting how he had tried to get her to abort their baby.

"So, do you know anybody I could get to, you know, take care of my wife? You know, kill her?" he stammered. When MacLean tried to brush the conversation aside, Stuart revealed that he had already asked his brother but been turned down. "All of a sudden he's got morals," Stuart said of his brother, then repeated his request. When MacLean told Stuart he was crazy for even thinking about such a thing, Stuart once again pretended he was only joking.

He then turned to his baby brother, Matthew, offering him a financial inducement, first $5,000, then doubling it to $10,000, for his help—almost a year's salary for an aimless and somewhat troubled kid still living at home. Matthew would deny to police that Chuck told him anything about killing his wife, claiming instead that his brother outlined a vague insurance scam. According to Matt Stuart, Chuck planned to stage a mugging, then file an insurance claim for the "stolen" items. What he wanted his brother to do was meet him near the crime scene and take away the property the mugger was supposed to have stolen.

—⁓—

Stuart set the date for the phony mugging for October 23, 1989. The night before, he drove his brother from Brigham and Women's Hospital, where the birthing class would be held, to the street a short distance away, where he told his brother to meet him at ten the following night. He even drew a map for his brother so that he could find his way home from the meeting site.

The morning of the murder, Stuart took three bullets from the safe at the fur store. He hadn't wanted to set up a paper trail by buying ammunition, so he was forced to commit the crime with just the three aged rounds that happened to be in the work safe.

One can only imagine how confused and terrified Carol Stuart must have been that night after the childbirth class at Brigham and Women's, when instead of heading home, Chuck drove into an unfamiliar neighborhood and suddenly parked on a desolate street and pulled a gun on her. Gunpowder residue on both her hands indicates that she may have grabbed the barrel or attempted to ward off its force in a futile attempt to save her life and her baby.

After shooting Carol, Stuart fired the second round into the roof of the car over the driver's seat, presumably to make it look as if that shot was directed at him. He had one bullet left, which he carefully aimed at his back, just above the buttocks. He was presumably hoping for a simple through-and-through wound, in through the love handle and out through the belly without hitting any vital organs. But to make the trajectory fit the story he was about to tell, he had to hold the gun awkwardly behind him, as if the shooter were in the backseat. Whether due to the adrenaline coursing through his veins, the awkwardness of the confined space, or perhaps the interference of his still-not-dead wife, he ended up pumping the final bullet directly into his intestines. He was enormously lucky. Only because the ammo was so old did it not continue its trajectory into his spinal cord.

In enormous pain and at risk of losing consciousness from blood loss, Stuart waited out the time until the appointed meeting with his brother and drove to the agreed-on rendezvous spot. He rolled down his window and threw Carol's Gucci purse into his brother's vehicle, with the gun, money, and jewelry inside—including the one-and-a-quarter-carat diamond engagement ring and the ruby-and-diamond band he pried off his wife's finger. As his brother screeched away, Chuck then called 911, remaining on the line a full thirteen minutes, claiming that he was driving around but could neither make out any of the street signs to help the authorities locate him nor find anyone whom he could ask for help.

Was he stalling, waiting for his wife and baby to die? He told the dispatcher at one point that his wife was "gurgling" and then she stopped. But in all those thirteen minutes, as recorded by the dispatcher, he never once addressed his wife or offered words of comfort to her. He did offer up, unsolicited, the claim that he had "ducked" as an excuse for why he was not as seriously injured as his wife.

At last a police cruiser spotted Stuart's car. Ironically, a television crew from the CBS reality show *Rescue 911* happened to be in the area riding along with paramedics, and captured nightmarish footage of the couple.

———

Stuart never veered from his plan even after the unexpectedly serious injury he had inflicted on himself. He had shown the preternatural calm of a psychopath once before, when their dog electrocuted himself by biting into an electric cord and Stuart barely raised an eyebrow, casually telling his wife to pull the cord out of the wall socket. Once his wife and baby died, he rarely mentioned them. However, he did talk excitedly about the new car he planned to buy with Carol's life insurance money as soon as he got out of the hospital.

Just after New Year's he did indeed buy that car, trading in the vehicle in which he murdered his wife. He was not the least bit abashed about appearing to move on with his life at lightning speed. He went out with friends to celebrate publicly on New Year's Eve.

He thought nothing of paying for the jewelry he bought for Debby Allen with a check drawn on the joint bank account he had shared with his wife. Shortly after leaving the hospital, he went to his salon to have his hair dyed, worried about the smattering of gray that was beginning to creep in. He actually seemed excited by all the attention and sympathy he was getting. With the fur store continuing to pay him full salary, he joked that he had picked a good time to take off work.

As suspicion and ire began to spread about Stuart's account of events, he was content to hide behind his family and a lawyer who had been serving as his spokesman. He did not, however, come through with the money he had promised his brother Matthew. Even after learning that his kin had betrayed him, Stuart seemed willing to continue his charade. He spoke with his attorney, and the phone numbers for several other attorneys were found in the hotel room where he stayed to avoid arrest the last night of his life. Shortly before jumping to his death, he visited a mini-mart for junk food in the wee hours of the morning, telling the clerk he might see him again "because I just might get hungry again." He never lost his appetite, right up until the very end.

——⁓——

The desire to eliminate an unwanted pregnancy by erasing the source of the problem is not an exclusively American phenomenon, despite what Theodore Dreiser may have believed.

Liana White, a twenty-nine-year-old medical clerk, was four months pregnant with her second child when she disappeared on July 12, 2005, in Edmonton, Alberta. A woman on her way to a morning workout came across Liana's Ford Explorer at 5:45 A.M. in a parking lot near a baseball field a short distance from White's home. The driver's door was wide open, and the contents of Liana's purse were spilled out in a trail leading away from the vehicle. Most disturbingly, a pair of women's shoes sat just outside the open door, as if the person who had been wearing them was snatched right out of them.

This was no false sighting or a case of someone attempting to reconstruct a time line after the fact. The passerby was so concerned that she called police before going on with her workout. Data from the key card she had to swipe to get into her gym backed up her report that the car was in the lot before 6 A.M.

Officers quickly managed to track down Liana's husband, Michael, a twenty-eight-year-old mechanic who would soon become known in the media as the "Scott Peterson of Canada," at the trucking company where he worked, and he rushed home to speak with them.

The couple met at an Edmonton nightclub in 1998 while White was serving in the Canadian military. They had been married for five years and had a three-year-old daughter, Ashley.

Unlike Scott Peterson and many other eraser killers, Michael White seemed appropriately distraught for a man whose wife appeared to have been the victim of foul play, and cried as he made a missing persons report to police. Family and friends described him as a gentle giant, a "teddy bear" incapable of violence. When asked straight out by a detective if he had anything to do with his wife's disappearance, he was indignant.

"How can you ask me that?" he said. "I love my wife. There's no way I could ever hurt her or anyone else."

White offered his own theory. Someone must have been hiding in the back of the SUV when she left for work, he suggested, saying that he frequently forgot to lock the garage door.

The time line he gave detectives, however, was problematic. He said his wife had risen at her usual time of 5:55 A.M., and left home at 6:15 for her 7:00 A.M. shift in the neonatal unit of a local hospital. How could Liana have gone missing before she had even gotten up?

The investigators were bothered by something else White said. Later that afternoon, when detectives asked to search his home, White told them he had spent some time cleaning and "tidying up" the house after he had returned home that morning. As with Scott Peterson's obsessive vacuuming the day after his wife went missing, why was White concerned with cleanliness at a time like this?

The most suspicious thing, however, was the crime scene itself. The shoes looked as if they had been carefully arranged, one right next to the other, not what one would expect if they had been haphazardly cast off in a struggle. Liana's wallet had no cash in it, which pointed to robbery as a possible motive. But the place it was found also seemed set up for discovery, not where a fleeing thief could have tossed it. Detectives also noticed that, just as in the Hacking case, the driver's seat and mirrors in Liana's car were not in the position they should have been if the car had last been driven by a five-foot four-inch woman. They were positioned as if to accommodate someone much taller, such as her six-foot three-inch husband.

Was this really a crime scene at all, they wondered, or something staged to send them off in the wrong direction? The community was already gripped with fear over the possibility that a serial killer was operating in its midst, as the bodies of twenty murdered women, mostly prostitutes, had been found in farmers' fields and other rural areas around Edmonton over the last thirteen years. Was Liana his latest victim, or is that what someone else was hoping police would think?

The next day, White alternated between periods of high drama and curious detachment. Choking back tears, he pledged in a television interview that he would find his wife. "Liana, hold tight," he said, speaking directly into the camera. "I will find you." A short while later he asked detectives if he should return to work, as if he had nothing more important to do with his time.

Police set up surveillance of White the following day after reviewing footage from the security camera outside a nearby bar. At around five o'clock on the morning she disappeared, the tape picked up a car just like Liana's traveling away from the White home in the direction of the parking lot. It was difficult to make out the driver, but it was clearly not Liana. Twelve minutes later, the tape showed a man matching Michael White's distinctive appearance—Caucasian, hulking build, shaved head, goatee—running back toward the house. This was even more troubling considering that White had told them he hadn't gotten out of bed until after his wife left for work.

That night, police followed an unsuspecting White as he went out to pick up his daughter from a friend's house. On the way, he stopped at a field and retrieved two plastic garbage bags secreted in the tall grass. Without ever looking inside them, he brought the bags back to his house and put them out on the curb for the morning's trash pickup.

An undercover officer hitched a ride on the garbage truck the next morning and collected the bags instead. Inside, police found their true crime scene, or rather what was left of it: clothing, paper towels, sponges, and latex gloves, all soaked in blood, and a broken lamp that matched one in the White's bedroom.

It was beyond ironic. White had gone to great pains to erase any evidence that he had killed his wife in their home. Then, fearing that the evidence was about to be discovered (because police had told White the night before that they were going to begin searching in that area), he brought it back to the scene of the crime. Exhibiting the extraordinary hubris of an eraser killer, he thought he was still in control, that he had everyone fooled. It never occurred to him that the police would be watching his every move.

Detectives were now convinced that White had staged a crime that had never occurred, to cover up one that he had committed. But they still had no body, no definitive proof that Liana was dead. As they awaited the results of DNA testing on the items from the trash bags, they got a warrant and searched his home. With the heat ratcheted up, White did something even more extraordinarily hubristic. He stage-managed the discovery of Liana's body.

White had insisted on conducting his own search for his wife, claiming he had special search training in the military and enlisting friends and family members to help him. Hoping that he might lead them to Liana, police actually encouraged his efforts, urging him to follow his intuition, the "psychic bond" between husband and wife.

On July 17, White and several members of his family, followed surreptitiously by surveillance officers, found Liana's body in a ditch off an isolated road a ten-minute drive from his home. She was lying face down, covered by leaves and branches, naked, her bra and panties discarded nearby to make it appear as if she had been raped. The search party had stopped their car in the area to talk, White said, and noticed the smell of decomposing flesh. They saw a leg sticking out of the brush, with Liana's telltale tattoo of a blue dolphin on the ankle.

White fell to his knees and sobbed. Then he asked someone to jot down the license plate numbers of passing cars, saying he thought that the killer might return to the scene of the crime.

Chillingly, he had found her just as he had promised in that television interview. In his mind—because he had staged her corpse to make it appear that some stranger killed her, some depraved sex criminal—there was no harm in finding her body. In fact, he needed her to be found, now that the focus had turned to him. He wanted the case to be closed, to give police a different motive, one that pointed away from him.

Just five days had passed since Liana disappeared. Yet left in that ditch, exposed to the elements, her corpse had been so scavenged by animals and maggots that it took months to complete an autopsy. She had been stabbed twice in the back and also had cut marks on several fingers, indicating that she fought for her life and may have been trying to run away from her attacker when she died.

The medical examiner could not determine the exact cause of death because so much of her body tissue was missing. He believed that she most likely died from an injury to the neck, either from stabbing or strangulation—in part because he was able to rule out other causes. The degree of insect infestation in the neck area led him to believe that there had been an open wound. Strangulation was also a possibility because Liana's hyoid bone, a small bone in base of the throat that is often broken during manual strangulation, was missing. He believed that abrasions on her backside occurred post-mortem, probably as a result of the corpse's having been dragged.

There was no evidence of sexual assault.

A few hours before finding his wife's body, White complained to the local newspaper, the *Edmonton Sun*, about being compared to Scott Peterson. In fact, he was very much like Peterson. In that interview, he was already speaking of his wife as dead, and described plans for her funeral. He seemed eager to move on, saying he had to "get back to normalcy" for their daughter's sake.

"Liana would want me to," he said.

He made another gratuitous remark about how clean detectives found his house on the day his wife disappeared, saying that his wife "hated mess." That was the same explanation Scott Peterson gave for why he claimed that his wife mopped the kitchen the day she disappeared—strange considering that their maid had cleaned the whole house just the day before.

White told the paper where he planned to search that evening—the very place he would find his wife—saying that was where he believed a body would most likely be abandoned. It was another eraser-killer prophecy that would come true.

White was the son and grandson of farmers. His life took a major turn at age ten, when his parents split and his mother married the farmer next door. On the surface, he was a polite and obedient child;

underneath, some darker traits were evident at an early age. As a teenager, he stole from relatives and friends. When caught, he would deny the allegations as convincingly as he would years later when charged with murder, with tears in his eyes and feigned sincerity.

He was prosecuted twice in the military for stealing equipment. One item, a computer, he gave to his wife as a Christmas present. When military police confiscated it, he told her they needed it back because it contained classified information. He only came clean with his wife on the eve of his court martial. He was fined and demoted but not discharged. According to her mother, Kelly, Liana told Michael that if he ever stole anything again, their marriage was over.

With the demotion they struggled financially. White left the military and found work as a mechanic. The couple managed to buy a small bungalow, but he still wasn't earning enough to satisfy himself or, he said, his wife. He began stealing again, this time tools from the trucking company.

Revealing perhaps more about his own mind-set than Liana's at the time of the crime, he claimed that his wife was tired of living paycheck to paycheck and that she wanted to "buy things, have things." Yet he said his wife didn't like him working so much overtime and asked him to cut back after she became pregnant with their second child, wanting him around to help her with their three-year-old, as she was still working full-time and was tired and ill from the pregnancy. He agreed, but he didn't seem that happy about it. The night before she disappeared, he stayed out late—not working, but drinking with a coworker.

Despite their financial troubles, Liana was clearly happy about having another child. She repeatedly checked a Web site on her computer that tracked the developmental stages of her pregnancy, and excitedly reported her findings to her friends. White claimed that he also very much wanted the baby his wife was carrying, but that seems less certain. He had long harbored the fantasy of one day buying the family farm and running his own machine shop. Another mouth to feed must have made those dreams seem remote.

And there was an even more serious obstacle to that goal. Liana's mother says her daughter had no intention of ever moving to the farm, where Liana felt that both she and her daughter were unwelcome among Michael's family.

The day Liana went missing, Kelly rushed over to talk with her son-in-law, but he wouldn't answer her questions. While she stayed up all night in the couple's bedroom, pacing anxiously, keeping vigil for her missing daughter, she could hear Michael snoring away in front of the television, sleeping like a baby. The next morning, she was shocked to overhear Michael say he had been unable to sleep a wink.

Ultimately, the Edmonton authorities amassed a wealth of evidence against Michael White, one of the strongest circumstantial cases ever presented in an eraser killing. They managed to do so, however, only because they acted quickly and astutely. If they hadn't moved rapidly, the security tape that refuted White's time line of the morning's events and served as a virtual eyewitness account of his dumping his wife's car and setting up the abduction scenario might have been taped over. If they hadn't set up surveillance on Michael when they did, the evidence in the trash bags, unimpeachable proof of his guilt, would have been lost forever, buried in the city dump.

They picked up on clues that didn't fit the supposed crime scene. They expertly worked their relationship with their suspect, ratcheting up the pressure as needed but also holding back on their suspicions enough to fool him into making mistakes and revealing his hand. They intuitively grasped something about his psychology and played into his ego, giving him enough rope to hang himself.

According to the theory presented by Crown prosecutors, sometime in the early morning hours of July 12, 2005, White killed Liana in the couple's bedroom, knocking over the bedside lamp during the attack. Criminalists detected traces of blood in the bedroom, hall, front doorway, garage, and the back of Liana's SUV—revealing the trail her killer took as he dragged her lifeless body through the house and drove her out to the ditch where he left her. The murder weapon, which has never been found, was ditched someplace else.

There was evidence that White did not randomly select the area where he dumped his wife's body. His next-door neighbor testified that he and White had once dumped a load of dirt in that same area while constructing a shared driveway. Many residents illegally dumped trash there. Liana's body lay near someone's discarded toilet. It was an ugly insight into his psychology. She meant so little to him that he would leave her body next to a broken-down toilet.

White then returned home to clean up the mess and went on another dumping run, stashing the blood-soaked items and shattered lamp in the grassy field. White apparently marked this site, preparing all along to return at some point and more carefully dispose of the evidence. Detectives later found the shade to the broken lamp propped up on a fence post like a beacon guiding his way to the exact spot where White had pulled over to retrieve the bags.

DNA tests matched the items in the trash bags to both Michael and Liana White. The clothing, which bore Michael's DNA, was stained with Liana's blood. Liana's blood was on the outside of the rubber gloves; his DNA was found inside the fingertips. The same brand of sponges and towels as those in the trash bags were found in the White home. Clothing identical in size and brand to the articles in the bag was also found among Michael's possessions.

A DNA expert testified that the odds that the blood on the gloves was from anyone other than Liana were 1 in 5.1 trillion. The odds that the DNA extracted from skin cells inside the gloves did not belong to Michael were even more astronomical: 1 in 8.7 trillion.

At five on the morning she vanished, White made his third foray, abandoning Liana's car in the parking lot and setting up the kidnapping ruse. In addition to the security tape, a neighbor testified that as he arrived home at five that morning from working a graveyard shift, he saw White heading out in his wife's car, speeding away as if in a big hurry.

White raised the usual defenses employed in eraser killings. The prosecution did not prove when, where, or how Liana died, White's attorneys contended, nor did it establish motive for why her husband would have killed her.

"He gained nothing from this crime," defense counsel Laura Stevens contended. "He lost everything." However, that argument fails to grasp (or purposely attempts to obscure) the peculiarly insidious nature of motive in eraser killings. The gain the killer is seeking is inextricably tied to the loss of his victim. Eraser killers think they will be better off without a particular woman or child in their life, without having to support them or share their estate or give up their home. They simply cannot abide for their victim to go on living.

The defense ridiculed the evidence against White, casting the mistakes he made in staging, his inconsistent statements, his inexplicable behavior, and even the hard physical evidence as proof not of guilt but of innocence. It was another argument invariably made by defense attorneys in eraser homicides, but a logically specious one: that a cunning killer would not make mistakes that would give him away. As eraser killers go, Michael White was not a particularly sophisticated or adept one. But even the best are often tripped up by their own hubris, by their abiding belief that they are above scrutiny, and by the sometimes warring aspects of their psychology.

If White were lying, Stevens argued, he should have been able to come up with a better explanation for the blood in his home and on the items in the trash bags than the far-fetched tale he told in court. If he were guilty, he wouldn't have left incriminating evidence lying around just waiting to be discovered.

"There have to be a thousand better places to get rid of evidence than an open field," she said. "It doesn't make any sense."

And if Michael had stabbed his wife to death in their home as the state contended, "that place should have lit up like a Christmas tree," said Stevens—referring to forensic tests with the chemical luminol, which causes blood to glow when viewed under a blue light. However, the articles in the trash bags proved that a major cleanup job had taken place. They also found traces of blood on a bottle of bleach in the house.

When police confronted White with the contents of the bags, he initially claimed not to recognize anything. He later came up with an explanation that attempted to cover all the evidence. He blamed it on his three-year-old.

While playing horsey in their bedroom with a coat rack as her steed, White said, Ashley accidentally hit her mother in the face and broke the lamp. Liana suffered a bloody nose, and White put on the rubber gloves to attend to her because his hands were dirty from his mechanic's work.

Liana wanted to go to the hospital, but Michael didn't want to take her. Like a "cold-hearted idiot," as he described himself at trial, he didn't want to spend the day in the ER because her nose wasn't broken. They fought about it as they walked through the house, leaving the blood trail. Liana gave in and later cleaned up the mess. She must have dumped the bags in the field herself, which they had used before to dump car parts, yard clippings, and other debris.

He said the nosebleed incident occurred three weeks before his wife disappeared—a time frame that defies credulity, considering that the towels in the trash bags were still wet with blood when police discovered them. What also defies credulity is the astounding number of missing women who are alleged to have had innocent yet blood-provoking accidents in their homes right around the time they disappeared.

The blood pattern on the recovered clothing contradicted White's account. A pair of men's pants found in the bag were soaked in blood all the way up to the waist. A nosebleed that copious would have been fatal. Blood on a sock (as well as the bedroom wall) revealed a high-velocity spatter pattern, consistent with someone's being struck, not a dripping nose.

When lab technicians checked the pants pockets, they discovered something even more eerie and highly significant. Stuffed inside was a piece of cardboard emblazoned with the brand name Extreme Edge—which appeared to be packaging for a knife. White was charged only with second-degree murder because police said they did not have evidence that the crime was planned. But the fact that White was apparently carrying a newly purchased knife in his pocket at the time of the killing certainly makes it appear that the murder was premeditated.

White's explanation for his bizarre retrieval of the garbage bags was as implausible as his nosebleed story. Because he had allegedly used the field before to dump trash, he assumed without ever opening the bags that they must belong to him, and brought them home to dispose of them properly—what his attorneys characterized as a "Good Samaritan" act.

He also backed off from the time line he had given for when Liana left home that morning. He told police the day she disappeared that he had spoken to Liana as she left for work at 6:15 A.M. He described what she was wearing, her mood, and plans they talked about for later in the day.

Now he said he was asleep when she left and just assumed that she departed at the time she normally did. However, that revision did nothing to explain his appearance on the security video an hour earlier.

"That's not me," he simply stated when a detective showed him the security footage after his arrest. When the videotape of that interrogation was played at trial, it was as if he were daring the jury with the old adage, "Who are you going to believe, me or your own lying eyes?" He grew out his hair for the trial, perhaps hoping that jurors would not recognize him as the man on the tape.

Later in the taped interview, White lost his cool. Like Scott Peterson, he seemed to think the police were pursuing him out of personal jealousy. "Is this because I found her and you guys couldn't?" he screamed at the detective. At another point—perhaps revealing his true feelings for his wife—White railed about being charged with the "friggin' murder of my goddamn wife."

As damning as the "circumstantial" evidence was in this case, the defense still tried to cast it as a specious form of proof.

"Michael White is going to stand right there and take that Bible and take that oath and what he tells us will not be circumstantial," cocounsel Robert Shaigec announced in his opening statement. He wanted the jury to believe that the word of the accused was direct evidence, beyond reproach, but that circumstantial evidence—even when it came in the form of hard scientific evidence—could not be trusted.

On the stand, White blamed some of the inconsistencies in his various statements and testimony on the shock of finding his wife's body, and simply refused to account for others. The entire case against him amounted to much ado about nothing, or as he put it, "It all has to do with a nosebleed."

As the prosecutor led him through each element of the crime and its cover-up in a series of leading questions—You killed your wife, didn't you? You dumped her vehicle, staged the robbery?—White responded with roughly the same polite but unequivocal response: "No sir, I did not."

The jury did not believe him, finding White guilty and recommending that he serve at least fifteen years in prison before being considered for parole. The minimum penalty for second-degree murder is ten years.

He was not prosecuted for killing his unborn child because in Canada, unlike in California at the time of the Peterson murder, a fetus is not considered a life.

The day after the verdict was delivered, an even more horrific fact was revealed, evidence the jury had not been allowed to hear. Ashley, who was home with her parents at the time of the murder, may have witnessed some portion of the crime or its aftermath.

According to testimony delivered during closed-door hearings, the girl, just five at the time of the trial, told her grandmother and a few family friends that she was awakened by a noise and found her mother lying on the floor. She also described seeing blood on her mother's neck and her father cleaning up blood on the floor with towels. The judge excluded any testimony about the girl's statements as hearsay and a threat to White's receiving a fair trial.

Michael White was sentenced to life with the possibility of parole in seventeen years. That means he could be freed before his fiftieth birthday.

—⁓—

If the fact of an approaching pregnancy and the accompanying responsibility and perceived loss of freedom are an impetus for some men to kill, what exactly is the narcissistic dream for which they are willing to execute their wife and unborn child? For eraser killers who have been caught, we often don't know, because they haven't begun to live out their ultimate fantasy. The best clue to this question may be found in the case of the eraser killer who killed not an unborn child but three young children and his wife, then proceeded to live out what to him was an exotic dream existence.

A little more than a year before Scott Peterson committed his pregnant wife to the murky depths of San Francisco Bay, a twenty-seven-year-old Oregon man fashioned a similar fate for his wife and three small children. Christian Longo, a once-devout Jehovah's Witness, strangled each member of his family one by one. Then he stuffed the bodies of his wife, MaryJane, thirty-four, and their two-year-old daughter, Madison, inside suitcases and threw them into Yaquina Bay off the coast of Newport, Oregon, near the pricey condominium he was renting. In an apparent attempt to further cover his tracks by not disposing of all his victims in the same place, Longo tied rock-filled pillowcases to the ankles of his other two children, Sadie, age three, and Zachery, four, and dumped them from a bridge into an inlet a few miles up the coast.

Familicide, or family annihilation, is a crime almost exclusively perpetrated by men. (There have been a few notorious cases of women, such as Susan Smith and Andrea Yates, murdering all of their children but *not* their spouse.) In case histories, men who kill their entire families are invariably described by those who knew them as loving husbands and devoted dads right up until the day of slaughter.

Behind that well-honed façade, however, is usually a long history of secrets and lies: mounting debts, clandestine affairs, and legal or other personal problems that they have managed to keep hidden from almost everyone they know. In fact, it is often the discovery or imminent discovery of their secrets and the unraveling of their lies that precipitate a fatal explosion of violence.

Because family annihilators often take their own lives as well, however, many psychologists and criminologists have tended to view their crimes through a surprisingly sympathetic prism: as the desperate deeds of broken men who believe they are delivering their families from a greater suffering. Whether or not one believes there is ever any truth to such a viewpoint, there is no question that Christian Longo fully intended to get away with murder and enjoy the fruits of his crimes even as he cast his murderous actions in just such altruistic terms.

On the day he was arrested for erasing his wife and children, Longo told police, "I sent them to a better place." However, unlike some men who kill their whole families, he did not then take his own life in order to join his family in this "better place." Instead, he skipped out on hundreds of thousands of dollars in debt and pending theft and forgery charges, assumed the identity of a real *New York Times* reporter, and fled to a Mexican beach resort—where he promptly took up with a pretty German photographer.

A better place, indeed.

The young German woman, Janina Franke, had no idea that the guy romancing her in the Yucatán was a married man who had just wiped out his entire family. Longo claimed that he was divorced and had no children, that he had no time for relationships because he was on the road so much chasing stories. After Franke told him she had come to Mexico to photograph the Mayan ruins, hoping to jump-start her career as a photojournalist, Longo said he had come to write about the same thing. For her, it was a perfect opportunity, as the man who convincingly presented himself as a well-traveled and well-connected journalist could open doors and advance her career. They spent several days collaborating on a project that he assured her he could get published in the *Times* or *National Geographic*, in addition to snorkeling and hitting the disco—until the FBI burst into their cabana and arrested him.

Apparently the Hemingwayesque life of a foreign correspondent appealed to Christian Longo more than the daily drudgery he experienced as a maxed-out dad and coffee barista (a job he was forced to take after losing his business cleaning construction sites).

"I could live out a dream," he later explained to the actual reporter whose identity he had stolen: that of the professional adventurer he used to fantasize being while reading the *Times* travel pages at the Starbucks where he worked.

———

While he was living out his fantasies in Mexico, the body of little Zachery floated to the surface. Divers found his sister, Sadie, with the pillowcase of rocks still weighting her down. A woman who babysat for the Longos a few days before the murders saw the children's pictures in the media and identified them. When police went to the condo, they found it empty except for two stuffed animals. A massive search was mounted. Divers searching the water near the condo discovered the two suitcases with Madison and MaryJane inside.

Longo was placed on the FBI's "Ten Most Wanted" fugitives list. A Canadian tourist informed the FBI that she had seen him in Cancún; he was traced to the hostel where he was staying and captured a little more than two weeks into his "new" life.

Curiously, he pleaded guilty to killing his wife and Madison, but mounted a strange and patently ludicrous defense regarding the other two children. He claimed that when he finally came clean with MaryJane about his secrets, she became distraught, strangled their two older children, and tried to kill the third. In a rage at her actions, he insisted, he finished the job, killing his wife and toddler.

Neither judge nor jury bought his story, convicting him of first-degree murder and sentencing him to death by lethal injection. In fact, there was considerable evidence that Longo had been planning for some time to kill his family and start over with a new identity. Police found information on Longo's computer from "Hitman On-Line," a how-to guide to murder available only in pirated Internet versions because its publisher was sued by the family of a woman whose ex-husband used the guide to hire a hit man to kill her and their quadriplegic son. They also found clippings of obituaries with notations in Longo's handwriting that seemed to indicate that he was compiling data to create a new persona.

Deceit and fantasy were nothing new to Longo. He had lied to his wife for years, hiding the truth from her about his affairs, his failed business, his lavish spending, the checks he forged to keep creditors at bay, the property he stole to keep up appearances. When the family car broke down and he couldn't afford to fix it, he swiped a new one from a dealer's lot. He once stole a powerboat, telling his wife he won it in a contest. He even stole to pay for the ring he had given MaryJane when he asked her to marry him.

The telltale signs of the pathological narcissist emerge with the details that a year before the murders, when MaryJane confronted him about e-mails he had written to another woman, Longo told his wife that he didn't love her anymore because she hadn't been any "fun" since having children. In Longo's view, it was his wife who had broken faith with him by bringing kids and the responsibilities and obligations of parenthood into their lives.

In a chilling twist on the eraser killer pattern of getting rid of the belongings and mementos that represent their dead victims, Longo actually started the "divestment" process before the killing. For months leading up to the murders, Longo had quietly disposed of baby clothes, family photos, and other personal items—the last of which he threw into a dumpster just before fleeing to Mexico.

Even by his own self-serving account of events—that his wife had started the killings—Longo did not attempt to resuscitate his children, get help, or call police. Instead, he finished the job, got rid of the bodies, then went for coffee and returned some rented videos. It was as if he were just checking another errand off his list on his way to bachelor paradise, the lives of his wife and children of no more consequence than returning a delinquent video.

PART THREE

A Psychological Autopsy of a Classic Eraser Killing

CHAPTER EIGHT

A Watery Grave

So much has been written and said about the Peterson case that we may be tempted to think there is nothing more we can learn from it. Yet for most people it remains a crime without context, something so seemingly diabolical and inexplicable that they cannot imagine that anything like it has ever happened before or since.

Even the jurors who convicted Peterson did not seem to grasp what the case was really about. In finding a lesser degree of culpability for the murder of Conner than for Laci, they treated Conner's death as collateral damage in the killing of his mother, as if he were just along for an unfortunate ride. Although medically speaking that may be true—Conner suffocated after his mother stopped breathing—there is ample reason to believe that Scott Peterson wanted to get rid of the baby as much as he wanted to get rid of his wife, if not more.

In a book published by seven of the jurors after the trial, they said they based their second-degree verdict in the killing of Conner on a lack of evidence of premeditation and malice, such as the absence of tool marks on Laci's uterus. To think that Scott would have needed to hack into his wife's womb to show that he planned and intended for his child to die reflects both a misunderstanding of the law and a misperception of what all available evidence indicates was the motive for this crime.

There is also a continuing myth, argued even by some who believe Peterson killed his wife and child, that he was unfairly convicted because there was no "real" proof. That the case ended in conviction was extraordinary—not because the evidence was lacking, however, but because of the battle waged both inside and outside the courtroom to exploit the fragility of our legal system in the face of eraser crimes.

—~~—

When Laci Peterson woke up on June 9, 2002, she just *knew* that her dream had finally come true. For the last year and a half, the twenty-seven-year-old had been trying, unsuccessfully, to conceive a child with her thirty-year-old husband. As a girl she had lost her right ovary and fallopian tube to a tumor and had grown up fearing she might never be able to have a baby. She even tried to convince herself for a while that she didn't want children. But now she did, desperately. She had been timing her ovulation and was about to consider more direct fertility methods when she suddenly sensed that she just might be pregnant.

Two days before, Laci had confided to one of her closest friends that her period was late. René Tomlinson, who had known Laci since their sophomore year of high school and had herself struggled for two years to get pregnant, knew far too much about false alarms, and cautioned Laci to be patient. "Sometimes your body plays tricks on you," Tomlinson warned. But Laci could not help but get her hopes up. That very next day, June 8, Laci hosted a baby shower for her friend, at that time eight months pregnant, and tried to imagine herself in René's shoes.

At the crack of dawn on June 9 she could wait no longer. Laci jumped out of bed and ran out to the store to buy a home pregnancy test. By seven that morning she had awakened every member of her family and each one of her girlfriends, unable to contain her joy.

"Emma's going to have a playmate!" she exclaimed to Tomlinson, who had already named the daughter she was carrying. Laci was ecstatic. Their children would grow up together, she said, just as they had.

Scott's reaction was strange, but not overly alarming. When Laci tried to rouse her still sleeping husband to give him the news, he seemed irritated, claiming he was hung over from the night before. As the pregnancy progressed, however, he seemed as happy as Laci, building a table for the baby's room, attending Lamaze classes with his wife, and even accompanying Laci to her prenatal appointments.

It was only in retrospect that anyone close to Scott or Laci was able to recognize clues to his real feelings about impending fatherhood. Only when it was too late did they learn of the steps Scott had taken to cut himself loose physically and psychologically from his wife and child, a path that grew into an increasingly determined plan as her February 10, 2003, due date drew closer.

When Laci learned during a sonogram in September that she was going to have a boy—she couldn't wait to find out that news either—she made another excited round of calls to friends and family. After much debate, Scott and Laci decided on the name Conner. They joked that that they liked the initials C. P., which mirrored the initials of their alma mater, Cal Poly, where they had met and fallen in love.

Laci stopped working as a substitute teacher in her seventh month of pregnancy to concentrate on the impending arrival. She and Scott converted a spare bedroom in their Modesto, California, home into a beautiful nursery, decorating it in a nautical theme. A mobile with tiny sailboats dangled tantalizingly above the dresser-cum-changing table. A lamp whose shade was adorned with pictures of lighthouses glowed comfortingly next to a rocking chair. A stuffed seal, a starfish, and a rubber ducky wearing a sailor's cap perched on shelves. Everything was ready, just waiting for the baby.

As a final loving touch, Laci hung a life preserver protectively over the crib, emblazoned with the words "Welcome aboard." Only Scott knew that the child would never see a new boat, though he would ride in one just once.

—∿∿—

It was after 11 A.M. on December 24, 2002, by the time Scott Peterson hitched the fourteen-foot aluminum fishing boat to his

Ford F-150, towed it out of the strip mall warehouse he rented for his fertilizer sales business, and began the ninety-mile drive from Modesto to the San Francisco Bay. That was a pretty late hour to be setting out on a solo fishing trip, or so it would seem later that night to police.

Avid fisherman typically head out well before dawn, when the winds are lighter, and fish, whose self-preservation instinct drives them away from the sun into deeper water as daylight advances, are still near the water's surface. Scott also brought the wrong fishing poles and tackle for what he would later claim he was fishing for: sturgeon.

To catch sturgeon in the turbulent waters of the San Francisco Bay, you need a sturdy saltwater pole, a long line weighted with a sinker to remain stationary on the bay floor, and fresh bait to lure these keen-smelling bottom-feeders from the herring roe, clams, and shrimp they hunt. The two rods Scott had with him were for freshwater fishing. The brand-new ultralight stream-fishing pole Scott had purchased four days before would be far too light to catch a sturgeon. The second rod was missing the crank on its reel. And the artificial lures he oddly selected for the excursion were never taken out of their sealed packaging.

You also need to be tightly anchored to catch sturgeon, skittish fish with a bite so soft you could never detect it in a moving or even gently rocking boat. Scott brought one homemade five-pound cement anchor, wholly inadequate for anchoring in the rough bay current. What's more, it wasn't even attached to a rope or chain.

The central bay, where Scott was headed, was also the least likely place to find sturgeon that time of year. During the winter months, sturgeon migrate up into the rivers and estuaries that feed into the bay, following the herring spawn to feast off their eggs. They can be found in the bay in December, but only in its farthest reaches. If he just wanted to "get his boat in the water," to try out his new toy, as his lawyer would argue at trial, there were a dozen lakes within a sixty-mile radius of Modesto. If he really wanted to catch sturgeon, the Sacramento–San Joaquin River Delta, much closer to home, was a better bet.

Most significantly, the boat Scott bought on December 9 for $1,400 cash—a boat not another living soul knew he owned save for its seller—was not up to the purported task.

The San Francisco Bay is like a mini-ocean, with treacherous currents and unpredictable swells that can easily overwhelm a small open boat. Sturgeon, armor-backed behemoths with prehistoric roots, can grow as tall as a man and weigh up to fifteen hundred pounds. A hooked sturgeon can mount an epic battle for survival, dragging and even capsizing a boat. Trying to land a struggling sturgeon alone in a boat designed for placid lake and river fishing would be foolhardy even on the most tranquil of waters. To attempt to do so in the bay verges on the suicidal.

"Going out on San Francisco Bay in a fourteen-foot boat, particularly at that time of year, that's almost like a death wish," said a sport-fishing boat captain who has plied the bay waters for twenty-five years. "I wouldn't do it."

A few other factors made Scott's fishing alibi seem even more implausible. It was Christmas Eve, a day most people spend enjoying the company of those they hold nearest and dearest, or madly dashing to malls and supermarkets to finish their Christmas shopping and prepare for holiday feasts. Scott would tell police he made a spontaneous decision to go fishing that morning because he had a free day, leaving his pregnant wife to mop the house, bake Christmas goodies, and prepare for a Christmas Day brunch she was planning to host for her whole family. Yet he had plans that night to have dinner with his wife and in-laws at six, and even more pressingly had promised to pick up a specially ordered gift basket for Laci's beloved grandfather that afternoon at a Modesto fruit market, which was closing for the holiday at three.

That meant he would be driving three hours round-trip for no more than an hour of fishing. He also would tell police he opted to fish that morning because it was too rainy and cold in Modesto to golf, his favorite pastime. Why, police wondered, would someone choose a cold, rainy day to take a new boat out on its maiden voyage, especially on the wild and wooly waters of the San Francisco Bay?

Scott Peterson never picked up the fruit basket that afternoon. He didn't need to, because he wasn't planning on spending Christmas Day opening presents with Laci's family. Nor was he planning to sit down to a warm family dinner with Laci and her mother and stepfather on Christmas Eve. He did, however, speak to Laci's mother, Sharon Rocha, that night shortly before the couple was supposed to arrive for dinner, and his words, so strange and abrupt, chilled her to the bone: "Laci's missing."

———

The entrance to Highway 99, the major freeway that cuts through Modesto, was just half a block from his warehouse, but Scott chose to take Highway 132, a rural route that cuts through twenty miles of strawberry fields, nut groves, vineyards, apple orchards, dairy farms, and grazing land of the verdant Central Valley until it finally connects up with Interstate 580 on the outskirts of the greater Bay Area.

It's a scenic, if lonesome, drive past ramshackle barns and crops watched over by crows. For most of its length, Highway 132 is just one lane in each direction. There'd be no nosy truck drivers peering down into the bed of his pickup wondering what was under all those patio umbrellas he was hauling, no bored Highway Patrol officers noticing that he hadn't registered the boat trailer he was pulling.

Scott wasn't interested in "trying out his boat" in any bodies of water close to home. He had carefully selected the destination more than two weeks before, a day before he bought the boat and "confessed" to his unsuspecting girlfriend that he had, in fact, been married but had "lost" his wife—a prophecy that had now come true.

On December 8, as forensic analysis of his computer would later reveal, he searched the Internet for places to launch a boat on San Francisco Bay, zeroing in on the Berkeley Marina and clicking on a map and driving instructions. He also accessed a real-time map of the direction and velocity of currents in the central bay, zooming in on a particular area near Brooks Island.

Up until the morning of the trip, however, evidence now indicates that he was considering an even more forbidding destination, a place from which his wife and child would likely never have emerged. On the same day that he researched San Francisco Bay, he also searched the Internet extensively for places to launch a boat directly into the Pacific Ocean. He was looking specifically for launch ramps south of the bay near the town of Watsonville. That was strange because Watsonville is not even on the coast. Then, just before logging off on December 8, he zoomed in on a driving map to Moss Landing.

No one commented on this part of his searching at trial, but it struck an alarm bell for me. Located about midway between Santa

Cruz and Monterey, and the only coastal launching point near Watsonville, Moss Landing is the site of an astounding geological anomaly. Beginning just a hundred yards offshore and extending sixty miles out to sea, the continental shelf drops away precipitously into a yawning underwater chasm equivalent in size and scale to the Grand Canyon. Carved out over twenty million years by earthquakes and avalanche-like sediment flows, the Monterey Submarine Canyon plunges more than two miles below the ocean surface at its greatest depth into a sunless abyss. Just a half mile off the Moss Landing jetty the water is already two hundred meters deep.

"You can scuba dive right over the mouth of the canyon, which is pretty creepy," says Lisa Borok of the Monterey Bay Aquarium Research Institute, located in Moss Landing. "Suddenly the sand disappears down a black hole."

There is no deeper water as close to shore, easily accessible by boat, anywhere else in the continental United States than there is at Moss Landing. Scott could never have taken his small open boat into the ocean outside the Golden Gate, where huge amounts of water rushing in and out of the narrow mouth to San Francisco Bay create treacherous swells. But Moss Landing, at the center of the gently crescent-shaped Monterey Bay, is one of the most protected places along the coast.

Gary Greene, a marine biologist with the Monterey Bay Aquarium Research Institute and professor at the Moss Landing Marine Laboratories, an arm of the California State University system, believes that a weighted body dumped into Monterey Canyon would probably never be found. In addition to the sheer depth of the site, sand and other sediment that washes down the canyon tends to bury objects or carry them away. Half a dozen times over the last few years, scientific instruments set on the sea floor near the mouth of the canyon have been swept away, some never to be found again. A great number of predators, including great white sharks, also forage in the canyon.

"This is one of the best studied canyons anywhere," says Greene. "Researchers are going out all the time with remote-operated vehicles, but it would be serendipitous to find a body in the canyon. If it was the size of a whale you might find it, but probably not a human—unless you were really looking and you went out right away, before it became fodder for other organisms or was buried or carried farther down the canyon."

Before Scott left home on Christmas Eve morning, someone logged onto his computer at 8:40 A.M., using his logon, and immediately checked the weather forecast for San Jose, the largest city south of the San Francisco Bay. Police believe Laci was dead by then. But even if she were still alive at that time, she would have had no reason to check the weather outside Modesto, as she had no plans to leave town that day. This could only have been Scott, and the only reason he would have been concerned about the weather in the South Bay is that he was planning on driving in that direction.

Afternoon rain was predicted for both San Jose and the Central Coast. Perhaps the forecast scared him off, or the longer drive—two and a half hours each way, making it difficult for him to get back in time to "find" Laci missing before their scheduled rendezvous with his in-laws. If he had dumped his wife's body at Moss Landing instead of in the San Francisco Bay, he might very well be a free man today. But Scott Peterson did not commit the perfect crime. No one ever does. He made mistakes and decisions that ultimately gave him away.

After picking up the freeway, Scott climbed up and over the hills that separate the valley from the Bay Area via the Altamont pass, known for its surreal hilltop wind-generator farms and a 1969 rock concert that ended in a fan's senseless murder. He passed "Club Fed," the federal prison in Pleasanton that once housed fugitive heiress Patty Hearst and was the scene of an inmate's daring 1986 escape by helicopter. He continued past a Babies "R" Us store, where Laci had registered for shower gifts, and a miniature golf course, where he might have taken Conner for his first whacks. At a fork in the highway marked by a hilltop church with three enormous crosses, he headed the last few miles toward Berkeley. He exited the freeway and drove down University Avenue toward the bay, following the directions he'd gotten from the Internet to the public launch area at the far northeast end of the marina complex.

The Berkeley Marina is usually a bustling place, the largest marina in the Bay Area and, with a thousand berths, one of the largest in California. On Christmas Eve, however, it was like a ghost town. Fishing season was still months away. No one booked a charter trip or party boat out of the Marina Sports Center that day. No one came into the waterfront manager's office. Between December 23 and December 27, only three people paid to launch boats from the public piers.

Scott Peterson was one of those three. He fed five $1 bills into the "iron ranger" at the top of the ramp, and the machine spit out a receipt stamped with the date and time: December 24, 2002, at 12:54 P.M. That same day, Marina groundskeeper Mike Ilvesta came upon a man with brown hair who looked to be in his thirties struggling to back his trailer down the ramp.

There was only one other truck and trailer in the parking lot, but it was situated in such a way that the two vehicles were lined up end to end in front of the ramp, blocking Ilvesta's path as he attempted to drive through the lot. He had to wait about twenty seconds while the embarrassed-looking driver tried several times to align his boat trailer with the pier, bumping into the pier at one point.

"I saw the truck and trailer mostly, and I caught a glimpse of the guy's face, smiling. But it was so brief I wasn't able to identify him to the detectives that came down, to pick him out of a photo lineup," Ilvesta told me several weeks later. But the truck and trailer he described matched Scott's: "A four-door Ford pickup, extended cab, goldish in color. What made it stick out in my mind was that the trailer was so much smaller than the truck. We usually see bigger boats at the marina."

As is the case with most eyewitness descriptions, there are some problems with Ilvesta's recollection. He thinks the boat was already off the trailer and that Scott was in the process of taking it out of the water when he happened by, but places the time at about 12:45 P.M. That would match up with the time Scott was preparing to launch his boat, but the incident he recalls matches Scott's own description of what happened when he was leaving. In any event, there is little question that this was Peterson, as Scott himself told Det. Craig Grogan of the Modesto police the next day that some Marina maintenance workers "got a good laugh" when he backed the trailer into the pier.

One of the biggest mysteries in the Peterson case, the question most often asked by those who argued his innocence, is why Scott Peterson told police he went fishing in the bay on Christmas Eve if he had dumped his wife's body there. Such an argument assumes, however, that killers are perfectly rational and logical, too smart to make mistakes or do anything that might ever get them caught. In reality, the fact that Laci's and Conner's bodies washed up where Scott placed himself on Christmas Eve, ninety miles from where his wife supposedly disappeared, excluded virtually any other reasonable scenario for how they got there. Even his attorney, Mark Geragos, concedes that this insurmountable fact is what got his client convicted.

So why would a guilty man place himself at the "scene of the crime," or at least at his chosen disposal site, volunteering the launch fee receipt to police that very night as proof of his whereabouts?

I think there are two explanations. Either he was so confident in the measures he took to weigh down his wife's corpse that he thought it would never be found, or once he knew he had been seen at the bay, he was forced to change his alibi.

Police believe that Scott was planning to say he spent the day golfing at the county club just outside Modesto, which he joined three weeks before Laci disappeared. That's what he told Laci's sister he planned to do on Christmas Eve when she cut his hair on the night of December 23 and he offered to pick up the gift basket she and Laci had ordered from Vella Farms, which is very near the country club. And when the search began for Laci, he told two different people that he had been golfing, apparently not having the new alibi quite fixed yet in his mind.

———

Being seen at the bay was his first mistake, the slip-ups on his alibi another.

As fate would have it, Mike Ilvesta was not the only person to have seen Scott that day at the bay. This other sighting, something that has never before been reported, was by Heather Hailey, a caretaker on Brooks Island, a small island in the central bay about two nautical miles northwest of the Berkeley Marina, near where Scott Peterson said he did his fishing that day. This second eyewitness, who got a much better look at Peterson than Ilvesta, posed an even bigger problem for Scott. The fact that she could place him at a specific location on the bay may be the reason Scott was forced to incriminate himself even more damningly—admitting that he was in the exact area of the bay where a tides expert later calculated that Laci was dumped, on the basis of where the remains of Laci and Conner washed ashore.

Very few people, even lifelong Bay Area residents, had ever heard of Brooks Island before the arrest of Scott Peterson. Unlike the much-visited destinations of Angel Island and Alcatraz, Brooks Island is restricted to visitors as a designated bird sanctuary, inhabited only by the couple who serve as its caretakers, Hailey and her boyfriend, Roy Tedder. No one else is allowed to step foot on Brooks Island without a permit from the regional parks department, which administers the island in conjunction with the federal Department of the Interior, in order to protect the habitat of marine birds that nest there.

The Spanish originally named the island Isla de Carmen—eerily, the name of a famous, if fictional, woman who was murdered by her lover. For a while it was inhabited by people who raised fruit, grazed cattle, and fished for oysters. It later became a private hunting reserve where swells like Bing Crosby came to shoot pheasant. For many years early in the twentieth century, the island was quarried for stone used for, among other things, constructing one of the cellblocks at San Quentin, the prison that houses California's Death Row.

Some 373 acres of rock and sand half a mile long, Brooks Island is shaped like a gun, with the main part of the island making up the handle and a long sandy spit extending due west forming the barrel. The caretaker's residence and private pier are located where the "hammer" on the gun would be. Near the base of the handle is another much smaller island called Bird Island, basically a large rock that juts up out of the bay, on which sea birds rest.

If one wanted to drop a body overboard, Brooks Island would be a pretty good place to do so. The water is shallow enough there to navigate safely in a boat the size of Scott's, but too shallow for most other boats on the bay. And the island provides a curtain of security, blocking the view of any prying eyes from the nearby Richmond shore.

Here Scott, due to unforeseen circumstances, made another mistake. Heather Hailey was out on the island Christmas Eve afternoon, looking for shorebirds in distress from oil residue that gets kicked up on top of the water after storm surges, when she suddenly noticed a small aluminum boat close to shore.

"The windward side of the island is pretty much riddled with rocks and boulders," explained Hailey, who was not called to testify and whose sighting has never before been made public. "It's too rough because it's shallow in there and catches the current bad. Fishermen don't go over there. I only see two or three boats a year in that vicinity."

The boat she says she saw that day matches the description of Scott's boat—twelve to fourteen feet, she estimated, with a black outboard motor. She couldn't see the pilot's face well, but could tell he was white, with brown hair and a medium build. When she locked eyes with him, something strange happened.

"As soon as he saw me, he pulled his boat around Bird Island and made a dead stop," Hailey told me. "I thought maybe he was going to try to land and go camping because of all the stuff he had piled in the boat. So I sat down on the beach, and we had like a ten-minute staring contest."

The man didn't wave or smile or shout a greeting. And he wasn't fishing. "He just kind of kicked back and was looking at me as I was looking at him," she said. After she decided he wasn't coming onto the island, she headed back toward the caretaker's residence. By the time she got home, the boat was no longer in sight.

A month went by before Hailey realized that what she saw on Christmas Eve might be important. "We can't get a newspaper out here, and we don't watch much TV news because it's so depressing," she said. "So it wasn't until sometime in January that I saw a picture of Scott Peterson's boat. That's when I called Modesto police."

There is one problem with Hailey's recollection, like Ilvesta's. She believes she saw the boat about an hour before sunset, which occurred at 4:55 P.M. on Christmas Eve. Scott appears to have left the marina by 2:15 P.M., when activity on his cell phone resumed. Hailey conceded she could be wrong about the time. It was overcast that day, so it may have seemed darker and later than it was when she saw the boat. But she is certain she saw it on Christmas Eve.

With so little activity on the bay that day, and with Scott admitting to being near Brooks Island, it is hard to believe there could have been anyone else in a boat that small in the same place on the same day. I believe that the fact that Heather Hailey got a good long look at Scott, that she seemed suspicious enough to report him to someone, made Scott realize that he had to admit not only to being at the bay but also to being in a part of the bay that the police otherwise would probably never have searched.

However unforeseeable, getting spotted near the place where he dumped the body was perhaps the single biggest mistake Scott made, and one that would potentially prove fatal for him.

The San Francisco Bay covers sixteen hundred square miles and holds five million acre-feet of water at mean tide. One could never search it all, and police would have had no reason to look around Brooks Island, an unlikely place to dump a body or even to pretend to be fishing. In fact, it initially seemed much more likely to the detectives investigating the case that Scott would have dumped his wife into the deeper waters of the shipping channel, a designated transit lane for major ship traffic that cuts through the center of the bay west of Brooks Island and out the Golden Gate.

Although police never did find Laci's body during their searches, the months they spent scouring the waters near Brooks Island put pressure on Scott that caused him to make more mistakes. At the same time that Scott was insisting that police were wasting manpower, that there was no reason Laci would be in the bay, he compulsively revisited the scene.

On at least six occasions in the month after Laci's disappearance, Scott returned to the Berkeley Marina, each time in a different car, often one he rented just for the trip. He never spent more than five or ten minutes at the marina, never checked in with the scene commander, never spoke with the dive teams. He just observed from afar, driving out to the lookout points and cruising up and down the frontage road that looks out on the bay.

By mid-January, Scott began staying on and off at the home of his half sister, Anne Bird, in the Berkeley hills, in an attic bedroom with a view of Brooks Island. In late February, after police served a second search warrant on his home, Scott began looking to move secretly to the Bay Area, hoping to live incognito in a room with a bird's-eye view of his wife's watery grave. Using the name Cal, Scott answered ads on the Internet bulletin board Craigslist and checked out several apartments in the Berkeley and El Cerrito hills, raving to his sister about the "spectacular view." Although both cities have a view toward Brooks Island, the El Cerrito hills look directly down on the Pt. Isabel shoreline where Laci's body would eventually wash up.

"One day he told me he and Laci were going to name the baby California and call him Cal for short," Anne Bird explained. "Then he started leaving all these messages for people from my house, and they returned his phone calls asking for Cal. He said he didn't want his name on a lease, he just wanted to rent a room." Anne was shocked. Did Scott think he would not be recognized, that he could just slink away from Modesto and start a cool new life in the "happening" Bay Area?

—⁓—

Scott believed he could get away with murder. He still believes that, even after his conviction, telling supporters how the defense held back in *this* trial, how very soon he'll be exonerated at a second trial. In truth, it could take five years or more before any court begins to review his case, more than twenty before his appeals are exhausted. Yet truth, not to mention humanity, has little hold on a man who could anchor his pregnant wife to the bottom of San Francisco Bay with homemade concrete weights and then watch over his handiwork like an omnipotent God.

Why would Scott Peterson want to gaze out on the bay, reminding him every day of his ghastly act? Did he simply want a better way to keep tabs on the progress of the investigation so that he could head for the border if the bodies were found, as he appeared to be doing when they were discovered? Or did he enjoy, like so many spousal killers, the feeling of power and control he exerted over his wife—knowing she was anchored to the bottom of that vast blue bay in what he hoped would be her final resting place?

Peterson believed that with charm and guile and faultless manners he would never be held accountable, never even be suspected of killing his wife and child. After all, women "go missing" all the time. And in many cases, without a body, without hard and compelling evidence, police are not able to make an arrest, much less sustain a conviction. That is a lesson he learned up close in his college days, a sad fact he hoped to turn to his advantage.

Who would care about another missing woman? Who would really bother to look for her? He figured that on Christmas Eve there would not even be a detective on duty, that it would be days before someone higher than a beat cop was assigned to the case of Laci Peterson. By then the trail would be cold, or so he hoped. And there were always the usual suspects on whom to cast suspicion: parolees, sex offenders, and vagrants. There were certainly plenty of those around.

Scott Peterson greatly underestimated the Modesto Police Department, just as he would the prosecutors assigned to try his case, the lover who would see through his lies, and the family and friends who would never stop looking for Laci or seeking justice in her name. He believed that he could charm, control, and outwit everyone around him because he had been doing it for much of his life.

San Quentin State Prison sits directly on the shore of San Francisco Bay just seven or so nautical miles northwest of the spot where Peterson sealed his fate. Ironically, barring a successful appeal, he will have a bay view for the rest of his life—albeit only what he can make out through the grimy, nearly opaque windows along his prison tier.

CHAPTER NINE

Keeping Secrets

Scott Peterson was raised in a blended family, a self-described "Brady Bunch" whose personal mythology masked an unacknowledged river of pain. To Scott's peril, and even more to the peril of his victims, his family has never come to grip with its secrets: a legacy of loss and abandonment that has played out over three generations.

Just a few days before Christmas in 1945, when Scott's mother, Jackie, was just two years old, her father was murdered. John Harvey Latham, thirty-six, was working late at the tire and salvage yard he owned in downtown San Diego when he was bludgeoned to death with a rusty pipe. An employee arriving for work the next morning found him lying in a pool of blood just outside his office door. Latham's wallet was missing, along with the day's receipts.

Latham had called his wife, Helen, around nine that night to say he was on his way home. When he failed to show up, she did not report him missing, however. As she later told police, he sometimes "stayed out with the boys."

An autopsy determined that Latham died from a single blow to the back of the head that fractured his skull. Police theorized that the killer lay in wait for him as he emerged from his office and hit him with the three-foot length of pipe found next to his body. They questioned and briefly detained an African American employee Latham had fired two days before the murder, Robert Sewell. But without any hard evidence the case went unsolved for four years, until police received a tip that Sewell had bragged to friends about the crime. He was rearrested in 1949 and after three days of interrogation confessed.

Like Scott Peterson, Sewell had his defenders who believed an innocent man was being railroaded. The case became racially charged. The NAACP hired a lawyer to defend Sewell after friends alleged that police had beaten the confession out of him, and held a defense rally in his honor the night before the trial began.

Sewell was, nevertheless, convicted and sentenced to life in prison. Two years later he died of natural causes at San Quentin.

Jackie has no memories of her father. His death was so sudden and traumatic that her mother refused ever to talk about him, and it wasn't until Jackie was an adult and found his school yearbook that she learned what he looked like. At times, Jackie said, she felt as though she had never had a father at all.

Her mother's silence came at a terrible price, both for her children and for herself. Helen Latham suffered from a painful, debilitating, and incurable disease, scleroderma, a progressive hardening of the skin and the tissue surrounding the internal organs. The condition is sometimes known as "Lot's wife disease" after the biblical character who turned into a pillar of salt, because it feels as if the body is turning to stone.

As with all autoimmune disorders, in which the body attacks itself, stress can cause the condition to worsen. Jackie and her siblings believe that the trauma of their father's murder caused their mother to suffer a long, slow death—a progressive imprisonment inside her own body—that played out over the next fifteen years.

"We were told it was because she didn't release the feelings she had when my father died, because she kept it all inside," Jackie explained in the penalty phase of her son's trial. "She had four young children to raise and could not . . . break down, and so her organs broke down.

They calcified, basically, until she died a very horrible death [after] years of being bedridden."

Unable to care for her children, Helen Latham placed Jackie and her three brothers in Nazareth House, a Catholic orphanage in San Diego that had once been the Spanish mission's school for Indian children. In her penalty phase testimony, Jackie gave only a faint description of the harshness of life in the orphanage, and most of that actually came in response to defense cocounsel Pat Harris's questions.

The children subsisted on whatever food the Poor Sisters of Nazareth, the English and Irish nuns that ran the orphanage, managed to beg for them: outdated breads and cereal, with an occasional treat of eggs from the chickens they raised. They learned "discipline" from kneeling in prayer and cleaning toilets, were punished for misbehavior in Mass with flicks to their ears. Jackie, who suffered from frequents bouts of pneumonia as a child and today uses supplemental oxygen for diminished lung capacity, was often kept quarantined from the other children.

"And every time I've tried to characterize that as being a rather tough existence you've always told me 'our needs were met.' What do you mean by that?" Harris asked her.

"I felt fortunate I had a roof over my head and three meals a day and was educated," Jackie replied. "There was no hugging or anything like that but my mother, somehow, got that through to us. I don't know how. But we knew that God loved us and that just took over everything."

Jackie's younger brother, Robert, described how the boys were not able to spend time with their sister, as the sexes were kept strictly separate except during church or class. "We would see each other through the [playground] fence mainly and say hi. I can remember one time when the boys were throwing dirt clods at the fence and they were showering down on the girls and I saw my sister there. I . . . reached through the fence and asked if she was all right. But it was a good place. There was a lot of care."

The picture of Nazareth House related by former residents currently suing the San Diego Archdiocese is much darker than that related by the Petersons, one of Dickensian cruelty and deprivation. Irwin Zalkin, an attorney representing close to one hundred victims alleging clergy abuse in San Diego, says the Nazareth House cases are the worst he's seen at any single facility in the range and enormity of physical and psychological abuse.

"It was an orphanage, where pedophiles and people with other issues had easy access," said Zalkin. "These kids were completely unprotected and vulnerable, absolutely powerless. There was no one they could go to."

One of Jackie's brothers repeatedly ran away from Nazareth House, only to be brought back by authorities every time he tried to go home. Jackie's middle brother, Patrick, the only Latham sibling not to testify at Scott's trial, has described the place as a "prison."

As each of the Peterson children reached high school age, they left the orphanage and were reunited with their mother. Although they were happy to be back home, life continued to be difficult. They hadn't seen much of their mom in years because it was difficult for her to travel to the orphanage. Now they had to take care of her. That role fell mostly to Jackie, as the only girl, who was also expected to do all the housework and serve as de facto mom to her brothers. And they only had a little Social Security money to support them.

Robert Latham recalls one Thanksgiving or Christmas when he and Jackie split a TV dinner. As usual, Jackie put a happy face on things, joking that it tasted good "if you put enough ketchup on it." But her childhood had ended long ago, and she would never get it back.

Helen Latham's last outing was to attend her daughter's high school graduation. She died the following January. The children began to disperse, first to work and then to the draft. Jackie got a good-paying job with PSA airlines, but after she got pregnant at eighteen her boss fired her.

"If you weren't married it wasn't acceptable," Jackie explained at trial. "And you couldn't draw unemployment if you were pregnant in those days. So it was a very hard time but it was of my own making and I got through it. My son was adopted by a very nice family. My doctor had people waiting for a child and he talked to me and counseled me and told me that was the best thing to do."

Jackie described the relationship that produced Don Chapman, the first child she gave up for adoption, like this: "I was naive and young and I got with someone that told you they loved you and wanted to marry you, and it just wasn't so. And I think I got involved because I wanted a father and a family."

Just a year later she was pregnant again, this time by her brother's best friend. "He was someone I trusted and we went together for a long time and we were in love," Jackie explained, offering the court a sheepish apology for sounding "like a broken record." But after he moved to Los Angeles for a teaching job, he fell for a coworker. She never even told him she was pregnant.

"I knew he would have married me and I didn't want to marry someone that was in love with someone else," she said. So the doctor arranged an adoption for this child, too, a girl who would be named Anne Grady by her adoptive parents. (After marrying, Anne would take her husband's surname, Bird.)

Three decades later, when Don and Anne found their birth mother, Jackie would tell Anne that she went into hiding for the duration of her pregnancy. Only her middle brother, Patrick, and the woman she lived with knew of her condition until a month before Anne was born, when Anne's birth father somehow found out. He offered to marry her, as she predicted, but she turned him down. Jackie was shocked and dismayed that the news had gotten out. She described her brother to Anne as "like a vault. He would never say anything to anyone."

It was a strange and hurtful thing to tell a child she had given away, and Anne wondered why her mother considered her birth such an ugly secret. But it was revealing. Keeping secrets was a family trait, one Jackie's son Scott would perfect to a pathological extreme. Scott may also have adopted the notion that children were a burden, that children were disposable—at the very least, that to have or keep a child was a decision one could make unilaterally, without consulting the other parent.

A year after Anne was born, Jackie had a third child, whom she named after her father. Jackie said she kept John because she was finally happy enough in her life to be a parent. (Other family members, however, say she considered putting him up for adoption as well but was talked out of it by her doctor.)

She raised John by herself for five years until she married Lee Peterson in 1971, a divorced father with three children of his own whom she met in a community college history class. The nuns had drummed into Jackie that she would not be able to go to college because she would have to take care of her sick mother, which only made Jackie more eager for an education. Lee Peterson was pursuing a degree in transportation management thanks to the G.I. Bill.

"She is the best thing that ever happened to me," Lee said of Jackie at trial. "I'm the grouch, and she wakes up happy every morning."

Like Jackie, Scott's father also seemed to be driven by a childhood of deprivation borne out of a sudden, unexpected reversal of fortune.

Lee's father, Arthur, the last of twelve children of Norwegian immigrants, was raised in a Minnesota farming community that was the setting for the television series *Little House on the Prairie*. Lee's mother, Marie, immigrated to Minneapolis from Lithuania by herself at age fifteen to work in a factory making underwear. Arthur tried his own hand at farming but failed. He moved to the big city of St. Paul, where he first delivered telegrams by bicycle for Western Union, then went to work for Royal servicing typewriters.

Arthur and Marie met at a dance. During World War II, they owned a corner grocery store, one of the family's more prosperous times, which Lee recalls with a child's enthusiasm.

"It was great because we could bring our friends in once a day and they could have a candy bar, or ice cream, whatever they wanted." His parents managed to save enough money to own a home for the first time and decided to build one. They bought a lot and, because there wasn't much lumber available right after the war, bought an old farm to harvest wood for construction.

"That's when the family got derailed," as Lee described it at trial. The contractor, as well as Lee's parents, failed to take into account the extremely high water table in the "Land of 10,000 Lakes." When the first rains began, the basement filled up with three feet of water, and there was no way to get it out.

"So the house was essentially useless," said Lee, who was seven or eight at the time. "My folks lost the house and the farm they had bought for the lumber, and just went totally broke."

It took the family years to recover. They lived in a series of cabins and shacks without running water at old tourist resorts that had fallen into disrepair. His mother, bitterly unhappy, cried a lot. Lee felt ashamed of his tattered clothes and tiny homes and wouldn't invite other kids over. His father, who Lee describes as lacking in ambition and business acumen, thought things were fine as long as they had food to eat and a roof over their heads. His mother couldn't stand living the way they were. When Lee was twelve she started working as a domestic, sometimes taking Lee along to the homes of her wealthy clients.

"It was a real treat to go along because [at one house] there was a boy about my age and he had tons of toys, all the goodies," Lee recalled. "He let me dress up in his cowboy suit and just experience things I had never seen before."

When Lee wanted a baseball mitt, his mother told him he had to earn the money for it. So he began doing yard work for neighbors in the warm months, shoveling snow in winter. "It was a good life lesson," Lee said, and the establishment of a strong work ethic he would try to pass along to his own children.

Lee described his parents as loving, but they showed their son little if any physical affection. Even when Lee left for the Navy after graduating from high school, they didn't send him off with a hug or kiss; they shook their son's hand. At trial, Lee would try to attribute Scott's lack of emotion after his wife and child went missing to an inherited family stoicism, what he termed a "Scandinavian trait."

"When something happened you were supposed to pick yourself up, figure out what was wrong, and go fix it . . . do whatever needed to be done," Lee said of his upbringing.

That description contrasted sharply with excuses Lee and Jackie had given for why Scott steadfastly refused to grant media interviews or make public pleas for his wife's return for the first month she was missing—until his affair with Amber Frey became public knowledge and the Rocha family turned against him. He was simply too emotional, they said, too distraught to stand before the cameras. Jackie had even claimed that Scott was suicidal in the wake of his wife's disappearance.

Five months before the end of his enlistment, Lee married his high school sweetheart, Mary Kaminski. They settled in Minnesota and had three children: a daughter, Susan, and two sons, Mark and Joe. Lee worked in the electronics field for several years before switching to sales for a series of trucking firms, largely because it afforded him the opportunity to play golf with customers. Lee picked up the game at age twenty-five after a coworker invited him to play, and it quickly became his abiding passion.

The family relocated to San Diego in 1967 in search of better weather and better opportunity for advancement. After a few years, the marriage faltered and the Petersons divorced. The children went to live with their mother and spent weekends with their father, but they say that Lee found an excuse to drop by and see them as often as he could.

"I had a great deal of guilt over not being there for them every night tucking them into bed and that kind of thing so I tried to make up for that by being there a lot," he said. The college he was attending three nights a week was just a few blocks from where the kids were living, so he'd stop by and play with them for a while or take them out to eat. It was at that college that he met Jackie.

Like Jackie, Lee had a big investment in the future of their union, a need for their blended family to be one big happy Brady Bunch, everybody working together and playing together, living out a communal dream.

When Scott Lee Peterson was born on October 24, 1972, almost a year to the day after Lee and Jackie married, his arrival seemed to cement the connection Jackie had longed for. At last she was married, to a man who truly loved her, and now they had a child together, a living embodiment of that bond.

In her eyes Scott was the perfect child, the golden boy who could do no wrong. She even called him that, the Golden Boy, a title Scott seemed to relish. Both she and Lee would lavish on Scott the rewards and privileges they had not been able to offer their earlier children, when their personal and financial situations were less secure.

Jackie was determined to put the pain of the past behind her. According to Anne Bird, none of the Petersons knew anything about the children Jackie had given away. They did know she had grown up in an orphanage, but Jackie gave few details. All the pain of the past was locked up, buried away. From now on, everything would be perfect. It had to be.

—⁓—

A favorite Peterson family legend is that Scott didn't learn how to walk until he was two years old because someone was always carrying him. Never was a child more wanted. "He was a joy from the moment he was born," says Jackie. "He was perfect," says Lee. "He woke up smiling and went to bed smiling."

Susan, Mark, Joe, and John were twelve, ten, nine, and six when Scott was born, but even they seemed to recognize his exalted status. Susan treated him as though he were her own child, vying with Jackie to feed him, change his diaper, push his stroller. She even bathed him twice a day when she was visiting because, she says, she enjoyed it so much.

"He was like a live baby doll to me," she said. When Joe saw his baby brother for the first time through the nursery window, he squealed to everyone within earshot, "He's mine."

Just two weeks after he was born, Scott almost died. He came down with pneumonia and had to be hospitalized in an incubator. According to the Petersons, doctors feared he might not pull through, but he recovered. John's first memory of his brother was in the hospital, Lee lifting each of the kids up so that they could peer through a window at their sick brother.

Yet for all their love and adoration, Jackie and Lee once forgot their young son in a restaurant. As Jackie described the incident to Anne Bird, Scott was such a good, quiet baby that they forgot they had brought him with them and had to be chased down outside by their waiter. "Ma'am, you left your baby," he called after Jackie.

With the exception of the restaurant incident, Scott's parents kept their son exceedingly close to them—to the point of enmeshment, some might say. Their happiness, their identity was in many ways derived through him.

Jackie once told a reporter that she and Lee were "enslaved" to Scott. It was a startling and bizarre choice of words, uttered without any rancor or resentment. Rather, it seemed to be an expression of some immutable family hierarchy, of what Jackie felt they owed Scott. At trial, the Petersons' exacting recall of the most minor details of Scott's life—his golf scores, his stint as a school crossing guard, his perfect attendance award in grade school—seemed almost fetishistic at times, especially when their idealized image of Scott was so at odds with the man captured on the Amber tapes and other police wiretaps.

It became clear over the course of the trial that the Scott everyone thought he or she knew did not exist. Or there were two very different people inside one man: the perfect son, brother, and friend who couldn't harm a flea, never got angry, was kind and generous to a fault; and the man behind the mask, a black-hearted monster, who used charm and cunning to get what he wanted and didn't care who he hurt in the process, who went through the motions of life without ever really feeling anything.

Jackie owned a designer dress shop called The Put On when Scott was born, and she set up a crib for him in the back room. As he learned to crawl, he had the run of the shop—until he bit a customer on the toe. Jackie served as den mother to Scott's Cub Scout troop, and mother and son studied piano together.

When Scott was still a toddler, Lee started his own business on the side, building customized wood packing crates for hard-to-ship items like computers. After a few years, San Diego Crating and Packing began to take off, and Lee was able to quit the trucking business. Jackie came aboard as bookkeeper, and set up an area in the shop for Scott and his toys. Eventually all the children would work for the family business at some point, including Scott. (Son Joe runs the company today.)

The business did so well that the family was able to move to progressively nicer and nicer areas around San Diego as Scott was growing up, from the posh lakeside Scripps Ranch to Rancho Santa Fe, an ultraexclusive development dotted with private golf courses, equestrian trails, polo fields, fashionable shops, art galleries, and gourmet restaurants. Lee described the move to Rancho Santa Fe, reportedly the richest community per capita in America with multimillion-dollar homes on minimum two-and-a-half-acre lots, as the culmination of a dream come true.

"It was like the very pinnacle," he said. "You have made it once you got there." Other aspects of their lifestyle improved as well. Lee got his pilot's license and bought his own plane. At one point, Lee was driving a Ferrari and Jackie a Rolls Royce.

Lee was still fairly young, only thirty-three when Scott was born, but he treated him like a late-in-life child, a little buddy with whom he could pal around, a near constant companion. Joanne Farmer, a longtime friend of Jackie's, recalls Scott following his dad around like "a shadow, wanting to do everything Lee did." Jeffrey Cleveland, who worked at the Peterson crating company for nine years, said Scott seemed to have just "sloughed off from Lee." John, the only other child living in the house while Scott was growing up, described his half-brother as a "little miniature dad," who even as a boy dressed like Lee in khaki pants and golf shirts.

Lee took Scott along with him on sales calls, saying Scott's mere presence "gave [him] confidence." When Scott was appointed a school crossing guard in the fifth grade, Lee would park and watch his son from a distance, marveling at how seriously Scott took the responsibility. By the time Scott was in high school, his father made it a point to be home by the time Scott got out of school. Lee would have snacks waiting for him, then the two would play golf together nearly every day.

Lee endeavored to instill his children with his passion for hunting, fishing, and especially golf, believing that the family would spend more time together if they all shared the same interests. All the kids took golf lessons, but Scott showed the most talent, beating his dad by the time he was a teenager.

One wonders, however, how much Scott really enjoyed the game. As a young boy he preferred fishing, bringing his pole along and bailing after a few holes to go fish in the river that ran through the golf course. Even as a teen, Lee seemed to feel the need to motivate Scott, promising to buy him his own Ferrari if he shot par. He accomplished that feat at sixteen, but Lee bought him a used Peugeot instead—"because it was safer," said Jackie.

Where other parents display a bronzed baby shoe or their child's handprint preserved in clay, Lee has a place of honor in his den reserved for Scott's first golf club: a sawed-off 3-wood they referred to as his "slugger."

While his family enjoyed the fruits of his success, Lee, as a self-made man and something of an adventurer, set a high standard to follow. Just as he had to work for the baseball glove he wanted as a kid, he expected his children to earn their own spending money. When he was still in the trucking business he would take the kids in with him on weekends and pay them to wash trucks, clean bathrooms, sweep up, and perform other odd jobs.

"We didn't go for lunch or get ice cream or do anything until we were done with the day's work," Joe Peterson recalled. Lee saw business in a very straightforward way: you told people what you were going to do, and you did it. He expected his kids to work hard and be accountable. Scott tried to emulate his father's entrepreneurial streak. He always had some kind of little business going on in the garage: assembling golf clubs, silk-screening T-shirts. But his real job, as Lee saw it, was golf.

"We told him 'Your job is to get good grades and practice your golf and become a professional golfer,'" Lee testified in the penalty phase. In exchange, they would support him while he pursued his that goal.

Lee also made his disappointment known when his children failed to live up to his expectations. He fired his eldest son, Mark, from the family business, and the two had barely spoken for more than a dozen years at the time Laci disappeared. As a teenager, John Peterson was sent away to live with other relatives when he wrecked one of Lee's cars.

But Lee and Jackie seemed to have a different standard for Scott. He could do no wrong in their eyes, and when he did they were always there to bail him out. "Perfect" was the word they used most often in describing Scott, even after he was charged with murdering his wife and child. Mark was shocked to learn from police how financially generous Jackie and Lee had been toward his half-brother over the years. Even he had bought into the mythos that Scott was the family success story, a self-made man like his father.

———

From an early age, Scott seems to have developed a strong need to please, to be whatever anybody wanted him to be. His brother Joe called him "Trooper" because of how strenuously he would try to keep up with the big boys. He took with good humor anything they could dish out, be it John's elaborately staged practical jokes (like the time he convinced Scott that a giant marauding squirrel was hiding in their backyard), or Mark and Joe's using Scott as a target for practicing their tennis serves.

With his parents and other adults, Scott displayed impeccable manners. Joanne Farmer remembers Scott at age eleven or twelve serving cookies at his parents' holiday parties, a perfect gentleman conversing with the grownups, expressing interest in what they had to say.

"My kid was in the canyon lighting bonfires, but Scott wasn't that kind of boy," recalled Joan Pernicano, another longtime friend of Jackie's, whose son, Andrew, was in Scott's Cub Scout troop. In eighth grade, Scott was voted "Friendliest Student" by his classmates. That was quite an honor, according to his best friend at the time, Britton Scheibe, because Scott wasn't "in the upper echelon of what you would consider the cool kids."

Apparently Scott was already becoming adept at charming people, at making them feel, as his cousin Kelly Beckton described it, "like the rest of the room melts away because he is paying attention to you." No one could ever remember Scott losing his temper, not even when he missed an important shot in a golf tournament. He was always even, steady, cool, in control—preternaturally so.

Like so many others, Anne Bird was once charmed and flattered by her brother's myriad kindnesses and the laserlike focus that made it seem as though he "hung on your every word and made you feel as if you were the center of the universe." Now she mourns for a child she feels was "raised like some sort of puppet," so busy pleasing others that he never learned who he really was and what he really wanted.

Scott attended University of San Diego High School, a Catholic school that required students to complete one hundred hours of community service in order to graduate. Scott volunteered as a designated driver for the campus's chapter of Students Against Drunk Driving, tutored the homeless, and visited senior centers, even "adopting" one particular woman and inviting her to school for Grandparents Day.

He took particular interest in an orphanage the school aided in Tijuana. Even after his service was completed, Scott continued to visit the orphanage, volunteering to drive other students there and deliver food and clothing.

Perhaps Scott was using good works as cover to get out of the house, take a road trip to Mexico, sample a little freedom. Or perhaps he was searching for answers, trying to understand something about his mother's life, about himself, about family secrets.

At Uni High, as it was called, Scott played on the golf team with future PGA star Phil Mickelson. After Mickelson graduated, two years ahead of Scott, Scott became team leader and was twice named most valuable player. Scott was so confident in his abilities—some teammates would say arrogant—that he had the words "Watch for me" printed as his senior statement in the school year book. (With an unfortunate typo that took on a creepy significance after he was charged with murder, his year book motto went on to say that "Great things and good deads await all of us.")

As good as Scott was, however, he never played at the level of Mickelson, who won the junior world title while still in elementary school and the Masters in 2004. It is one of the sad ironies of this case that while the man known as "Lefty," one of the most beloved figures in golf history, was exulting in winning the game's most coveted title, his former teammate was in a courtroom picking the jury that would condemn him to death.

Although the Petersons portrayed Mickelson as a good friend whom Scott invited to play at the family's country club, Mickelson says he doesn't remember Scott at all. And although Mickelson grew up much more humbly than Scott, he now lives happily with his wife and children in a luxurious Rancho Santa Fe villa, while Scott is confined to a prison cell.

Scott followed Mickelson to golf's collegiate mecca, Arizona State University. Here the facts as related by the Petersons grow murky. In the early days of Laci's disappearance, Jackie told reporters that Scott went to ASU on a golf scholarship. Even his high school teammates believed that to be true. After school officials said that Scott never received a scholarship, the story changed.

During jury selection Lee Peterson said that Scott was invited to try out for the team and told that if he showed enough promise, scholarship money might become available. At trial, the story morphed further. Lee testified that Scott boarded with team members and played one match. However, both current ASU officials and Steve Loy, who was the coach of the golf team at the time Scott was a student there and is now Mickelson's agent, maintain that Peterson never played golf there.

Yet another version of the story emerged after the trial. The father of professional golfer Chris Couch says that he got Peterson kicked off the team. Couch, national junior champion at the time, beating out Tiger Woods for that title, was being heavily recruited by ASU. According to his father, Chip Couch, Scott was assigned to show the seventeen-year-old around campus but instead took him out drinking and skirt-chasing. Chip Couch says he was so upset to find his son hung over when he picked him up at the end of the recruiting trip that he complained to the coach. He says the coach called him back and told him he threw Scott off the team. Chris Couch ended up going to the University of Florida instead, where he made the winning putt to win that school the national collegiate championship.

Scott dropped out of ASU before the end of his first semester and moved back home with his parents. Why he did so is another matter of dispute. Scott told the Modesto police that he didn't like the coach, didn't think his talent was adequately respected. Scott's sister, Susan Caudillo, told me shortly after Laci went missing that she thought Scott was just not ready to make the break from his parents.

At trial, Lee testified that Scott realized he was out of his depth at ASU, which won the NCAA golf championship in 1990 with players like Mickelson and another future pro, Per-Ulrik Johansson from Sweden. "They were unbelievably good. And I think Scott said, gee, I'll never be that good."

But why give up so easily, effectively abandoning his dream without really giving it a shot? Scott didn't even stay through the golf season, which runs until June. And why drop out of college altogether? Even if he didn't make the team, or was booted off, a degree from Arizona State would still be worth something.

Anne Bird has heard from some of Scott's cousins a far different explanation about why Scott left ASU so precipitously: that Scott got a woman pregnant, an African American woman, and that "Jackie was upset because she didn't want him to shame the family."

"I heard two different versions," Bird said, "one that Jackie and Lee went out and one that just Jackie went out and pulled Scott out of school, paid this woman off, and had her get an abortion. Maybe they just gave her a little money to move on with her life, or maybe they didn't pay her at all and just paid for the abortion. [But] the reason I heard was that he was shaming the family so they pulled him out of Arizona State."

While Scott was on trial, a seventeen-year-old boy contacted Bird and some members of the media claiming that he believed Scott was his father. The boy's mother died a few years ago, but a friend subsequently told him that she had gotten pregnant by Peterson while visiting San Diego. Bird is skeptical, because the young man has refused to get a blood test. And Scott would have been just fifteen when the child was conceived.

"Maybe he's just trying to get some notoriety," Bird says. But in both pictures the boy sent her, he looks uncannily like Scott. And when Bird wrote Scott in jail about the boy's claims and forwarded his letter, Scott's only response was a low-key "that's weird." No outraged denial, no "that couldn't possibly be true." If either of the stories Anne Bird heard is true—an abortion in Arizona, an unacknowledged child conceived in San Diego—it could help explain how Scott came to believe that women and their children are expendable, that he bore no responsibility for a life that he helped create.

———◊◊◊———

When he moved back home after dropping out of Arizona State, Scott worked for the family company for about six months. Lee retired, turned the business over to his sons Mark and Joe, and he and Jackie moved to Morro Bay, a coastal town about halfway between Los Angeles and San Francisco and just a few miles from San Luis Obispo.

Scott chafed at the ordinary laborer work he was hired to perform, such as building crates. He had bigger ambitions; he wanted to go out on the big jobs, bring in clients, and Joe, who was in charge of the shop, didn't think Scott was ready for that. So Scott left and moved in with his parents in Morro Bay. Their house was just a few blocks from the Morro Bay golf course and a restaurant called the Pacific Café, both regular haunts of Jackie and Lee and both places Scott would find employment. After eighteen months out of school he enrolled at the local junior college, Cuesta College, where he once again was a star on a golf team, a big fish in a little pond.

Jackie and Lee contend that one day when Scott was twenty he surprised them by declaring out of the blue that his parents had done enough for him and that from then on he was going to support himself.

"You don't owe me anything," Jackie says he told them.

He moved into an apartment his dad characterized as an "Animal House" with some of his Cuesta College teammates, a bachelor pad with artificial turf laid out on the roof for practicing their golf shots. The Petersons bragged after Scott's arrest that he insisted on paying his own way through school, working two, even three jobs at a time in order to do so. The truth, as so often in Scott Peterson's life, may be more complex. Although he did sometimes work multiple jobs while he was in college, graduating didn't seem like much of a priority to him. It ultimately took him eight years to get his bachelor's degree. (Oddly, when police searched his home after his arrest, they found several phony diplomas on the wall, from schools Peterson never even attended. One claimed he had earned a divinity degree, very strange for someone who until he met Amber showed no interest in religion. He claimed Laci had bought them for him as a gag gift, but no one had ever heard that she had done such a thing.)

After the humiliation in Arizona, Scott likely craved more freedom and independence from his parents. He may also have felt that he could not expect their financial support, as he was no longer on the path to becoming a professional golfer. Around this same time, however, the Petersons began to suffer significant financial problems. A relative said the family was living far beyond its means, with creditors calling night and day attempting to repossess their home and cars. The mortgage on the Morro Bay house went into default in 1992, and tax liens were filed in 1990 and 1992. (The debts were eventually satisfied and the default rescinded in 1994.)

Lee testified that about two years after he turned the reins of the crating company over to Mark and Joe, the business began to suffer, and he had to go back to San Diego for about eighteen months "to get it cranked back up again," which apparently included firing his eldest son. He then returned to Morro Bay and started a similar business, Central Coast Crating, with Scott. They each put up $3,500 as partners and started finding clients. This could partially explain why it took Scott so long to finish college.

Yet despite his surface industriousness, Scott seemed to be going through the motions: halfway continuing to pursue golf, halfway following in his father's footsteps, halfway trying to be his own man. But he would always fall back on his parents' help when he really wanted something—a house, a golf club membership, money to survive on the lam. Scott would, ultimately, do almost everything in life halfway. Half in, half out, no real commitment—that is certainly how he approached marriage and fatherhood. He had no clear purpose because he had no true sense of himself.

But he sure could fake it: the perfect son, the perfect husband. He could be whoever anyone wanted him to be.

CHAPTER TEN

Too Good to Be True

Laci Denise Rocha was born on May 4, 1975. She grew up with one foot in the country, one foot in the city, in a loving family but one also riven by divorce. Laci was just a year old when her parents, Dennis and Sharon Rocha, split after seven years of marriage. A year later, Sharon's cousin Gwen Kemple and Gwen's husband, Harvey, set Sharon up on a blind date with a construction worker buddy of his. Although they've never actually married, Sharon and Ron Grantski have been a couple ever since.

After Sharon and Dennis divorced, Laci and her brother, Brent, lived with their mother in Modesto but spent every other weekend with their father on their grandparents' dairy farm, located about twenty-five minutes outside the city. Dennis subsequently remarried, and six years after Laci was born had another daughter, Amy. When Dennis's second marriage broke up, Amy, too, spent weekends at the Rocha family dairy. To the children it was a magical place with barns and horses and a coyote pup named Princess as the family pet.

"It was a great place to grow up," said Brent, who was four years older than Laci. "We rode four-wheelers out there, went swimming in my grandparents' pool. There were tons of places to play. You kind of create your own things to do when you're out in the country." At age nine, Brent went to live full-time with his dad, but he always remained the protective older brother.

When the Rocha family came to believe that Scott had killed Laci and publicly broke from him at a January 24, 2003, press conference, it was heart wrenching to hear the sense of guilt and responsibility Brent felt for not protecting his sister from a danger no one could have perceived. It stood in stark contrast to the complete lack of conscience and denial of responsibility Scott showed with regard to his wife's murder.

Laci was very close to her paternal grandparents, and Brent saw his sister as a younger version of their grandmother: loving, centered, thoughtful. Laci inherited her grandmother's passion for cooking and from both sides of her family an appreciation of the land and its bounty. (Her maternal grandfather was a foreman on a fruit and nut farm in the same small town of Escalon where the Rocha dairy was located.)

Even as a child, Laci liked to work in the garden and dreamed of one day owning her own flower and herb shop. One of Brent's fondest memories of his sister is as an earnest little girl trying to help feed the cows while wearing her dad's oversized rubber boots, slipping and falling in the mud and manure. No one laughed harder at moments like that than Laci herself.

"She was always fun to be around," said Amy. "I was the little sister who wanted to tag along, and she let me."

Laci inherited her broad dimpled smile from her mother. Sharon remembers Laci even as an infant smiling each morning when she came to take her out of her crib. Once she learned to start talking, she never stopped. One of her girlfriends nicknamed her Chatty Cathy. Her stepfather called her J.J. for Jabber Jaws. Once on a car trip when Laci was little, he made a bet with her to see if she could go thirty seconds without saying anything. She agreed, then immediately asked if the time was up yet. After she was killed, Ron was left with the pain of wondering if his good-natured teasing had hurt Laci's feelings.

Laci was good at just about anything she put her mind to. She was popular enough to make the cheerleading squad, but was also a good athlete and an excellent student. By the time she graduated in 1993 from Modesto's Downey High School, film director George Lucas's alma mater, Laci had developed the tight-knit circle of girlfriends who would work so tirelessly to find her when she went missing. Just as she and her siblings had done on the farm, Laci and her friends created their own fun. They tee-peed each other's houses, videotaped themselves making mock commercials, and threw raucous slumber parties in which the first person to fall asleep would have her bra frozen. They shared everything together, even their first hangover. When one of the girls sneaked a bottle of champagne into one of the sleepovers, they all vowed to make it to school the next day, but Laci was the only one who managed.

"She would never let us forget that," remembers René Tomlinson. "Laci was in all the smart classes, and she was so dedicated." In Laci's mind it was simpler than that. They had made a pact. A deal was a deal. When she set her mind to something, she was determined to see it through. It was the same way she would one day embrace the concept of marriage.

Laci and Brent were the first in their family to graduate from college. While Brent went off to law school, Laci chose California Polytechnic State University in San Luis Obispo, a state college specializing in agricultural studies, where she majored in ornamental horticultural. Laci's passion and creativity stood out among her peers. She won her department's Outstanding Freshman award and was one of just thirty students across the nation selected for an endowed internship to train in the floral industry. She was elected president of the horticulture honor society and hired to manage the campus flower shop.

Laci had been involved in only one significant relationship before meeting Scott Peterson. She was a fifteen-year-old high school sophomore when she started dating William "Kent" Gain, a seventeen-year-old senior who had recently moved to Modesto from the Bay Area.

From the outside looking in, they made a picture-perfect couple: he dark-featured and handsome as a soap star, Laci gorgeous and magnetic. He moved to San Luis Obispo with her when she went away to college, and they shared a cottage during her freshman year. While Laci studied, he worked in a warehouse and surfed. They dated, according to Gain's exacting computation, for "3 years, 4 months, and 7 days." He says he asked her to marry him, but Laci told him the time wasn't right.

Inside, the relationship was anything but perfect. Kent had a temper, and Laci confided to friends that Gain yelled at her, demeaned her, and angrily pushed her once during an argument. At the end of her freshman year, they broke up, and he moved out. When Laci disappeared, Brent Rocha was concerned enough about Gain that he suggested police check him out as a suspect.

What the police discovered about Gain shocked everyone. Kent and Laci's relationship had been more violent than she had ever let on. But he could not have been involved in her disappearance because he had an airtight alibi: he was in prison in Washington State serving a fifteen-year term for shooting a subsequent girlfriend in the back.

On January 17, 1999, five years after Kent and Laci broke up, Gain shot his twenty-four-year-old live-in girlfriend, Grace Ho, with a .44-caliber pistol. Gain admits he was arguing with Ho at the time, but insists the shooting was a drunken accident, that he simply dropped the gun and it went off. However, shortly before the shooting, Gain had called another girlfriend and told her he was going to hurt Ho. That girlfriend was on the phone to 911 at the exact moment Ho was shot. (Gain was also on the phone with another friend venting about how mad he was at Ho when the friend heard the gun go off.)

Nevertheless, a jury rejected the charge of attempted murder and convicted him of first-degree assault. His lawyer had argued that Ho suffered no permanent, life-threatening injury, although that was due to sheer luck. The defense also claimed that Gain was too drunk that night to consent to a search of his apartment or waive his rights against self-incrimination.

Gain eerily posted several impassioned messages to the Web site set up by Laci's family and friends after she went missing. He has the words "In Memory of Laci Denise Rocha" tattooed *Memento*-style across his chest and calls the tattoo his "shield." He claims he still loves Laci and has pictures of her in his cell, as does Scott, but he insists he is nothing like her husband. "He never deserved to be with Laci," Gain says.

To try to prevent future eraser killings, and domestic homicides in general, it is important to look at these cases from the victim's point of view, to see if there were warning signs of impending danger, if there was anything the victim could and should have done to protect herself. That both of Laci's long-term relationships involved men capable of such extreme violence is one of the most unsettling facts in the Peterson case, but it probably says more about the shocking prevalence of intimate partner homicide than it does about Laci repeating any kind of dysfunctional pattern.

We do now know that Laci kept some aspects of her relationships secret and was willing to tolerate, at least for a while, abusive behavior from Kent. She also knew about at least one of Scott's affairs and remained married to him—although there is no evidence that she knew of, or tolerated, ongoing cheating.

This leaves open the possibility that there could have been some prior acts of violence in the Peterson marriage that Laci kept hidden. But neither the police nor anyone else has uncovered any evidence of that, and the fact that Laci did break off an unhealthy relationship with Kent Gain, that she refused to marry him, more likely indicates that she recognized the danger in a more typically abusive man like Gain.

Scott Peterson seemed to be as different from Gain as one could possibly be: successful, ambitious, kind, considerate, solicitous in the extreme. The only person around Laci who had any reservations about Scott prior to Laci's disappearance is Dennis Rocha, who says he found his son-in-law cocky and patronizing. But even Dennis sensed nothing disturbing in Kent Gain, who had visited the farm often with Laci and appeared to him to be a nice young man.

———

Laci was nineteen when she met Scott in the summer of 1994 at the Pacific Café, shortly after breaking up with Gain. She had been into the restaurant several times with a friend, whose boyfriend also worked there. Never shy when it came to getting what she wanted, Laci made the first move. One day, she wrote down her phone number and asked her friend's boyfriend to give it to Scott. Believing his coworker was playing a joke on him, Scott threw Laci's number in the trash. But after being convinced otherwise, he retrieved the piece of paper and called her.

On their first date, Scott took Laci deep-sea fishing on a catamaran. Laci got horribly seasick and refused ever to go fishing with him again. That fact ate away at Sharon Rocha as police searched the bay for her daughter's body.

"Laci always got motion sick . . . and you knew that and . . . you put her in the bay," Sharon railed at Scott during her victim-impact testimony at sentencing. "You knew she'd be sick for all eternity."

Despite an unpleasant and embarrassing first date, Laci was awed by Scott, who seemed like a combination of Jay Gatsby and Ernest Hemingway. He wasn't even twenty-two yet, but he owned his own business, drove a Porsche, and oozed self-confidence. He was dashing and daring and exceedingly romantic. He looked like he was going places. He looked like he had his life together.

Scott was drawn to Laci's fun-loving, outgoing personality. It complemented, and camouflaged, his more reserved, guarded nature. According to his sister Susan, he was also impressed by Laci's adventurousness, "that she was willing to try almost anything, that she wasn't high-maintenance."

Scott would claim in his "damage-control" interview with Diane Sawyer that he fell in love with Laci on one of their very first dates. He said he realized he was in love as they were driving down the highway one day, and he couldn't stop smiling "because she was there." In truth, Scott was begging another girlfriend, an eighteen-year-old waitress he worked with at the Pacific Café, to come back to him for a couple months after he started seeing Laci.

Lauren Putnat had dated Scott for about a year and a half, but broke up with him after he started talking marriage. Lauren was one of the few women who recognized that Scott was too good to be true, who saw his romantic excesses as too studied, as an imitation of love.

Scott could turn as cold as ice when he was through with a woman, but as the rejected one, he showed extreme emotion, crying and pleading with Lauren for a second chance, and attempting to make her jealous by inviting Laci to the restaurant while she was working. The more she denied him, the more jealous and persistent he became, until she moved away and ceased all contact with him.

Scott didn't tell Laci anything about Lauren Putnat. But he did tell her that he had lived with a woman while he was at Arizona State, a woman he said was several years older than him.

Laci decided right away that Scott was "the one" for her. After they had dated only a few times, she called her mother and told Sharon that she had met the man she was going to marry. About a month later, Sharon came down to Morro Bay to meet Scott at the Pacific Café. Scott staged a breathtaking tableau.

"He greeted us at the door with this huge grin, looked at Laci and said, 'I have a special table for you,'" Sharon recalled. On the table were a dozen red roses for Laci and a dozen white roses for me. I was very impressed."

Neither Laci nor Sharon knew that Scott's grand romantic gesture was a stock one, practiced and honed to perfection. Equally as constant in Scott's dating history, all the way back to high school, were cheating and lying. And Scott didn't just lie when he was caught. He lied gratuitously. He lied outlandishly. He lied even when faced with absolute proof to the contrary.

When Scott was a senior at Uni High, he wooed sophomore Stephanie Smith with flowers and expensive gifts, including a ring for Valentine's Day—when all the while he was cheating on her with another classmate. When friends told her that they saw Scott holding hands with the other girl and had seen her driving his car, Scott came up with the most preposterous explanations.

"I hold hands with lots of my friends," he said. And he had simply traded cars with the girl for a day so she could try his out—a very similar explanation to the one Lee Peterson gave under oath for why he had Scott's truck, with GPS locator attached, and Scott was driving Lee's, in the days leading up to his arrest.

"That's something we did all our lives," Lee testified. "We like cars and we like, you know, to drive different cars."

Even after Scott had wooed and won Laci, he continued to break out the roses to pursue other women. He showed up with twelve bouquets of a dozen roses each for his first date with Janet Ilse, a Cal Poly sophomore, who had no idea Scott was married until she walked into his house one day and found him in bed with Laci.

Katy Hansen found out Scott was married when Laci came up and gave him a big kiss as she and Scott sat together at their Cal Poly graduation ceremony. A week after being outed at the ceremony, apparently hoping to rekindle the relationship, Scott sent Katy a dozen pink roses with the cryptic note "No job, no home." Was he pretending that Laci had thrown him out and he was now free to be with Katy?

Scott's lies to his last extramarital girlfriend, Amber Frey, would become legendary, as would the cheesy *9½ Weeks*–style rosebud seduction he used to distract Amber from his admission that he had been married but had "lost" his wife.

What Scott didn't say was even more telling. He would talk about his passion for golf, his inflated ambitions—he told Katy Hansen he planned to run for mayor of Fillmore, California, a city in Ventura County where his friends Mike and Heather Richardson live but where Scott never has. But he rarely revealed anything personal or honest about himself.

Whereas his parents and siblings relished talking about Scott and his accomplishments, however minor, he hardly ever talked to anyone about his family. He spoke so little of them that Katy Hansen assumed he was an only child. He told Laci that his family was "dysfunctional." Anne Bird was disturbed by how, in all the time he stayed with her after Laci's disappearance and when she visited him in jail, Scott never once talked about his wife or child with any emotional resonance.

"Everything was on an historical level, like he was repeating something from a history book," she said. "He would talk about things that happened—like how he hiked up a hill in Mexico to get some fresh fruit for Laci, or recipes, or things that were going on in jail—but nothing about feelings, or being sad that Laci was missing. Nothing on an emotional level."

Laci and Scott moved in together a few months after they started dating. At one point they shared a house with another couple. For a few years, they rented a tiny bunkhouse on a ranch near a fish-stocked pond, around which Laci would walk McKenzie, the golden retriever puppy she gave Scott as a Christmas gift.

After drifting in and out of school for several years, Scott eventually enrolled at Cal Poly, where he majored in agricultural business—a curious choice for someone without any apparent affinity for rural life. He did well in his classes, graduating with a B+ average and making the dean's list three times, without ever applying himself too strenuously. He started work on his senior thesis—choosing the rather self-evident topic "Attributes That Consumers Desire in Fresh-Cut Salad"—just two days before it was due, and aced it.

Scott began schooling Laci in the finer things in life. When Brent went to San Luis Obispo to check out the guy Laci was so smitten with, he found a "good guy, a good-natured person" who really seemed to care about his sister. He was struck by the changes in Laci, how worldly she was becoming.

"She wasn't the typical college student going to keggers," he recalled. "Going to dinner was an event for her, where they'd pair the wines up with the meal—a little more cultured atmosphere than we are used to in the Valley. She loved to cook exotic meals. She grew so much and she taught me so many things."

Amy Rocha first met her future brother-in-law when Laci brought him to one of her middle school cheerleading practices. (Laci had volunteered to teach her sister's squad some cheers.) Amy became so fond of Scott that she considered him both like a brother and as the type of man she hoped to find one day for herself, words that would later sicken her. Ron Grantski was impressed as well. "He was the kind of guy you wanted your daughter to marry," Ron believed at the time. "He seemed like a perfect son."

There was at least one sign that something was amiss, however. The industrious young man, lauded by his parents for holding down up to three jobs at a time, was fired from the Morro Bay golf course for stealing. He told Laci that it was all a misunderstanding and that he had straightened everything out—the same thing Mark Hacking told his wife about the medical school to which he had never even applied. If it was a mistake, if everything had been "straightened out," why didn't Scott get his job back? Laci believed him. She seemed outraged that he had been accused of something he hadn't done, just as his family (and hers, too, initially) would be when he was accused of her murder.

In late 1996, about two and a half years into their relationship, Scott and Laci got engaged. In engagement photos taken on the beach, they dressed identically in white shirts and jeans, Scott already seeming to merge his identity into Laci's—just as he had once styled himself as a miniature version of his father.

Without being asked, Scott would transform himself, chameleon-like, into whatever he thought people wanted him to be. He gave up meat while dating vegetarian Janet Ilse. For Amber he started reading the Bible and analyzing parables—this from a man who told Amber when they started dating that he wasn't religious at all.

Around the time of his engagement, Scott learned something about his mother that must have rocked his already fragile sense of identity. Don Chapman, the first child Jackie had given away, had lost both of his adoptive parents and grown estranged from his adoptive sister. Craving a familial connection, Chapman searched for his birth mother and managed to locate her address in Morro Bay. He sent her a certified letter, which Jackie opened in front of her family, completely unaware of its contents.

The secret she had kept for more than thirty years was suddenly revealed, and Jackie was left utterly shaken. Although she would later contend to Anne Bird that she had confided in her husband early in their marriage, other relatives say absolutely no one in the Peterson family knew that Jackie had given up two children for adoption.

Whatever Jackie's initial feelings might have been, by the time she met Don they had a warm reunion, and he soon met Lee and the other kids. But even then Jackie apparently didn't tell her family about the second child she gave up for adoption, until Don made contact on his own with Anne and encouraged a reunion with her as well.

Anne had never felt any great need to connect with her birth mother. She had been mildly curious in high school and had gone as far as researching Jackie's name in county records. But when she discovered that her mother had married and had other children, she didn't pursue it any further. She felt very loved and secure in her adoptive family, but after giving it some thought agreed to let Don give Jackie her number. Jackie called the next day, and a few weeks later they met in a San Diego hotel.

They had a somewhat awkward first meeting. Jackie asked a series of odd questions—"Do you like mushrooms? Colorful clothes?"—as if the bond between mother and child came down to a simple list of shared tastes. She offered no real explanation for giving Anne up, much less an apology, other than saying, "the nuns never talked to me about sex."

The details she did give Anne were somewhat gratuitous and painful: how she hid out for the duration of her pregnancy and couldn't remember much about Anne's birth at all. Conversely, she waxed rhapsodic about her Golden Boy from that very first meeting.

Anne's relationship with her birth mother remained superficial, if pleasant, for a while, but it eventually deepened. After Laci disappeared, Jackie would come to depend on Anne as a sounding board and would entrust Scott to his new sister's care when the investigation heated up, asking Anne to provide Scott with a safe harbor at her Berkeley home away from the prying eyes of the police and media back in Modesto.

Just as Jackie adamantly insisted, right up to trial, that she had had a happy childhood, the Petersons claim not to have been the least bit ruffled by the revelation that Jackie had given up her first two children.

"We had a bigger family now and they were such nice folks that it was just easy to take them into our family," Lee Peterson contended under oath. On the family tree he drew for the jury in court, however, he misspelled Anne's name as Ann. Interestingly, she only knew Lee as "Pete" until the case hit the news, a name she was told by other relatives he assumed after the family got into financial straits.

It is hard to believe that Scott, who enjoyed such a place of primacy in the family pecking order, was not thrown by the news that he now had two more siblings with whom he had to share his mother's love. If it is true that his mother persuaded him to get rid of his own first child, the impact may have been even more severe. If so, he kept those feelings buried, as he would so many others. By the time he met Anne, he embraced her like a long-lost friend.

"This better not be a one-time thing," he said at their first meeting. "I have plenty of brothers, but I'm kind of short on sisters." In fact, Scott seemed to be enthralled with Anne, as if he were recognizing a missing part of himself.

—⁓—

Scott and Laci were married on August 9, 1997, in a spectacular garden ceremony at Sycamore Mineral Springs resort, an historic hotel and spa tucked into the hills between San Luis Obispo and the coast. It was an incomparably serene setting, with open-air hot tubs dotting the hillside and suites bearing names like Excellence and Virtue. A babbling brook, fed by a waterfall, ran underneath the gazebo where they exchanged vows. Laci planned everything to the last detail, from the flower arrangements, which she designed herself, to the sugar-coated lemons and limes decorating the tables, to the flower petals marking the aisle.

Laci was pretty as a princess in a wedding gown with train, hip-length veil, and silk opera gloves, Scott dashing in white tie and tails. Laci's brother and sister were in the wedding party along with several of Laci's girlfriends, and Scott's nephews and nieces served as ring bearers and flower girls. Oddly, Scott asked none of his brothers to be in his wedding, even though he had served as his brother John's best man. Instead, he asked Mike Richardson to stand up for him, a college friend with whom he had only recently become acquainted.

In wedding photographs, Laci is the picture of poise and grace, smiling broadly as Scott looks at her with the adoring gaze her friends recall so often seeing. Scott, always a suave speech maker, toasted his new in-laws for entrusting him with their "perfect daughter." (Scott had always been unfailingly polite to Sharon and Ron, asking for their blessing at the time he and Laci got engaged.) At the end of the day, Scott literally swept Laci off her feet and carried her upstairs to their room. They honeymooned in Tahiti, and to everyone who knew them seemed destined for a lifetime of happiness.

"Laci was in love; she had met the man of her dreams," said Renee Garza, a friend of Laci's since kindergarten. "At her bachelorette party all she talked about was how wonderful he was."

"They were doing the things we always wanted to do," said Ron Grantski. "They were living our dream."

The dream was only an illusion. Scott's dark side emerged even on his wedding day. The groom drank heavily and was seen by resort manager Roger Wightman before the ceremony sitting at the hotel bar hitting on one of the waitresses.

Within months, Scott was engaged in the first of at least three affairs police were able to confirm during the Petersons' five-year marriage. Scott told his sister Anne Bird that he had casual sexual encounters during his marriage as well, claiming to have had sex with two different women on a single airplane flight.

Just before trial, a relative told a reporter that Scott had had as many as half a dozen extramarital affairs. Presumably that admission was meant to boost Scott's defense. If he didn't kill Laci to be with any of these other women, why would he have killed her for Amber?

No such "supercad" defense was ultimately mounted, however, the risks of such a strategy being obvious. The only girlfriend to testify was Amber. The defense acknowledged that Scott did have an affair early in the relationship and that Laci found out about it but told no one—a fact they used to support Scott's astonishing assertion, first to Diane Sawyer and then to other reporters, that Laci knew about his affair with Amber because he told her so himself.

At some level, however, Laci may have sensed even before they were married that she was making a mistake. The night before her wedding, Laci had called her mother around midnight in near hysterics and said she didn't know if she should get married.

Earlier that evening at the rehearsal dinner, Laci had been all smiles. Now she was sobbing into the phone, claiming she didn't want to lose her ethnic surname. Laci was certainly proud of her Portuguese heritage, but was this really what was upsetting her? She didn't have to change her name at all if she didn't want to. It was as if she somehow knew that by tying her fate to Scott Peterson she would lose herself forever.

———

Scott's first affair, with Janet Ilse, began while he and Laci briefly lived apart. Laci graduated four months after they got married, in December 1997, and was offered a job with a wine distributor in the Carmel area. Scott still had another semester to go at Cal Poly, so Laci rented a mobile home in Prunedale, a small city just east of Moss Landing and north of Salinas, and Scott drove up on weekends to see her. Meanwhile, Scott moved into a house with three other Cal Poly students—none of whom had any idea Scott was married until Laci called one day and identified herself as his wife.

Just as he would with Laci and Amber, and as many eraser killers do, Scott pushed his relationship with Janet to a serious level very quickly. He lavished her with expensive gifts: jewelry, clothing, fabulous dinners. (She provided police with a picture of herself, looking pleased but a little startled, holding the dozen bouquets Scott gave her on their first date.) He talked about taking a vacation with her to Mexico and about moving in together. Janet and her roommate even double-dated with Scott and one of his roommates.

After five months of dating, Janet showed up late one night unannounced and found him in bed with Laci, who had herself come for a visit. Distraught at his apparent betrayal, Janet lit into Scott, but he just stared back at her unemotionally, uttering a meager "I'm sorry." One of Scott's roommates finally intervened and drove her home.

"How could he cheat on me?" Janet asked. "He's not cheating on you with her; he's cheating on her with you," the roommate explained.

A week later Scott showed up at Janet's and expanded ever so slightly on his apology. "I'm sorry you found me in bed with Laci," he said, but still showed no apparent empathy for her pain, nor remorse for his deceit. How he dealt with the situation with Laci no one knows. She never told anyone about it. But his cheating continued unabated.

———~~~———

Scott seemed to thirst not only for sexual conquest but also for the romantic trappings of a relationship, however studied and artificial. Psychologists refer to this as a sex and love addiction, and like all addictions it is generally fueled by feelings of inadequacy. Janet Ilse told police that Scott was insecure about whether he was sufficiently endowed to satisfy a woman. She heard from one of his roommates that after they broke up, Scott engaged in a strange bit of sexual acting out, drunkenly exposing himself one night in a bar.

When police served a second search warrant on Scott's home two months after Laci went missing, they found him driving away with an overnight bag. Packed inside were Scott's wedding ring, a bottle of wine, and a bottle of Viagra that Scott had ordered from an online pharmacy in January 2002. Whether he truly needed the drug to perform or simply used it to enhance his experience is unknown. But the fact that he felt the need to carry a ready-made seduction kit, even with no assignation planned (as far as anyone knows), is telling.

The overblown romantic gestures, the extravagant gift-giving, the lies and exaggerations about his wealth and ambitions all seem like overcompensation for low self-esteem—the flip side of narcissism. He needed to dazzle women, to overwhelm them, to be idolized. Laci worshiped him, but the love of one woman wasn't enough.

Shortly after his relationship with Janet, or maybe even simultaneously, Scott began seeing classmate Katy Hansen. Katy asked Scott straight out if he had ever been married. No, he told her, just as he would tell Amber.

The next day, however, he confessed to Katy that he had lied. He then immediately lied again, claiming that he was divorced. He then told a half-truth, saying his "ex-wife" lived in Salinas. As with Janet Ilse, Katy had no reason to believe Scott was lying. He wore no wedding ring when he was with her. She saw no photographs of Laci or any of Laci's things at Scott's house.

She was blindsided with the inescapable truth when Laci came up and planted a lei and a big kiss on Scott at graduation. Scott introduced the woman who kissed him simply as Laci and never spoke another word to Katy, other than the written missive he sent her a week later with the pink roses.

But a picture taken of Scott on graduation day, still wearing his cap and gown and orchid lei, is chilling. It reveals what I believe to be the actual face behind the mask: the fury of Scott denied. In the photo, Laci smiles proudly at the camera, her arm clasped firmly around Scott's shoulder. Scott does not reciprocate her embrace and stares grimly into the camera, his eyes masked by sunglasses but his lips pressed together in disgust. Laci has spoiled his party, and he is not happy about it.

I saw that same look of suppressed fury on Scott's face only one other time—on the third day of trial, when he looked over his shoulder and glared for a long moment into the front row of the gallery where the Rocha family was seated.

It was the only time during the entire trial that Scott ever looked into the audience, other than the perfunctory smile and nod he would make to his family on the other side of the courtroom each time he walked in. I happened to be sitting directly in his line of sight that day, and I stared back, astonished, trying to figure out to which member of the family he was directing such rage.

After a while I could see that it wasn't one of the Rochas Scott was staring down but the detective seated next to them: Craig Grogan, the lead investigator who had methodically built the case against him. The testimony at that particular moment was exceedingly minor, but the witness was saying that Grogan had misinterpreted something she said.

Scott felt the same contempt toward the police that I believe he felt toward Laci at his college graduation. They had ruined his game, but now, at last, he had his day in court, and he believed absolutely that he would beat them.

His rage against Grogan and fellow Modesto police detective Al Brocchini, one of the other chief investigators, was ugly and personal. Both men are short and stocky, and a year before trial Scott's father was characterizing the case against his son as a "pissing match" between a short stumpy cop and his tall handsome son.

Exactly which of the two detectives Lee was referring to with that description is unclear. Yet his thinking betrays an incredible bit of reductionism—as if the case against his son were no more than a state conspiracy built on penis envy. In fact, it was Scott who seemed to be sexually obsessed with the detectives, making derisive comments about their size and potency.

Laci must have at least suspected something was going on between Scott and Katy Hansen, but she probably had no idea until graduation day. During the ceremony she told her friend Heather Richardson that Scott was "acting single." She didn't elaborate, but later that night, after a celebratory dinner, Heather overheard Laci yelling at Scott in the bathroom. She heard no response from Scott.

Katy told police that her relationship with Scott had not yet become sexual. Perhaps Scott convinced Laci it was just a friendship. Maybe Laci blamed herself for their physical separation or attributed his behavior to a period of adjustment. Or maybe, as the child of divorce, Laci was determined to make her marriage work at all costs.

Other than her brief comment to Heather, she never told anyone about this episode. Although the plan had been for Scott to join her after graduation, she instead quit her job and moved back to San Luis Obispo. Little did she know that Scott tried to win Katy back with flowers and a note hinting that his wife was no longer in the picture. Nor did she know that Scott had told Janet Ilse that he never wanted to have kids because they would get in the way of his lifestyle.

CHAPTER ELEVEN

Seeds of a Plan

‍‍‍he least fortunate of all erased persons fall into a black hole in the criminal justice system, a bizarre netherworld in which they are considered neither alive nor dead. The investigation into their disappearance is never officially closed, but as months and then years go by, it remains neither active nor productive.

Contrary to the impression created by the popular TV drama *Without a Trace*, crack FBI agents are not sitting around waiting to leap into action when someone files a vexing missing persons report. In general, police departments are reluctant to jump into an investigation, sometimes reluctant even to take a report, because of the roughly eight hundred thousand Americans reported missing in any given year, the vast majority turn up on their own within a few days or weeks.

Over the last two decades, major reforms and safeguards have been instituted nationwide regarding police handling of reports of children abducted by strangers, a tiny subset within the much larger number of children taken by one parent or the other in the midst of a custody dispute. There is now widespread recognition that children abducted by strangers are in mortal danger, often murdered within hours by their kidnappers, so time is of the essence.

The system often breaks down, however, with older teens or young adults, whom police are more likely to treat as runaways or as people who have simply dropped out of sight temporarily—say, to ditch an exam they have not prepared for or to take a road trip without informing mom and dad. It is a sad and little known fact that Ted Bundy was able to kidnap and kill dozens of young college students in several states before he was caught, in part because many of his victims were initially deemed to be runaways.

While Scott Peterson was living and working and going to school in San Luis Obispo, his normally sleepy little college town was hit by an inexplicable crime wave. In a span of less than three years, three young women, all college students, seemingly vanished into thin air. It was perhaps the most baffling cluster of mysterious disappearances anywhere in the country, considering the area's otherwise exceedingly low crime rate and the fact that none of the women was in any high-risk category for criminal victimization.

The town was gripped by fear. For years you couldn't go anywhere in San Luis Obispo without seeing a young woman's face on a missing persons poster, couldn't open a newspaper or turn on the TV news without hearing one of the girls' names. Speculation and rumor ran rampant. Many wondered if a serial killer was operating in their midst, someone like Ted Bundy with a penchant for pretty coeds. Because of San Luis Obispo's proximity to the Pacific Ocean on one side and the sprawling and sparsely populated coastal foothills on the other, it was easy to imagine how bodies might go undiscovered forever.

Like everyone living in San Luis Obispo at that time, Scott Peterson became well versed on the subject of vanished women and the inner workings of a missing persons investigation. At a formative stage in his life, as he was grappling uneasily with the strictures of marriage and adult responsibility, he saw how easy it was to make a woman disappear and for a suspect far less savvy than himself to avoid being charged with murder. He learned how poor police work in the early stages of an investigation could prevent a suspect from being arrested, much less convicted, even when authorities were absolutely convinced he was guilty. He heard investigators disparage circumstantial evidence and proclaim that unless their suspect chose to confess there was nothing they could do to him.

Before he had any desire or notion to erase someone from his own life, he came to believe that murder cannot be proved without a corpse.

Whereas the lack of empathy and conscience that leads someone to feel entitled to take a life are believed to be the result of both nature and nurture, the idea that one can carry out a "perfect murder" is learned. In the abstract, the story Peterson would later spin to cover his own wife's murder, that a grown woman was snatched off the streets just blocks from her home, seems ludicrous. In light of what he learned in college, it makes perfect sense.

—⁓—

The first disappearance to strike San Luis Obispo took place right on the grounds of his campus. Kristin Smart, a nineteen-year-old Cal Poly freshman, was last seen just a few hundred feet from her dorm as she walked home from a fraternity party in the early morning hours of May 25, 1996.

Rachel Newhouse, a twenty-year-old Cal Poly junior, disappeared on November 12, 1998, while walking home from a party at a popular downtown bar. Her blood was found the following morning on a pedestrian bridge over a set of railroad tracks, the route she would have needed to take to get home.

Just four months later, Aundria Crawford, a twenty-year-old student at Cuesta College, the community college Scott Peterson also attended before he transferred to Cal Poly, was kidnapped from her apartment. A screen had been removed from a bathroom window, and traces of Aundria's blood were found inside the duplex.

Although thousands of dangerous men are incarcerated just a few miles from campus at a state prison and a maximum-security hospital that treats the criminally insane and sexually violent predators, murder is almost unheard of in San Luis Obispo. During the last decade, only three to seven murders a year have been committed in the entire county, in most years none within this city of forty-four thousand. Those that do occur generally fall into the typical range of disputes over drugs or money or the escalating violence of domestic abuse. Three young college students vanishing in the night was something very different and extraordinarily alarming. Young women began packing Mace, flocked to counseling sessions offered by the colleges, and signed up for self-defense classes.

"Norman Rockwell doesn't live here anymore," a grim-faced police sergeant told hundreds of anxious students who took time out during finals week to attend a safety seminar at Cuesta College after the third young woman disappeared.

Seeking to quell a growing sense of panic, police announced that they did not believe there was any connection between the cases. Yet they continually linked the first two victims by the fact that they had been drinking on the night they vanished, as if they were somehow complicit in their own disappearances. At a press conference three days after Crawford vanished, Captain Bart Topham of the San Luis Obispo police differentiated Aundria from Kristin and Rachel by saying, "She doesn't drink, she's not a partyer."

In fact, it was the second and third cases that turned out to be related. Rachel Newhouse, characterized by the police as a "partyer," was in fact a straight-A student and student body officer in high school who came to Cal Poly to study nutrition. Aundria Crawford had to give up her first love, ballet, due to constant pain, switching her passion to horseback riding and barrel racing. She was working hard to qualify for transfer from Cuesta College to Cal Poly, where she wanted to study interior design, and hoped to own a ranch one day.

All the hopes and dreams of Rachel Newhouse and Aundria Crawford were extinguished when they had the misfortune to catch the attention of Rex Allan Krebs, a sex offender paroled to the area in 1997.

Krebs, who was eventually abandoned by an alcoholic mother after years of violent abuse from her husband, admitted to police and a psychiatrist who examined him that he hated women and felt the need to completely dominate them. He fits the classic profile of the sexual sadist, taking a step up from rape to sexual homicide. Although his victims were not his intimate partners by choice, he used the same kind of thoroughness and cleverness in erasing their bodies and covering up his connection to their disappearances.

Rex Krebs was leaving a bar just after midnight on Friday the 13th of November 1998, when he noticed a pretty young woman walking toward the Jennifer Street Bridge, which was the only way to cross the railroad tracks in that part of San Luis Obispo. A winding, mazelike staircase leads up to the enclosed pedestrian bridge, which is essentially a steel cage suspended three stories above the street.

In the eyes of a predator like Rex Krebs, it was a perfect place to trap his unsuspecting prey. By the time Rachel saw the man lying in wait for her, a terrifying Halloween skull mask obscuring his face, there was no way to escape his clutches. He knocked her unconscious, dragged her down to his pickup, and drove her to an abandoned cabin near the home he was renting in a remote canyon just a few miles from the beautiful resort where Scott and Laci were married. There he raped and killed her—although he would insist she accidentally strangled herself while struggling against her bindings.

A few months later, when Krebs caught sight of Aundria Crawford entering her apartment as he drove by on the way home from one of his other favorite watering holes, he knew he'd found his next victim. He cased her duplex on four different occasions, peering in the windows and watching her undress, before he worked up the nerve to break in.

On March 11, 1999, he decided to take her. He had a hard time squeezing through an unlocked bathroom window, injuring his ribs in the process. Aundria heard a commotion and went to investigate. But he quickly overpowered her, beating her, as he had with Rachel, until she lost consciousness. Then he transported her to his house, where he raped her and then strangled her to death.

Krebs might very well have gotten away with his crimes. Much of California's central coastline is undeveloped. A few miles away from the picturesque coastal highway and its resortlike towns, the pavement turns to dirt and gravel and the terrain to steep canyons and inhospitable brush. Krebs took advantage of his isolated surroundings, burying both girls near where he was living, in an area so remote that neighbors often went months without seeing each other, and accessible only by a treacherous unpaved road. In one of the graves, which was farther out into the woods, he took the extra precaution of placing wire mesh over the body to prevent it from being dug up and exposed by wild animals.

He burned his victims' clothes and threw away the shoes and clothing he had been wearing when he kidnapped them. He washed their blood out of his truck and carefully cut out carpeting and a seatbelt he couldn't wash clean. There were no eyewitnesses to the abductions. He left behind no fingerprints or other forensic evidence linking him to the crime scenes. They were close to being perfect murders.

He was caught, however, thanks in large part to an astute parole officer who followed his intuition—just as Modesto Police Detective Al Brocchini would follow his gut instinct when he was assigned to a report of a missing pregnant woman on Christmas Eve 2002, pressing the "grieving" Scott Peterson for a detailed statement, searching his home and warehouse, and preserving crucial evidence that might no longer have existed two days later when police returned with a warrant and Scott had hired an attorney.

David Zaragoza graduated from Cal Poly with the same major as Scott Peterson. But finding little opportunity in the agricultural field, he made a career in law enforcement. When he read in the newspaper about the disappearance of Aundria Crawford, one of the more than one hundred parolees he was assigned to supervise sprang to mind. Breaking into his victims' homes as part of a sex crime was the modus operandi of someone whose rap sheet he knew well: Rex Krebs.

It was something of a stretch to suspect Krebs in the case of a missing woman, however, as he had only ever been arrested for rape and burglary, not kidnapping or murder. Zaragoza took the initiative anyway to visit Krebs at his isolated residence. He found his parolee wincing in pain, a weightlifter's belt wrapped around his injured ribs.

Good investigators are quick to notice something unusual or out of place, and Zaragoza pressed the ex-con about his injury. Krebs claimed that he had tripped and fallen onto his woodpile. But Zaragoza's instincts were now more aroused, as he was aware that Crawford's kidnapper had crawled in through a window barely big enough for a grown man to pass through. He passed on his suspicions to the San Luis Obispo police, who in turn passed the information to the Department of Justice, the agency in charge of culling through lower-priority tips.

The investigation of Rex Krebs as a potential suspect could easily have ended here, as more than five hundred tips had already been received on the Crawford case, and more were coming in every day. Fortunately, the DOJ did follow up. During a search of Krebs's property, agents found BB pellets and got Krebs to admit to owning a BB gun that simulated a more dangerous weapon. That constituted a parole violation and meant that they could take Krebs into custody and begin trying to break him down.

Larry Hobson, an investigator with the district attorney's office, played a key role in this stage of the case. He worked to develop a relationship with Krebs, first asking for his expertise as a sex offender generically to help police solve the cases of the missing young women, then asking him to help himself by giving them information needed to clear him. As more evidence came in—including wiretaps of conversations between Krebs and his girlfriend, in which he admitted no guilt but failed to deny any involvement and continually probed her for information about the status of the investigation—the investigator went back at Krebs again and again.

For two months Krebs could not be broken. Then a second, more thorough search of his property cracked the case. Minute traces of blood belonging to Rachel were detected on the jump seat from Krebs's pickup truck, which he had removed from the vehicle for cleaning but had not sanitized thoroughly enough. And a small 8-ball key chain known to have belonged to Rachel was also found tucked away in his house, which he kept because he had a fondness for the number eight and considered it to have special significance. Now they had evidence that tied Krebs not only to Crawford but to Newhouse as well. When confronted with the forensic findings, he gave a detailed confession and led investigators to the women's bodies.

Krebs was subsequently diagnosed as an antisocial personality and as a sexual sadist aroused by women's suffering. Yet he seemed to have an insight about himself that Scott Peterson lacked. When Rex's girlfriend became pregnant two months after he killed Rachel Newhouse, he told her he didn't want the child.

"I don't have a conscience," he explained, simply and honestly. In a jailhouse interview the day after Rachel and Aundria's bodies were exhumed, Krebs told a reporter, "If I'm not a monster then what am I?" and said he deserved the death penalty.

In 2001 he was sentenced to death. He resides today on San Quentin's Death Row with Scott Peterson and about six hundred other condemned men.

—⁓—

Kristin Smart remains missing, but the circumstances of her disappearance are no longer a mystery to authorities. They are certain that she is dead. They believe they know when she died and where she died. For ten years they have had one and only one real suspect: Paul Flores, a fellow college student who promised to escort her home from a party. They have named him publicly. They have amassed considerable circumstantial evidence against him. But they have never arrested him, never charged him with anything because by the time they got around to taking Kristin's disappearance seriously, vital evidence was long gone and the investigation seriously hampered.

Unlike Rex Krebs, a seasoned criminal who would have gotten away with murder if not for good police work, the person police believe to be responsible for the disappearance of Kristin Smart is about as unsophisticated an offender as a detective would ever confront. Yet the Smart case is a textbook example of what happens when police botch a missing persons investigation, when inexperienced cops fail to recognize the likelihood that a crime has occurred, fail to preserve critical evidence, fail to bring pressure on a suspect within the narrow window of opportunity when he is most vulnerable to confessing or incriminating himself.

The catastrophic result of such failure is that Kristin's parents are no closer to finding their daughter today than when she disappeared more than a decade ago. Like Laci's parents, they have suffered an indescribable loss, but they don't even have the cold consolation of being able to visit their daughter's grave, much less any sense of justice having been served.

Watching the drama of the Kristin Smart case unfold was like a graduate-level course in criminology for Scott Peterson. He saw how critical timing is to police response, which could explain why he chose a holiday to disappear his own wife. He heard or read over and over again how mistakes police made in the first month after Kristin disappeared doomed their ability to bring charges.

Perhaps that knowledge, filed away in the recesses of Scott's mind, had something to do with why he promised Amber Frey that he would be able to spend more time with her at the end of January 2003—a month after his wife disappeared. He may have believed that if he could get through those first thirty days, he would be in the clear.

The Kristin Smart case gave Scott Peterson a blueprint for how to get away with murder. The plan he would later conceive to explain his wife's disappearance was not far-fetched after all. Women vanish. He had seen it over and over again in his safe little college town, the smiling faces of Kristin and Rachel and Aundria frozen in time on billboards and on countless fliers under the haunting words, "Where are they?" Some women are, in fact, kidnapped and killed by parolees and sex offenders. Some are never found, and no one is ever charged.

Scott didn't expect the police in Modesto to be any smarter or better trained than those who looked for Kristin. Yes, Rex Krebs was nabbed for the other two disappearances, but he made stupid mistakes—like saving that dime-store key chain and bloodstained car seat. And he confessed. He *led* investigators to those girls' bodies. Otherwise they never would have been found in so remote an area.

Actually, Krebs probably factored directly into Peterson's cover story. It was Scott who fed Det. Brocchini the theory that Laci might have been kidnapped by vagrants who hang out in the park near his home, some of whom have criminal records.

Just as one cannot fully understand the mind-set of Scott Peterson without looking at what he may have "learned" while he was in college, one cannot judge how the police handled the investigation into the disappearance of Laci Peterson without first looking at how authorities mishandled the Kristin Smart investigation. The contention that Modesto police "rushed to judgment" against Peterson must be considered in the context of what happens when investigators do not act quickly and aggressively in a missing persons case.

Because Laci Peterson was seven and a half months pregnant, happily anticipating the birth of her child, closely bonded to her family and friends, Modesto police correctly concluded that she would not have walked away from her life. They immediately suspected foul play and focused in on the last person to see her, someone whose behavior and affect was, from that very first night, suspicious. They moved heaven and earth to find her and, in the words of Al Brocchini, "to get whoever got Laci."

The system failed Kristin Smart. Cops more adept at writing parking tickets than investigating a potential homicide treated her like a lost bicycle—telling her friends and family to check back in a few days to see if she turned up. They did not follow up promptly on clues and contradictions that should have set off alarms. As precious time slipped away and evidence was lost forever, they viewed her behavior and character as more suspicious than that of the man who would become the prime suspect in her disappearance.

—∿—

On the Friday evening leading into Memorial Day weekend, 1996, Kristin went to a party at a home leased by fraternity members just a block from campus. She had been out with a group of friends earlier in the evening, but none of them wanted to go to the party, so they dropped her off, and she went in alone.

Tim Davis, one of the students at the party, noticed Kristin talking several times that night with a nineteen-year-old freshman food science major named Paul Flores. At one point there was a loud noise. When he looked to see what happened, he saw that the two had somehow fallen to the floor in the hallway, Paul on top of Kristin. He told police he didn't know whether Flores knocked her down intentionally or if they simply fell together, but when they got up, they separated.

At 2:30 that morning Davis was outside arranging rides home for some his friends when he saw Kristin lying on the lawn next door.

Davis assumed that Kristin had passed out, but when he approached her she was conscious and told him she was cold. (A person who is drunk usually feels warm, not cold.) He helped her up and arranged for a female student who lived in a neighboring dorm, Cheryl Anderson, to walk Kristin home. Just as they were about to leave, Paul Flores reappeared, saying he also lived in the dorms and would accompany the two girls home.

As they walked the quarter-mile route to the residence halls clustered on the eastern edge of campus, an unsteady Kristin leaning against Paul for support, the two stopped to rest.

"Just keep going, I'll get her home," Paul told Cheryl. But she did not feel comfortable leaving Kristin alone with Paul, so she waited, and they continued walking together. When they came to the turnoff Cheryl needed to take to go to her building, Paul asked Cheryl for a kiss. She refused. Paul then asked her if he could "at least get a hug." Cheryl again said no.

She left them about three hundred feet from Kristin's dormitory, Muir Hall. Paul's dorm, Santa Lucia Hall, was kitty-corner to Kristin's. All the residence halls in that area are identical three-story red brick buildings. In the state Kristin was in, she could easily have been steered into the wrong building thinking she was being led to her own room.

—◊—

Kristin had left a telephone message for her parents earlier in the week to report good news. A biology professor the previous term had misplaced her final exam and didn't believe she had actually taken the test. He had given her an incomplete in thc class, and she fretted about the situation all term. Now the professor had located the test, and she had been vindicated.

"I'll give you the details later," Kristin said, promising to call on Sunday, as she did every week. When her parents did not hear from her on Sunday, however, they were not alarmed, as it was a holiday weekend.

The following Tuesday, everything changed. Kristin's roommate, Crystal Calvin, called Kristin's mother, Denise Smart, in tears. Crystal had gone away for the weekend after Kristin left for the party. When she returned, she could tell that Kristin had never been back to their room. Her backpack was just as she had left it, atop her bed, her makeup partially spilling out. The roommates were not close, so for Crystal Calvin to be that emotional, Mrs. Smart knew something was terribly wrong. She began shaking uncontrollably. But her nightmare was only beginning.

Some of Kristin's friends had reported her missing to the dorm's resident adviser over the weekend. The RA contacted the campus police on Monday, but they refused to take a report, telling her to wait and see if Kristin showed up for classes on Tuesday. In their view, it wasn't unusual for a college student to leave campus without telling anyone, especially on a holiday weekend. Now it was Tuesday and Kristin was nowhere to be found, yet Denise Smart still could not get the university police to take a missing persons report on her daughter.

Kristin's father, Stan, left immediately for San Luis Obispo, where he would spend the next three months personally searching every culvert, tunnel, and creek bed in San Luis Obispo County—anywhere he thought he might find his daughter, dead or alive.

He told Denise to stay home in case Kristin called or showed up there. Mrs. Smart didn't leave her house for five weeks. She began working the phone, calling the FBI, having no idea who or what to ask for. She got passed to a sympathetic agent on the sexual assault task force who called Cal Poly and got the campus police to finally take a report.

There was little reason to believe that Kristin had taken off of her own accord. Her wallet, ID, and all her personal effects were still in her room. The only thing missing was her room key and the clothing she had on the night of the party: a T-shirt, shorts, and tennis shoes. She had no money with her, no checkbook, no ATM card, no credit cards, no car. She had not contacted any of her friends or loved ones.

There was, however, plenty of reason to suspect foul play. Paul Flores told police he left Kristin about fifty yards from the safety of her dormitory at 2:30 in the morning as he went toward his own, yet she never made it to her room. He denied speaking with Kristin at the party prior to walking her home, although other students saw him not only talking to her but also sprawled on top of her. (He later told a friend that Kristin was flirting with him.) He didn't tell police about pressing Cheryl Anderson for a kiss and a hug as the three of them walked home.

Most disturbingly, Flores showed up for classes on Tuesday sporting a black eye. He initially told police he was elbowed in the face while playing basketball on Monday with his best friend, Jeromy Moon. After Moon told detectives that Paul already had the injury when he saw him on Sunday, the day before the basketball game, Flores changed his story and said he bumped his head while installing a stereo in his car. He had told Moon, however, that he couldn't remember how he got the black eye—"I just woke up with it."

Flores told Moon something even more troubling. He claimed to have gotten a "blow job from some slut in the bathroom" that weekend at a Cal Poly party. Flores said that afterwards the girl started hanging on a bunch of other guys at the party.

Moon considered those words an empty boast. He believed that his socially awkward friend was actually a virgin. But the angry contempt toward women Paul's comment displayed should have sent up some red flags with law enforcement, particularly in connection with his mysterious injury, his inappropriate behavior toward Cheryl, and other disturbing information in his background.

In fact, Flores had a reputation at Cal Poly for making unwelcome advances toward girls at parties. Some students had taken to calling him "Chester the Molester" after a cartoon character depicted in a pornographic magazine, who hung around playgrounds hoping to lure children into his clutches. Flores's modus operandi, they said, was to hang around until the end of a party and offer the most intoxicated girl a ride home. Five months before Kristin's disappearance, a woman reported him to police after she found a drunken Flores on her apartment balcony. Another student claimed she found him peeping in her bedroom window an hour after he left a Halloween party at her house. He was known to drink heavily and was on the verge of flunking out of Cal Poly with a 0.7 GPA at the time Kristin went missing.

A mother told the Smarts that when Paul was in middle school he used a choke hold to render her son unconscious and then kicked him in the head while he was prone on the ground. Paul's father, Ruben Flores, contends that his son was jumped by other students and was only defending himself. Court records show that he and his wife paid $5,000 to the boy's family to settle a civil suit.

The university police didn't know many of these facts, though, because they didn't bother asking. They distributed fliers and searched the campus grounds, but they never investigated Flores, who as the last person to see Kristin would have been the first person any good detective would have checked out.

Instead of profiling potential suspects, they profiled Kristin, and not very accurately. In their eyes she was at best a flaky teenager who decided to blow off finals (she had that incomplete on her transcript, after all), at worst a deliberate runaway, but never a victim. They asked the FBI to check airline records to see if Kristin had used her passport, and passed on false sightings to her family.

"They would tell us this harebrained stuff," Denise recalled. " 'Kristin probably went camping.' 'She was seen at a drug store in town, so she must be staying with a friend.' I told them that would be totally out of character for her, that she is very close to her family, that she always calls. But you want to hang onto any thread, so whatever they say you try to believe them."

The incident report, prepared by the campus police on May 31 after only the most cursory investigation, reeks with condescension toward Kristin and specious psychologizing. Oddly enough, in a section of the form clearly intended for explaining how a bicycle was stolen, the investigating officer summarized the case thusly: "Victim attends party and does not return home afterwards, does not contact friends or family, and skips school."

He repeatedly writes how people described Kristin as "very drunk" and "flirtatious" at the party and concludes with these observations: "During the course of my investigation, I have spoken with many people who have been associated with Smart. They have all told stories that agreed with each other. The stories have all included the following information: Smart does not have any close friends at Cal Poly. Smart appeared to be under the influence of alcohol on Friday night. Smart was talking with and socializing with several different males at the party. Smart lives her life in her own way, not conforming to typical teenage behavior. These observations are in no way implying that her behavior caused her disappearance, but they provide a picture of her conduct on the night of her disappearance."

Three weeks later, campus police still did not believe that any harm had befallen Kristin. In a story published in the college newspaper on June 20, 1996, Investigator Mike Kennedy declared, "There is no evidence of any criminal activity. It doesn't look like she was the victim of a crime so we are pursuing this case as an adult missing under unusual circumstances." Unusual circumstances?

Cal Poly police were well acquainted with Stan Smart by that time, as he was on their doorstep virtually every day inquiring into the progress of their investigation and passing on whatever information he was able to turn up—such as the number of every pay phone on campus he thought Paul Flores might have used to call for someone to help him dispose of a body.

But it wasn't until a full month after Kristin disappeared that any officers came up to Stockton to interview Kristin's mother, siblings, or longtime friends—people who could give them a more accurate picture of Kristin than the one provided by strangers at a frat party, and a clearer sense of whether she was a runaway or the victim of foul play.

Unbeknownst to Denise, a reporter who had interviewed her didn't think she was "upset enough" and reported that to police. Shortly after their visit to Stockton, police called Mrs. Smart to tell her she had been eliminated as a suspect.

"They said 'We just want to let you know that after talking to you and friends and family we don't think Kristin ran away or that you were involved,'" Mrs. Smart recalled. It was now time to bring Paul in for extensive questioning, they said.

Now? Denise burned with outrage. "I know they deal with a lot of 'possibles,' people who turn out not to be missing. But you have to act; you can't wait."

—◆◆◆—

What happens or does not happen during the first few days of a criminal investigation—when leads are fresh, evidence has not been completely destroyed or hidden, and a suspect can be caught off balance—generally determines whether or not the case is solved.

Cal Poly police did not speak to Paul Flores until three days after Kristin disappeared, and then apparently did so only by phone, because they failed to note in their report that Flores had a black eye. Two days later a team of investigators did interview Paul in person and asked him how he sustained the injury, as did investigators from the district attorney's office the following day, but none of them photographed the wound to turn this potentially important finding into a concrete piece of evidence that could be submitted at trial. (Under purely fortuitous circumstances, a neighboring city's police department did photograph Flores a few days later and preserved a record of that evidence, but Cal Poly police knew nothing about that at the time.)

Another huge blunder was not preserving the apparent crime scene. Campus police did not secure Flores's dormitory room until sixteen days after Kristin went missing—after Paul moved out of the room and cleaned it thoroughly—and did not even enter the room to look around for another three weeks. The university says it did not have the right to do so, although campus authorities routinely inspect dorm rooms for health and safety reasons, such as having a potential fire source in a room.

Yet the university refused to yield jurisdiction to the county sheriff's department, an agency better equipped to handle a potential homicide investigation, until a month after Kristin disappeared—and only then as a result of pressure brought by the Smart family. Egos and jurisdictional turf battles eclipsed common sense, as more time and potential evidence slipped away.

The biggest opportunity lost by not acting quickly is one that could potentially have broken the case wide open within hours of Kristin's disappearance.

At the time Kristin vanished, Flores had an outstanding warrant for his arrest on file in an unrelated matter. Paul had been convicted of drunk driving, and while on probation for that offense had been caught driving with a suspended license. When he failed to appear in court for the probation violation, a warrant was issued for his arrest.

The police could have arrested him at any time on the outstanding warrant and taken that opportunity to press him about Kristin. Purely by coincidence on the Memorial Day holiday, while Paul was out with his friend Jeromy Moon, a police officer came to his parents' home in Arroyo Grande just outside San Luis Obispo to serve the warrant. That evening his father took him down to the police station to clear the warrant.

A mug shot taken by the Arroyo Grande police that night captures not only Paul's black eye but also scrapes on his hand—injuries that could have been inflicted by a young, athletic woman fighting for her life, or that he could have suffered while disposing of a corpse. When the police interviewed Flores a few days later, they also noticed that he had red, scraped knees, which an investigator described as consistent with a rug burn.

Confronted nearly a month later by investigators for the district attorney's office about his inconsistent explanations for the black eye, Paul appeared extremely anxious, writhing in his chair and clutching at himself nervously. The investigators believed he was on the verge of confessing when he suddenly ended the interrogation with a mocking frontal assault.

"If you're so smart, then tell me where the body is," he said before getting up to leave. They would never get the chance to question him again.

One can only wonder what might have happened if police had gone harder at him earlier on—perhaps in those first seventy-two hours when a warrant was hanging over his head—about injuries he still to this day has not adequately explained.

The university police, the agency that would initially have jurisdiction because she disappeared on campus, believed Kristin was heavily intoxicated that night—an opinion that seemed to color their view of her and every aspect of their investigation. Her parents fear she actually might have been slipped one of the so-called date-rape drugs, powerful sedatives that can quickly incapacitate an unsuspecting victim.

It is hard to believe that Kristin could have been so drunk that she not only collapsed to the floor in the middle of a party but also brought another person down on top of her. She had nothing to drink before arriving at the party at about 10:30 that night, according to the girlfriends she was with earlier in the evening. Drugs like Rohypnol and gamma hydroxybutyrate (GHB), modern equivalents of the old-fashioned "Mickey Finn," can drop a person like a stone within minutes of ingestion and make it difficult to resist a sexual assault.

The victim may quite literally never know what hit her. Colorless, odorless, and tasteless, the drugs are undetectable when dissolved into a drink, and have a powerful amnesic effect. They can also lead to coma and death, especially when mixed with alcohol: one danger is that they significantly depress respiration; another is that the victim may throw up while unconscious and then aspirate vomit.

The drug has been showing up increasingly at college bars and campus parties around the country since the 1990s. In 2002 a member of a Cal Poly fraternity—where juice spiked with GHB was so regularly consumed that it was kept in the refrigerator in Gatorade bottles—died from an overdose of the drug. The fraternity brothers dubbed the concoction "Faderade."

———

Within days of taking over primary investigative duties in the case, the San Luis Obispo Sheriff's Department conducted a second search of the campus—this time with cadaver dogs trained to pick up the scent of a dead body.

The dogs were certified through the California Rescue Dog Association, the same body that provided dogs during the search for Laci Peterson and establishes training standards for dogs and their handlers. Dog teams that have passed a series of tests and proven successful in the field are dispatched through the state's Office of Emergency Services.

So as not to bias the handler's ability to accurately read the dog's behavior, the handlers who participated in the search that day were not privy to any information about the suspect or what areas of campus might be of particular interest to the investigation. To further ensure the integrity of the search, detectives followed from a distance to avoid exerting any influence on either the dog or handler.

Wayne Behrens had already worked his Labrador retriever, Sierra, through two other dormitories without incident when his dog "alerted" outside the locked door to room 128 in Santa Lucia Hall—the room occupied by Paul Flores at the time of Kristin's disappearance.

A second team of dogs was brought to the dormitory. These two dogs, border collies named Cholla and Cirque, had previously worked an infamous abduction case, successfully picking out the car in which Richard Allen Davis transported the dead body of twelve-year-old

Polly Klaas, whom he had kidnapped from her Petaluma, California, home in 1993.

Their handler, Adela Morris, was told nothing about Sierra's reaction in Santa Lucia Hall, but was simply asked to search the building. She took the dogs in one at a time. Cholla twice came back to room 128, sniffing and scratching at the carpet outside Flores's door. Morris took Cholla inside to search the room, which was empty except for the furniture and fixtures belonging to the university. Cholla alerted on one of the two mattresses in the room, showing no interest in the other.

Morris then worked Cirque through the hall. Cirque also stopped at Flores's room, pawed the door, and barked. When Morris took Cirque inside the room, he alerted on the same mattress, pawing at it and even grabbing at the mattress with his teeth. A detective had the dogs walk through all three floors of the building to see if they reacted with such interest to any other rooms, but they did not.

The mattress and box spring cover were removed as evidence. Then a fourth dog was brought in to search the hall. Just as all the others had, Torrey, a boxer, stopped at Flores's room. Handler Gail LaRogue took Torrey inside, where he alerted in the corner of the room where the mattress had been. He also reacted to the end of the bed frame, the telephone, and one of two wastebaskets in the room.

The handler suggested testing Torrey on the wastebasket by placing it down the hallway with identical trashcans taken from other rooms. The dog went directly to the waste container from room 128.

The detectives were stunned. Four different dogs had picked up the scent of death in Paul Flores's dorm room. They were now convinced that Kristin was dead, that she had died in that very room, and that Paul Flores, at the very least, knew what happened to her.

What they didn't know—and felt they needed to know to bring charges against Flores—was how Kristin died. Was she murdered, or could she have died accidentally, perhaps from passing out and vomiting, as some claimed that Paul told a friend? And where was she now? Without a body, without blood or a weapon or some other hard evidence, the Sheriff's Department did not believe they could prove that Paul killed Kristin.

Cal Poly police insist that they did not have grounds to search Flores's dorm room before he moved out. But by the time of the cadaver dog search, a full thirty-five days had passed since Kristin disappeared—plenty of time to get rid of evidence and hide a body somewhere it might never be found.

"Much of the evidence was more than likely gone by Saturday or Sunday" of Memorial Day weekend, said Lt. Steve Bolts of the San Luis Obispo Sheriff's Department. And Flores was no longer cooperating. He had answered questions on three occasions during the first three weeks that Kristin was missing. He now had a lawyer and was refusing to speak to police at all or take a lie detector test. He has not spoken to anyone from law enforcement since and has never spoken publicly about the case.

The dog evidence enabled the Sheriff's Department to obtain a search warrant for Paul's parents' house in Arroyo Grande. (Paul had told police that his father picked him up on the Sunday after Kristin disappeared and drove him home for the rest of the Memorial Day weekend. Soon thereafter Paul moved back home.)

Searchers found nothing that would tie Paul directly to Kristin's disappearance or demise, such as the clothing she wore the night she disappeared, her room key, or her blood on some article of his clothing. However, they did find a collection of newspaper clippings about Kristin's disappearance.

In frustration, authorities tried to force a break in the case by convening a grand jury that October. They did not ask for an indictment. Rather they used the grand jury's subpoena power as an added tool for investigating the case. But Paul cited his Fifth Amendment right against self-incrimination and left the grand jury room within five minutes of arriving.

The Smarts were appalled. The person they believe killed their daughter and committed her to some unmarked grave could refuse ever to tell them where she is, and the law would protect his right to do so. Yet their daughter had not even the minimal status afforded the dead. She could neither testify against her killer nor offer her corpse as proof against him. Her family could not even get victim-assistance funds to pay for grief counseling because, legally speaking, no crime had occurred.

Once again the investigation foundered. A year after Kristin went missing, Ed Williams, the sheriff at that time, seemed to throw up his hands, telling a reporter for the local newspaper, "We need Paul Flores to tell us what happened to Kristin Smart. The fact of the matter is we have very qualified detectives who have conducted well over a hundred interviews and everything leads to Mr. Flores. There are no other suspects. So absent something from Mr. Flores, I don't see us completing this case."

In other words, the burden of responsibility for bringing this case to justice was not on the police but on the suspect, from whom they wanted a confession.

A year later, a sheriff's representative reiterated that pessimistic sentiment on national television during an interview on the ABC newsmagazine *20/20*. When asked why Flores had not been charged, Sgt. Bill Wammock said that the evidence they had been able to gather was circumstantial.

"We need more. It's unfortunate, but there are times that there's nothing there." Wammock concluded by making the same astonishing assertion Sheriff Williams had: "Short of Paul Flores telling us [what happened] or giving us reason not to focus on him, which is within his constitutional right, there is nothing else to look at."

"Who would ever say that about any case?" an incredulous Denise Smart asks. "Can you imagine standing up and saying 'Until someone admits he's the Unabomber that case will never be solved?' 'Until Scott Peterson tells us that he killed Laci that case will never be solved?'"

Paul Flores has never admitted to any knowledge of or involvement in Kristin's death or disappearance. However, according to the Smarts and their attorney, on several occasions during the past ten years a lawyer representing Paul has broached the possibility of a plea bargain in exchange for Flores leading them to Kristin's body. The first time, about a year after Kristin disappeared, the district attorney offered to let Paul plead to voluntary manslaughter—a killing without malice, committed in the heat of passion—and serve just six years in prison.

"You know what that means?" an FBI agent told Denise. "That's your confirmation that she is no longer alive, if he is willing to lead you to her."

It was a devastating realization, and Kristin's parents were deeply divided over what to do. After much painful reflection, Denise decided that nothing was more important to her than to get Kristin back, to be able to give her daughter a Christian burial and lay her to rest in a place of beauty and serenity. Stan had a harder time accepting what he viewed as little more than a slap on the wrist. He believed that wherever his daughter is, she is already at peace, and he wanted her killer punished for all the devastation his family has endured.

"I want my daughter back, but I want justice as well," he says. "I don't think we should excuse him for what he did." Ultimately, though, both parents agreed to support such a deal. However, Paul's attorney, Melvin de la Motte, didn't think Paul should have to serve any time. He would agree to nothing greater than an infraction—roughly the equivalent of a parking ticket.

At least three times since then, according to the Smarts' attorney, Paul's counsel has brought up the subject of a plea but has never followed through with any serious offer. The Smarts believe that comments by the Sheriff's Department like the ones in the local paper and on *20/20* killed any chance of Flores admitting culpability. As long as he kept his mouth shut, they seemed to be telling him, there was nothing the authorities could do to him.

Ironically, if Paul had accepted any one of the plea offers discussed, he would have finished his prison sentence long ago.

———

The investigation has continued, in fits and starts. But much of the activity has come about only at the initiative of the Smart family.

Patrick Hedges, the current sheriff, maintains that his department is still actively investigating Kristin's disappearance. Experts from other law enforcement agencies, including psychological profilers, have been consulted. One investigator is assigned full-time to the case, working tips that still continue to come in regularly, and Hedges says he remains optimistic that it will one day be resolved.

The Smarts want to believe that, but it is hard for them to put much faith in the system anymore. For a decade they have been stuck on an endless, sickening roller coaster ride, their hopes raised with each new lead, then dashed by each dead end. At times, according to Denise, an entire year has gone by without anyone from law enforcement calling them or returning their calls.

In desperation, the Smarts have waged their own campaign to keep pressure on Paul Flores, to let him know he will never be truly free—free of them—until he tells them what they need to know. Yet they still have been thwarted at every turn.

They filed a wrongful death lawsuit against Paul, not in hope of any monetary settlement, but to force him to answer their questions.

Instead, when deposed under oath, Paul refused to tell them anything other than his name and Social Security number.

"On the advice of my attorney, I refuse to answer that question, based on the Fifth Amendment to the United States Constitution," he responded to every other query, reading carefully from a scrap of paper placed in front of him by his lawyer.

In a Catch-22 from which they seemingly cannot escape, the Smarts can't proceed to trial on the civil suit without access to the evidence uncovered by the Sheriff's Department. But the sheriff has refused to turn over the records, contending that to do so would compromise the criminal case. Every few months a local judge privately reviews what progress has been made in the criminal investigation. As long as he is satisfied that the sheriff is actively pursuing the case, the records will remain confidential and the civil suit stayed.

When Paul was still living in San Luis Obispo, Stan and Denise attempted to speak to him at the gas station where he was working, but he retreated into the restroom and refused to come out. They have kept tabs on him and cost him several jobs by sending news clippings about the case to his employers.

When deposed in the Smarts' civil case, both of Paul's parents denied that they have any knowledge of their son killing Kristin or that they aided him in any way after the fact. They said he told them the same thing he told police, that he left Kristin outside her dorm and never saw her again. Recently, Paul's mother and her boyfriend (the Floreses are now divorced) have filed suit against the Smarts accusing them of a campaign of harassment and seeking damages for intentional infliction of emotional distress.

—◆◆—

For years after Stan Smart went back to his job as a school administrator, he spent every weekend looking for his daughter, pursuing any possible sighting, employing all manner of psychics. It was a ghastly, demoralizing quest. In desperation he followed the leads psychics would suggest, all amounting to nothing. The places his own instincts took him were equally grim. He searched lakes, dumpsters, even the agriculture school's slaughterhouse for "bones, sinew, hair," or any other trace of a human corpse. He became familiar with the smell of death from all the animal carcasses he discovered in the rugged canyons around San Luis Obispo, but found no sign of his daughter.

When he found out that a new performing arts center was under construction at the time Kristin disappeared, right across the street from where Cheryl Anderson left Kristin and Paul on their walk back to the dorms, he was sickened by the thought that she could have been interred in one of the trenches underneath the complex, sealed away for ever.

One of the most painful facts Stan learned was that the dumpster closest to Paul's dorm was emptied just hours after he got back to campus from the party. Authorities searched the landfill where refuse is taken, digging down through eighteen feet of garbage until they reached dated material from the day of her disappearance. Even that is not a foolproof method, however. Garbage does not remain in one place, ready to be exposed like an archaeological dig, but gets pushed to and fro as new trucks come in and add more refuse to the pile. Some of the investigators and the landfill manager think it is possible that Kristin's body was overlooked. That's certainly possible, considering that it took Salt Lake City authorities three solid months of concerted digging with the assistance of cadaver dogs to find the remains of Lori Hacking.

After several years of devoting every weekend to searching for his daughter, Stan Smart had to pull back a little, "to get on with life here. Otherwise, it just eats you alive."

Kristin's parents both say that the only way they have managed to keep going is out of concern for their two other children. Two weeks after Kristin disappeared, someone Denise didn't even know said to her, "You have to recognize that you have lost one child, and you don't want to lose all three."

At the time, those words felt monumentally presumptuous, "like a slap in the face," but Denise now realizes that they were something she needed to hear. The Smarts have worked hard to balance their efforts to find Kristin with the needs of their other children. Every birthday, holiday, or personal accomplishment makes them wonder "what if Kristin were here." But they make a point of honoring those occasions.

In 2005 Denise accompanied daughter Lindsey to Italy to celebrate her graduation from UCLA. They speak with pride of seeing their two surviving children nearly make the Olympic team. The only comfort they draw from Kristin's short life is that she packed a lot of adventure into that time. One thing she never got to do, which she dreamed of doing, was go to Australia and Fiji. Her brother, Matt, a pharmacy rep, visited those places in her honor.

"You're always in conflict: do I help my living children or do something for Kristin?" says Denise. They vow that they will never stop looking for Kristin, never stop trying to bring to justice the man who they believe took her life.

"People ask, 'How do you "do life" and still do this?' " Denise says of their efforts on Kristin's behalf. "It's not easy. It's a pain that never dissipates. Sometimes you have to pretend like it didn't happen."

CHAPTER TWELVE

A Collision Course

After Scott graduated from Cal Poly in June 1998, his parents moved back to San Diego. Lee sold his half of Central Coast Crating to Scott for just $3,500, the price of his initial investment. But Scott had no real interest in the shipping business and quickly sold off the company. Instead, he and Laci decided to start their own business, opening a restaurant in an abandoned bakery a few blocks from campus.

According to the Petersons, The Shack was based on a business model Scott devised for a class project. As business plans go, it was a pretty simple one and seemed like a can't-lose proposition: a sports bar with cheap grub and brew and different games playing on the various televisions scattered throughout the room. They ran the restaurant for two years, and as far as they ever told anyone, it was a success. But a lien for unpaid taxes was not satisfied until almost a year and a half after they sold the restaurant.

Whether or not the business was in financial trouble, the day-to-day drudgery of running a restaurant had grown old for Scott. Brent

Rocha remembers his brother-in-law telling him, "I don't want to spend my life flipping burgers."

Laci had her own reasons for wanting to sell the restaurant. The death of her beloved paternal grandmother to lung cancer in 1999 made her realize how much she missed her family and friends in Modesto. Her grandfather was suffering from dementia and would, within a few years, need full-time convalescent care. Laci wanted to be closer to those she loved. She was ready to start her own family, and wanted her children to grow up in the kind of community and around the people she so treasured.

One can't help but wonder if Laci also may have been reacting to lingering fears about Scott's infidelity. Perhaps she hoped that moving away from the site of his past indiscretions would remove Scott from temptation and cement his commitment to her.

She made a deal with her husband. If he agreed to move to her hometown, she promised that she would return the favor in the future, should he ever want to live closer to his family. His family maintains that relocating to the Central Valley was no real sacrifice for Scott.

"Because his major was in agriculture, it was an ideal place for that," his sister, Susan, said. "And Scott came from a big family so it was nice to have Laci's family around." Yet for someone weaned on country clubs and ocean-view estates, the move to landlocked, working-class Modesto must have been a shock to his system.

In May 2000 Scott and Laci sold The Shack. With no jobs or home to live in—truly, this time—they moved in temporarily with Sharon and Ron. They soon found work: Laci as a wine salesperson and later as a substitute teacher, and Scott with Tradecorp, a position he obtained with the assistance of one of his Cal Poly professors.

A Spain-based exporter of agricultural chemicals, Tradecorp was attempting to break into the American market. Scott was named manager of U.S. operations, a big title in an unglamorous field. He would at times try to make it sound even bigger, telling some people that he was the owner of Tradecorp, that he had "come out of retirement" to launch the start-up after making a killing selling a previous European venture. In reality he was a salesman, a company of one, driving around the Southwest peddling manure—albeit high-priced, new age–formulated synthetic manure with bionutrients and amino acids.

Unlike his sure-thing sports bar, this was risky business. Farmers are traditionalists, constitutionally averse to change. It would take someone with indefatigable drive and superb salesmanship skills to convince the average grower to take a new and more expensive approach than their fathers and grandfathers had before them and to believe that feeding their crops a diet of zinc and iron and calcium would ultimately produce bigger yields and more profits.

Under Scott Peterson's leadership, the company did not even make a dent in the market. In 2002, total sales for Tradecorp USA were a meager $124,000, and company accountants had to intervene to get Scott to pay delinquent taxes. A month before Laci disappeared, the executive director of Tradecorp told Scott that he needed to increase sales tenfold in order to reach the company's goal of breaking even in 2003.

Just as he had entered into marriage (and would later into prospective fatherhood) without the requisite acceptance of the responsibilities involved, Scott was not self-reflective enough to recognize that the job with Tradecorp was a bad fit. He was neither consumed by passion for the field nor disciplined enough to succeed at such a self-directed position. The title appealed to his ego, as did the freedom the job provided—freedom both from the oversight of his bosses, far away in Europe, and from his wife. He spent many nights away from home on sales calls, and traveled to Mexico, Egypt, and Europe for business meetings and conventions. As police would discover after Laci went missing, not all Scott's overnight excursions were work related. His job provided good cover for his secret life. He could see other women, and his wife was none the wiser.

At least one member of the Peterson family was not particularly happy about Scott and Laci's new life. Jackie Peterson privately referred to Modesto as "a little nothing town" and "the wrong side of the tracks." She would contend that Scott and Laci never intended to settle there permanently, that they were simply operating on a "five-year plan." She also seemed somewhat ashamed of Scott's chosen profession. After her son became a household name, she berated reporters for calling him a fertilizer salesman.

"He's the West Coast representative of an agricultural supply company," she corrected them. Nevertheless, she and Lee gave the couple $30,000 to purchase a $177,000 home less than a mile away from Laci's mother's house, a three-bedroom, two-bath fixer-upper on a leafy street that dead-ends on a large, rambling park.

The fifteen-hundred-square-foot clapboard and brick home, built in 1949, was exceedingly humble by California real estate standards.

But Laci saw its potential. With her decorating skills and Scott's handiness with tools, they quickly turned their home into a showplace for entertaining friends and family. They remodeled the kitchen into a chef's paradise. They had a hot tub and a kidney-shaped swimming pool installed in the backyard, and Scott built an outdoor barbecue and tiled wet bar for summer pool parties.

Several whimsical touches were pure Laci. She draped a canopy of mosquito netting over the bed she shared with Scott, creating a romantic harem-style effect. And she hung a large framed chalkboard on the wall near the dining room on which she would write descriptions of the elaborate dishes she served her guests, like the specials board in a fancy restaurant.

"She said they wanted their house to be the place where everybody hangs out, the place everyone would consider home," said René Tomlinson. "And it was home to a lot of us."

One of Laci's primary goals on returning to Modesto was to bring her old circle of girlfriends back together. They were all adults now, of course, with careers and mortgages, and several had children of their own. Yet Laci was determined to recapture the closeness they shared as kids. She reinstituted the tradition of slumber parties, hosting grown-up sleepovers when Scott was out of town. Laci was more worldly than most of her friends, many of whom had never left Modesto. But rather than holding herself above the group, says Tomlinson, "she brought the world to us."

She had taken cooking lessons in Tuscany after she and Scott were married, and she delighted and amazed her friends with her gourmet concoctions. She threw parties for nearly every occasion: Christmas, New Year's, Fourth of July, an annual Cinco de Mayo party with margaritas and Mexican food for her May 4 birthday. She was generous to a fault, her gifts personalized and thoughtful. She baked eye-popping cakes for all her friends' birthdays, each more spectacularly decorated than the last. Even after she became pregnant, she volunteered to do all the cooking for a friend's wedding.

Laci was the life of every party, the center of every gathering. After she went missing, her friends could not remember ever seeing her in a bad mood. They could find no photograph in which she was not smiling.

"She was just this amazing force," says Garza.

Laci's girlfriends were as taken with Scott as her family had been. When Scott and Laci entertained, he was the perfect host, bartender, and grill-master, catering to everyone's needs and oozing self-confidence. They marveled at the adoring, attentive way he looked at his wife, how he completed without complaint the running "honey-do" list of errands and projects she kept on the refrigerator door. Even at the slumber parties when the girls inevitably got around to complaining about their husbands or boyfriends, Laci never once had a negative thing to say about Scott.

"They really seemed to have the perfect marriage in every sense of the word," said friend Kim McNeely six weeks after Laci disappeared. "He doted on her. And she always referred to him as 'My Husband,' even to us, showing her pride in him, that he was her husband. She loved him and he loved her, so it appeared. They had a wonderful home; they were expecting this baby. It was everything we all wanted."

Scott was so good at focusing attention on others, at making whomever he was speaking to or waiting on feel like the center of the universe, that only in retrospect did Laci's friends realize they knew very little about him beyond his obvious passions for things like golf. Until confronted with incontrovertible proof in the form of his ongoing affair with Amber Frey that he was not the grieving husband he pretended to be, none of Laci's friends could imagine that he was capable of harming his wife in any way.

Laci's family defended Scott just as vociferously in the early weeks of the investigation. Only Dennis Rocha saw his son-in-law as something other than a perfect gentleman, devoted husband, and excited father-to-be. Dennis believed that, like Jackie, Scott looked down on humble Modesto, that he viewed the Rochas as unsophisticated farm people.

—⁓—

It is a well-known fact that opposites attract. We are often drawn, subconsciously, to the qualities in others that we lack in ourselves. On some level, we hope our partner will complete us, that through some kind of mystical alchemy two "halves" will make a perfect whole. Scott used just such language in one of the four carefully orchestrated interviews he granted in the days after Amber Frey was unveiled at a police press conference.

"You always look for someone who completes you, you know, that harmony," he told KTVU reporter Ted Rowlands, describing what attracted him to Laci.

Considering what it took to kill and then dispose of his wife in the fashion he had, could Scott ever have truly felt that way about Laci?

Two months before his wife disappeared, Scott told Shawn Sibley, the woman who would introduce him to Amber, that he had once found his "soul mate," but lost her. Was he talking about Laci, presaging her death just as he would when he "confessed" to Amber that he had "lost" a wife who was not yet dead? Might he have been referring to Janet Ilse, the woman he talked about moving in with while his wife was living out of town? Could it have been Lauren Putnat, the last woman he was seeing before Laci, whom he had asked to marry him and tearfully begged to take him back after she ended their relationship? Or was this proclamation just another lie, an artifact of his imagination?

If he was referring to Laci as his lost soul mate, she was already dead in his mind, a distant memory. Scott seemed to crave the great love his parents shared, but he was unable to sustain it. Relationships were only skin deep for Scott because he was only skin deep. Inside he was a mystery even to himself.

One of the things that first struck me as odd about Scott when I began reporting on Laci's disappearance was that he seemed to have few real friends of his own. Almost all the people in their circle were primarily Laci's friends. She collected friends like a magnet, but he had few enduring relationships—odd for someone who had been voted "friendliest" in his junior high school class. Not once during the entire trial did anyone other than immediate family members or infatuated strangers ever speak up in the press on behalf of Scott or sit in court to show his or her support. A few friends did ask for his life to be spared in the penalty phase. But just three were people with whom he had a significant ongoing relationship at the time of the crime.

In many ways, Scott had chosen to marry a woman very much like his mother. People who know Jackie Peterson describe her in terms nearly identical to those used to describe Laci.

"She laughs a lot, she's always looking on the bright side," Joanne Farmer, a friend of Jackie's for nearly forty years, said at the trial. "I don't think I have ever seen Jackie really, really down."

Laci and Jackie were each the center of their respective worlds. Jackie's brothers John and Robert describe their sister as the "heartbeat" of their family, bringing the Latham siblings back together after tragedy separated them as children and the responsibilities of adulthood scattered them around the globe.

Just as people saw Scott and Laci as a perfect couple that never argued, the same is said of Lee and Jackie. Laci and Jackie also shared a similar power dynamic within their respective relationships, at least on the surface. Jackie is the dominant figure in her marriage, with Lee the laconic cowboy, seemingly happy to take a backseat to his more assertive wife. This dynamic remained in place even after their son was accused of murder, with Jackie very much the driving force in her son's defense, both in public and behind the scenes. Laci "wore the pants" in her marriage as well.

In his daily life with Laci, Scott was passive almost in the extreme. He appeared content to bask in his wife's glow. Yet he must have resented the subordinate role he played so expertly. Murdering her, then hiding her body and pretending it never happened, is the ultimate passive-aggressive act.

After Scott was arrested, the Peterson family painted an idyllic portrait of Scott and Laci's marriage for *People* magazine, accompanied by smiling photos the Petersons provided of the two. Curiously, Jackie also provided *People* with a warm note Laci had once written to her for Mother's Day, which the magazine photographically reproduced in its five-page cover story. "You are a wonderful and caring person, friend, and mother," reads the note, which ends with Laci's signature and a smiley face. "I am fortunate to be gaining a mother-in-law like yourself. Thank you for treating me like your own daughter. I love you."

Yet, according to Anne Bird, Jackie was actually quite critical of her daughter-in-law. She complained to Bird about the "silly" way Laci dressed, about her perfectionist tendencies, even about things as particular as how Laci wrote thank-you notes. (It's hard to find fault with the example Jackie herself provided to *People*.)

At a Latham family reunion a year after Scott and Laci got married, Jackie made fun of the romantic trail of roses Laci had laid up to the door of the cottage she and Scott were sharing. Only Laci would do something like that, Jackie scoffed. Anne wondered what Jackie could find wrong with such a loving gesture. Didn't Jackie want Scott to have a wife who adored him?

The first time Anne met Laci, shortly after she and Scott got married, Anne commented to her mother about how pleased she must be with her new daughter-in-law. Jackie complained about

Modesto and said that she feared Laci would talk Scott into moving there. After a trip to Carmel with Scott and Laci, Jackie mocked Laci to Anne as looking "like Minnie Mouse" when she wore white gloves and a white scarf with a black coat.

That trip, a week before Laci disappeared, was the last time Jackie would ever see her daughter-in-law alive.

Anne was stunned by Jackie's harshness toward Laci. She concluded that in Jackie's eyes no one would ever be good enough for her Golden Boy.

Shortly after Scott and Laci moved to Modesto, Sharon Rocha got another tearful late-night call from her daughter. The couple had hosted a party that evening at which Laci's brother revealed that his wife, Rose, was pregnant with their first child. Laci desperately wanted her own children to grow up with Brent's, to have the kind of bond she and her brother shared.

Scott had been telling Laci for some time that he was not yet ready for kids. After the guests went home that night, he confessed that he didn't think he wanted to have children at all. Laci was devastated.

Just a month later, however, she claimed that Scott had reversed himself, saying he was now ready to start a family. In December 2002, she stopped taking birth control pills.

Had Scott really changed his mind so quickly on such an life-altering issue, or was he just appeasing his wife, pretending to go along with what she wanted but hoping it would never come to pass? After Laci went missing, Rose Rocha recalled a startling comment Scott made during her own pregnancy, when she asked him if he was ready for kids.

"I was kind of hoping for infertility," Scott responded. At the time, she thought he must be joking, but looking back she remembered that he wasn't laughing or even smiling when he said it.

Scott had reason to believe his wife might have trouble getting or staying pregnant. In addition to the fact that she had only one ovary, the year that they got married Laci had surgery to remove abnormal tissue from her cervix, the narrow opening to the womb that dilates during labor, allowing the baby to pass into the birth canal. Laci had been diagnosed as suffering from cervical dysplasia, precancerous cell changes that can develop into cancer if left untreated. These changes were severe enough in Laci's case that doctors opted for an aggressive form of treatment, cutting away the affected tissue around the cervical opening.

This procedure can weaken the cervix and cause it to dilate prematurely during pregnancy, resulting in miscarriage. A quarter of all miscarriages after the first trimester are the result of a weakened cervix. Laci was concerned enough that when she began to feel pressure internally from her growing fetus during her second trimester, she told her doctor she was worried that her cervix might not be strong enough to carry her baby to term.

Laci's belief that Scott had undergone a change of heart about wanting children was not merely wishful thinking on her part. He was with her when she announced to family and friends at a holiday party that she was going to start trying to get pregnant, and he nodded approvingly. He was certainly up for whatever it took sexually to try to get her pregnant. But there were other indications that he was deeply ambivalent about becoming a father.

There was the "hoping for infertility" comment in 2001, and the irritation Scott showed when Laci woke him up on the morning of June 9, 2002, to tell him that her home pregnancy test was positive. When they visited her mother the evening after taking the test, Laci could not stop talking about how excited she was. Scott said nothing about the pregnancy and looked decidedly unhappy. It was so awkward between the three of them that Laci felt the need to offer an explanation.

"Scott's having a midlife crisis," Laci opined, "because he's turning thirty and becoming a father all in the same year." Scott himself said something very similar to Laci's brother one day that summer as they lounged in the Peterson's new pool. As Brent recalled, Scott expressed a sense of both failure and dread about where his life was heading, stating that "he wasn't doing good at his job and that he had a lot going on—he's turning thirty, going to be a father."

Scott also appeared to be worried about the impact a baby would have on his sex life. He asked one of the fathers in their circle if couples ever had much sex again after they've had a child.

Laci was so happy finally to be pregnant that she began wearing maternity clothes before she needed them. When she did begin showing, she proudly pointed out her growing waistline. She chronicled each milestone of the pregnancy in a journal, noting the first time she felt the baby kick, the first time she heard its heartbeat, the "excitement and relief" she felt at seeing her child moving inside her during a sonogram.

At Laci's twenty-week sonogram, on September 24, 2002, she found out the baby's sex. Laci immediately called her friend Renee Garza, who had a kindergarten-age son. "Guess what I'm having?" she crowed, then immediately began discussing her plans for the nursery. She was pleased that the spare bedroom they had been planning to convert to a nursery was already a lovely cerulean blue. It seemed like a sign that everything was as it was meant to be.

Scott continued to send mixed signals. From the earliest days of the pregnancy, he seemed to be looking for a way out of his situation. Laci told a friend that Scott urged her to get a more extensive than usual sonogram and tried to get her to agree to an abortion if any birth defects were discovered.

It seemed as if he could not envision ever having a warm moment with his child. When Laci's aunt, Gwen Kemple, asked Scott one day if he was looking forward to playing catch with his son, he oddly replied, "I've got friends who can do that."

All summer long, as they sat out by the pool, Laci and her girlfriends had bantered about baby names. "Scott has to like it, too," she always reminded them. One day that fall, as Laci discussed names with her family, Scott suggested Ripley.

If it was a joke, it was in poor taste. There are three famous figures associated with that name: the man with the "Believe It or Not!" collection of freaks and oddities; Tom Ripley, the protagonist of a series of mystery novels and movies, a charming young man who turns out to be an utterly amoral killer (appropriating the attributes and identity of those around him to make his way in the world); and the eponymous heroine played by Sigourney Weaver in a series of science fiction movies, who first battles aliens, then becomes unwitting host to an alien baby, which she ends up killing in an act of murder-suicide.

According to Laci's baby journal, Scott did not feel the baby move until late October, when she was more than six months pregnant. She noted that he didn't show much excitement on that momentous occasion, but then tried to convince herself otherwise. "I know he really was," she wrote.

In fact, by that time, Scott and Laci were on very different trajectories. Laci was consumed with her role as wife and mother. She had recently inherited a large cache of jewelry from her late grandmother, and was in the process of fashioning a new wedding ring for herself. She instructed the jeweler to make sure and use all the gold and diamonds from the one Scott had given her so she would not hurt his feelings. She made one other demand: please have it ready by Christmas Eve.

Despite her growing pregnancy, she also wanted to throw an elaborate dinner party for seven couples to celebrate her husband's thirtieth birthday on October 24. But she had a hard time getting Scott to commit to a date. The last person with whom he wanted to commemorate that milestone was, it seems, his pregnant wife.

That very week, Scott began taking concerted steps away from his wife and unborn child. Three days before his birthday, while attending a trade show at the Disneyland Hotel, Scott met Shawn Sibley, a pretty blonde lab worker from Fresno. Despite the fact that she announced right away that she was engaged to be married, Scott flirted outrageously, continually pressing Shawn about how committed she was to her relationship. On their way to dinner, Scott asked her what moniker he could add to his nametag to attract women. Over dinner with a few other colleagues, the conversation Scott initiated turned so blue—discussing his favorite sexual positions and asking Shawn about hers—that the others eventually excused themselves in embarrassment.

When Shawn described her fiancé as her soul mate, Scott turned serious. "He said that at one point he had found a woman he thought to be his soul mate, but then he lost her," Shawn recalled at trial. Then Scott asked her, "Do you think there is only one person you are meant to be with forever?"

Shawn told him no, that she believed there were potentially thousands of potential soul mates for everyone. Scott went on, telling Shawn that he had had a lot of "one-night stands," that he was sick and tired of women who seemed to be "bimbos with no brains," and that he was looking for someone with intelligence for a long-term meaningful relationship. Did she have any single friends she could hook him up with? Scott continued to press Shawn about this after dinner over drinks in the hotel bar, and then in the hallway outside Shawn's room where they sat talking until the wee hours of the morning.

Her friend Amber came to mind. But Shawn told Scott she was reluctant to introduce them because Amber had been hurt before. Her last boyfriend had left her shortly after she became pregnant. (Her daughter, Ayiana, was now a year and a half.) After Scott assured Shawn that he was looking for a serious relationship, she gave him Amber's phone number.

The curious thing about all this is how directed Scott was. He did not fall into an affair or turn to someone he already knew for attention he wasn't getting from a distracted wife, as many men do when their wives are pregnant. Scott went out looking for someone to fall in love with—and not just a girlfriend, a soul mate! He solicited a long-term serious relationship. He was married, about to become a parent. Even if he might have been entertaining the idea of merely divorcing his wife, there is no longer-term relationship than parenthood.

How serious or truthful Scott was being, to Shawn or with himself, is unclear. He lied to Shawn about almost everything else. He pretended to be single, and claimed, among other things, that he lived in Sacramento, owned two homes, had a lot of money, and owned Tradecorp. How he ever hoped to establish any kind of ongoing relationship, to climb his way out of the hole he had already dug with such easy mendacity, seems incomprehensible. Nevertheless, he followed through and called Amber, setting up a date for November 20.

———

While Laci got together with her girlfriends to watch the reality dating show *The Bachelor*, Scott acted out the part in real life with an unsuspecting Amber. They met at a Fresno bar, where Scott got Amber to leave her car and come with him to his hotel, saying he needed to shower and change before going to dinner. He had come prepared for an evening of seduction. Out of his luggage he pulled a bottle of champagne and fresh strawberries to add to the glasses—a romantic gesture, however well practiced it might have been, that dazzled his date.

Over dinner at a Japanese restaurant, where Scott finagled a private room, he continued his litany of lies, embroidered here and there with bits and pieces of truth. He told her about his 1940s-era house but claimed to live in Sacramento, not Modesto, alone. He bragged about his great kitchen and how he loved to cook (although Laci was the gourmet chef in his household). He claimed to own a condo in San Diego (a complete lie), which he said he was thinking of selling furnished in a package deal with a Land Rover he had stored in the garage (actually the Land Rover was Laci's, which she was still driving in Modesto). He denied even having pets, saying he traveled too much to take care of them. (In addition to their dog, he and Laci had also taken in two stray cats.)

He said he was going on a weeklong fishing trip to Alaska with his father, brother, and uncle over the Thanksgiving holiday. That was a trip he had taken many years before when he was younger, to his uncle's hunting lodge. But he wasn't going this year. He would be spending Thanksgiving with his wife in San Diego, where his family was going to throw Laci a baby shower.

He also said he planned to spend Christmas with his family in Kennebunkport, Maine, which he claimed to be a traditional Peterson gathering place, then jet off on December 28 to celebrate New Year's with friends in Paris, followed by a month of business in Europe. The only truth there was that he was scheduled to go to Europe in January for meetings with Tradecorp executives—a trip Laci wasn't happy about because it was getting close to her February 10 due date. He was supposed to be spending Christmas and New Year's in Modesto with his wife. They had already made plans for New Year's Eve with friends. The strangest thing about Scott's lies was their specificity, the gratuitous detail. Kennebunkport? Did he pull that location from a news story about the Bush clan?

Amber couldn't help but be impressed by Scott's tall tales. Just as he had appeared to Laci, he seemed like a real catch: ambitious, impressive, and romantic to boot. He told her that he was eager to settle down but just hadn't found the right woman. They spent the night together at his hotel, and he assured her the next day that he did not consider what they did a one-night stand.

———

He called a few times before their next date, at one point pretending to be at the airport on his way to Alaska. Instead, Scott was traveling to San Diego and to Disneyland with Laci, his parents, and some of his siblings. Anne Bird recalls Scott as withdrawn and moody both on the excursion to Disneyland and when he came to collect Laci and her gifts from the baby shower.

On the Disneyland trip, Scott spent a lot of time on the phone on what he said were business calls. One day, as the extended Peterson clan gathered in Lee and Jackie's hotel room to exchange Christmas gifts, Anne's two-year-old son momentarily disappeared. Everyone in the room leaped to their feet to search for the boy—except for Scott, who just kept talking on his cell phone. Months later, Anne wondered if he might have been talking to Amber.

On December 2, Scott called Amber, saying he was back in Fresno on business and wanted to take her on a romantic hike. Planning ahead as always, Scott showed up not only with a picnic lunch but also with groceries to fix her dinner afterwards, all but ensuring him another overnight stay. They took Amber's daughter with them, and Scott apologized for not having thought to childproof his car.

At some point that day, Scott told Amber that he was so happy he couldn't stop smiling—the same words he would later use in his media interviews to describe the moment he knew he was in love with Laci. Was he drawing on some memorized stock image of love? Was he capable only of inferring emotions from a general physical state, rather than actually feeling them—a hallmark of psychopathy? Eerily, Scott described his expression to Amber as a "rigor-mortis smile." Perhaps it was just a malaprop, or maybe a revealing clue that even Scott realized that his face was merely a mask, with no genuine feeling below the surface.

At the end of their hike, they snuggled in his truck bed and stargazed until the night grew too chilly. Scott would later commemorate the romantic moment in a Christmas gift he had shipped to Amber's child: a battery-operated planetarium that projects the night sky onto the walls and ceilings of a darkened room. Whereas the defense portrayed this gift at trial as a cheap and meaningless trinket—and mistakenly as a present for Amber, not her daughter—it seemed to me to be quite meaningful. He certainly put more time and thought into it than what he said he gave his wife for Christmas, a Louis Vuitton wallet, which Laci actually bought for herself while shopping with her mother-in-law the week before Christmas.

On the day of the hike, Scott gave Ayiana another touching present: a pop-up book version of the classic poem *The Night Before Christmas*. In one of the most surreal moments of the trial, Scott's brother Joe would recount how it was a Peterson family tradition to read the poem aloud every Christmas Eve before opening their presents—Lee, Jackie, and each kid taking turns reading a page, then passing it on to another family member.

That Scott could call up such a warm childhood memory just three weeks before killing his own child—on Christmas Eve, no less, or a few hours before—is beyond comprehension. What makes the image even more chilling is that there is a distinct possibility that Laci actually bought that book to carry on the Peterson family tradition with Conner, as she and Scott had gone shopping for books for their baby around this time.

Scott went to great lengths not only to impress Amber but also to cover his lies. On the day of their hike, he brought along a photo of himself fishing, claiming it was taken on his fictional Thanksgiving trip to Alaska. She hadn't questioned his whereabouts, but he apparently felt the need to use a few props to sell his story.

The following day, Scott called Amber back, claiming that business required him to stay another night in Fresno. He cooked dinner for her again and took mother and daughter shopping for a Christmas tree. As they decorated it, Amber asked Scott straight out if he had ever been married. "No," he told her. "Ever get close?" Amber asks. "Never," he replied emphatically.

———

Scott Peterson did not wake up one morning and decide out of the blue to kill his wife. For months, maybe years, the idea was probably a dim fantasy, the dark stirrings of a restlessness and panic that had nothing to do with Laci and everything to do with him.

To the outside world, Scott seemed to be the perfect husband, but in his mind he was never "married," never committed to the notion of a wife and family. There was always a disconnection with Scott, a mental escape valve. Cheating, "acting single," a lost wife, a dead one: reality was what he said it was.

Scott could live the life of a footloose frat boy in San Luis Obispo, never mentioning the fact that he had a wife conveniently tucked away in another city. He could talk to Janet Ilse about moving in together while he was "happily married" to Laci. Even after moving to Modesto, he could go on leading a double life, lying to all who loved him without conscience or remorse. He could play the game, and he could end the game when he decided it was time for a new one.

Ultimately, Scott and Amber would see each other just five times—a fact the defense made much of at trial, insinuating that Scott could not possibly have developed feelings deep enough for Amber that he would have killed to be with her. But motive for murder is rarely that simple, or black and white. Scott's desire to get rid of his wife was not about replacing her with Amber or any particular woman. It was a more nebulous quest to make reality conform to his fantasies. His grandiose lies were projections of the life he wished he had, the person he wanted to be.

That quest began before Scott ever met Amber and grew in urgency as the baby's due date approached. But the fact that he went out looking for someone, and at least telling himself that he wanted a serious meaningful connection, is important. For what he planned to do, he needed to have the fantasy that a perfect relationship was his for the taking, that another woman was out there who would love him unconditionally.

The time Scott spent with Amber in Fresno was more like a parallel marriage than a purely sexual affair. He shopped and cooked for her, picked her daughter up from preschool, helped her relocate her massage therapy practice, cancelled plans to attend a Christmas party with Laci so that he could squire Amber to a holiday formal. Scott was making plans to move his warehouse from Modesto to Fresno. If not for the imminent arrival of a baby and Amber's growing suspicions about his marital status, Scott may have been happy to carry on with two separate "families"—neither having any idea the other existed.

In a pattern we often see with eraser killers, Scott's relationship with Amber intensified almost immediately. They may have had only five dates, but they spoke on the phone nearly every day, on some days exchanging more than a dozen calls between them. Between mid-November 2002 and mid-February 2003, when Amber asked Scott not to call her anymore, one of the very few days they did not speak to each other at all was on Christmas Eve—a fact that stuck out like a sore thumb when police subpoenaed Scott's telephone records.

In their conversations, Scott idealizes Amber for all the things he is not. He marvels at her ability to connect with people, raves about her sense of touch. She is both a mother and a professional massage therapist, an object of reverence and fantasy. His attraction to her seems almost Freudian. On Christmas Day, just hours after killing his wife and child, he asks Amber to sing to him, the next time he sees her, one of the lullabies she sings to her daughter.

Finding her at such a pivotal juncture in his life must have seemed like a miraculous gift to him. She believed his fantasies, thought he really was a guy with multiple homes and a jet-set lifestyle. He lied to her shamelessly, but in some ways he was more honest with her than with anyone else he knew—certainly more than he was with his wife. Within a month of knowing her he told her that he did not want to have any biological children, was thinking of having a vasectomy, and invited her to come with him to speak with a doctor.

One of the most puzzling questions in the Peterson case is why a man who did not want a child, who killed to prevent that child from ever being born, would take up with a woman who had a small child of her own. Whereas Scott showed little interest in his unborn son, he was tender in his interactions with Ayiana. Perhaps this was simply because he did not seriously plan to spend his life with Amber. Or maybe a child who did not belong to him, who was already born, who was a girl, was less threatening to him. She would not grow up to compete with him, to challenge, rebel against, or outshine him, as a son might. Or maybe it had something to do with the fact that Amber had already crossed the parental Rubicon yet was still 100 percent available to him emotionally and sexually, in a way he could not imagine his wife ever being after their baby was born.

Whatever the reason, that Amber had a child in no way vitiates the impending birth of Conner as paramount motive for the murder. How otherwise could a man with a baby on the way, a son he had felt move inside his wife's belly and seen on an ultrasound, so cavalierly declare as he did to Amber on what would turn out to be their final date, "I don't really feel I need a biological child. Assuming that you and I are together, the one child I could see in my life is Ayiana"?

Those were not mere words or halfhearted sentiments. He was prepared to take the steps necessary to make sure there would be no more children with Amber or any other woman. He was adamant about having a vasectomy, even when Amber became tearful, telling Scott that she definitely wanted more kids and that he was too young to make such a potentially irrevocable decision.

Scott's two lives were headed on a collision course. His wife had decided she did not want to return to work after the baby was born, and Scott's job may have been in jeopardy. In the weeks leading up to the murder, he appeared to be scrambling for money. He ordered his credit report, and ran ads on eBay and visited pawnshops with his wife to sell off some of her grandmother's jewelry. Two days after

Thanksgiving, Laci took her newly inherited jewelry to be appraised, telling the jeweler her husband wanted to know how much it was worth. When given an estimate of at least $100,000, Laci remarked that Scott would be very happy to hear that.

Yet that very same week he thought nothing of joining a local country club—where he would later sneak off to play golf and work out while everyone else he knew searched frantically for his missing wife. His parents paid the $23,000 membership fee, but Scott had to come up with nearly $400 in monthly dues. Laci appeared to have some qualms about that decision, if not for the expenditure it involved than for what it seemed to indicate about Scott's priorities.

"Now I'll see you less than I already do," she groaned, when they told Sharon and Ron over dinner one night in late November about the purchase. Scott feebly told Laci she could come with him—not likely any time soon with an infant in tow.

Another sore point between Scott and his wife was his failure to pay Laci's health insurance premiums and prenatal bills. Laci was so aggrieved by the situation that a friend overheard her during the summer ask Scott whether he cared about her and the baby. He didn't pay the delinquent bills until the insurance was days away from cancellation. Interestingly, the day he wrote the check was December 23, the last day anyone saw Laci alive and the day police believe she was most likely killed. Perhaps he was afraid a debt like that would look suspicious after her disappearance.

Whatever wish or fantasy Scott may have harbored for escaping his marriage and impending parenthood, a concrete plan to achieve that end began to take shape in early December, when the wall Peterson had carefully constructed between his two lives began to collapse.

In an offhand conversation with coworker Mike Almasri on Friday, December 6, Shawn Sibley happened to mention the name of her new friend, Scott Peterson. Almasri said he had met Scott, had interviewed with him in June for a sales position at Tradecorp. He was very taken by how young Scott looked and asked him how he came to be running an entire U.S. operation at his age. Scott told him he got the job after moving with his wife to Modesto.

His wife? Shawn was apoplectic. She immediately called Scott and angrily confronted him: "Tell me I didn't just set my friend up with a married man!" At first Scott simply denied the fact outright. "Must be another Scott Peterson," he said coolly. But Shawn was not appeased. After she called a coworker of Peterson's for more information, Scott called her back in tears.

"I'm sorry I lied to you earlier," Scott stammered. "I had been married. I lost my wife. It's too painful for me to talk about." Shawn was too taken aback to ask him what happened. He begged Shawn to let him tell Amber. She agreed, but warned him that if he did not do so by the following Monday, December 9, she would tell Amber herself.

The next morning and again in the late afternoon on Saturday, Scott searched online want ads looking for a boat. He called a man named Bruce Peterson about the fourteen-foot Gamefisher he had listed and made arrangements to come see it the following day.

Saturday night Scott and Laci went together to a Christmas party. Friends remembered how gallant Scott seemed, telling them how Laci had offered to sleep on the couch so as not to disturb him, as she was struggling with the latter stages of pregnancy. "Isn't my wife great?" he said, beaming at Laci—adding that he, of course, declined her offer. Even as he set into motion a diabolical plan, he remained on the surface the adoring husband, ever grateful for such a wonderful wife.

Scott had paid for and picked up the boat Monday morning. Shortly after noon he called Amber, telling her that he was in the area and wanted to see her. When he arrived he looked very establishment in a blue suit, his membership pin for the Rotary Club affixed to his lapel, but he acted like a scared cornered animal. Scott was such a practiced fabulist that he could lie without thinking, but he was outside his comfort zone here. For once he was not completely in control of the situation, not sure if he could sell this one, and he actually seemed to be experiencing fear. Amber could hear his stomach making noises as he paced the room. Then he began to cry.

He used the same words he had told Shawn, that he had been married but "lost" his wife. He said he lied because it is was so painful to talk about that it was easier for him to act as if he had never been married. He seemed so distraught, literally choking to get the words out, that Amber too was afraid to press for any details. She did ask him how long it had been, and he said that these were the first holidays he would be spending without his wife.

Amber was so impressed by what she considered his genuine grief that she took his hand and comforted him, assured him that she was not mad. How could she be when he had suffered such a terrible loss and made such a painful confession? When he saw that she was buying his story, he quickly regained his composure. She asked him if he was ready for another relationship, and his response was emphatic: "God, yes!"

Strangely, Scott claimed to have spent the previous weekend sailing on the bay with some friends. "I just had a horrible weekend, and it wasn't fun for anybody because I had this on my mind," he said, although withholding any mention of Shawn's confrontation and ultimatum.

For their last date on December 14, the night of the Christmas formal, Scott was back to his old practiced self. He showed up at Amber's door with three dozen red roses, then pulled off one bud and began rubbing the petals around her breasts. During the week, Shawn had confessed to Amber what she had learned about Scott, and Amber interrupted Scott's seduction to ask if he would have made his confession to her if Shawn hadn't forced his hand. He claimed he had planned to tell her the truth when he returned from his business trip to Europe at the end of January.

"I live a certain lifestyle, and I can see you living that lifestyle, too," Scott told her. He then cryptically added that he was in the process of making some big decisions and hoped that when he returned from his trip, she would say yes to whatever he asked of her without question.

Scott rushed off the next afternoon, telling Amber he was headed to Arizona and New Mexico on business. In fact, he had to get home to have dinner with his wife and in-laws. The four of them happened to have a long conversation that evening about fishing. Ron Grantski is such a fishing fanatic that he keeps a pole in his car at all times, just in case he happens to find himself near a good fishing spot. Sharon hardly ever goes with him, but she had accompanied him that morning, and they laughed at the description of her gamely trying to pass the time reading the newspaper and ward off the morning chill while Ron happily fished. Scott mentioned nothing about having just purchased a boat. Neither did Laci, even though the defense at trial would claim she knew all about the boat, had even been to the warehouse to see it.

It was the last time Sharon Rocha would ever see her daughter. Laci proudly showed her the nursery and wanted desperately for her mother to feel the baby kick, mentioning how impatiently Scott would always snatch his hand away when she asked him to feel Conner move inside her. Sharon kept her hand on Laci's stomach for a long time, but never did feel the baby stir. She finally laid her head against her daughter's belly and spoke to the grandchild she would never get a chance to know.

"Hello, little Conner," she said. "I can't wait to meet you."

The lie Scott used to cancel plans with Laci the night before in order to take Amber to the formal dance was that he had to pick up his boss at the San Francisco airport. There had been very high winds that night, and when Sharon asked him how the drive had been, he quickly changed the subject, turning on his well-practiced charm. Just as he had at their wedding, he raised his glass, toasting Sharon for giving him her wonderful daughter.

CHAPTER THIRTEEN

Sex, Lies, and Audiotape

I don't believe that Scott Peterson ever loved Amber Frey. I doubt that he is capable of truly loving anyone. But he needed her to love him, to believe in him in order to maintain the illusion that even after committing an unspeakable crime he was still the Golden Boy—the sensitive, chivalrous, rose-bearing knight.

For the first two weeks after the murder, before Amber let Scott know that she was aware he had a missing wife, she was his refuge from the maelstrom swirling around him. She was like a blank slate, or so he believed, untouched by the horror he had set in motion, the only person with whom he could carry on his pose of normality. With Amber he could continue to play out his fantasies and be whoever he wanted to be.

It was stunning to sit in court and listen to his tape-recorded phone calls with Amber as the jury was hearing them. After two and a half months of often confusingly presented testimony—one of the inherent difficulties of putting on a circumstantial case—here was Peterson himself speaking in a way he never would have had he chosen to take the stand. Until she forced him to give up his ruse by leading him to believe a friend was about to tell her his true identity, he regaled her with richly atmospheric tales of his fictitious European revels: the quaint cobblestone streets, the magnificent churches, the rich French cuisine that he fretted was turning him into "Pudge Boy."

In between the elaborate lies are moments of truth so revealing they seemed like free association. He rhapsodizes about the book he was reading at the time Laci disappeared, Jack Kerouac's *On the Road*, a tale of the ultimate rambling man, commenting on "how I never had a prolonged period of freedom like that from responsibility." He raves about what he termed "the best movie ever made," *The Shining*, a Stephen King story about a man who goes mad and attempts to kill his wife and young son. He quotes a line from the Ron Howard film *A Beautiful Mind*, in which a mentally disturbed and socially inept math genius approaches a woman without any attempt at romantic seduction and says exactly what is on his mind: "I don't know what I have to do for prevention, but I'm trying to get to the point of intercourse as fast as I can."

"That's somehow appealing, just to, you know, cut the crap," Scott says. "Just the clarity of saying, hey, screw the rest of it, let me just tell you what I want."

"Love doesn't mean two people can be together forever," he tells Amber at another point. When she tries to insert a serious note into Scott's boyish babblings, suggesting it must be hard for him to be spending his first holidays without his wife, Scott cuts her off curtly, and perhaps with more honesty than he intended. "Well, I don't think about it," he says. He is capable of compartmentalizing even the act of murder.

Knowing when these tapes were recorded and what was really going on in Scott's life at that time induced a dizzying sense of cognitive dissonance. What was most damning was what was clearly *not* on Scott's mind: any sense of concern for his missing wife and child. He was a man without a care in the world.

Curiously, Scott's need for Amber seemed to grow into near obsession *after* she let him know she was on to him. Rather than breaking off contact with her—which he surely would have done if she meant nothing to him and should have done if he had followed his lawyer's advice and the dictates of common sense—he subjected himself to her relentless interrogation, hour after hour, day after day, week after week. Why did he keep coming back for more?

I believe that in a strange way, Amber was the closest thing he had to a confidant. I say strange because he remained to the end deceitful and evasive with her. Yet as he became increasingly isolated by the suspicion surrounding him, an odd intimacy developed between them. He was desperate to make her believe him, to keep her on his side, to win back her affection and approval, but he knew he was not fooling her. Amber might have been working for the police, but her feelings were raw and direct. There was a realness between them, however painful, that Scott hadn't shared with another soul.

Although Scott never admitted any involvement in Laci's disappearance, he refused to answer even the simplest questions and instead offered strange and cryptic deflections. A typical exchange, from January 7:

"Amber, you don't know all the facts."

"Well, then why don't you share them, Scott?"

"I can't."

"Why?"

"I can't tell you everything now."

"Scott, from what I gather, the whole nation is wanting to find Laci."

"Definitely. She does not deserve, you know, she's—"

"She does not deserve what?"

"She was abducted, disappeared, and she needs to be found . . ."

". . . That all too familiar silence," Amber interjects sadly after Scott drifts off into silence. "I know why I'm silent, but why are you so silent?"

"Because I said what . . . what I can say and what I need to say. . . . And if that is not enough for you, it's not enough for me, but it's right for now."

He uses bizarre logic and tortured, abstract syntax. At one point he insists that he never cheated on Amber (apparently overlooking the glaring fact that he was married). At another point he tells Amber "I have always told you the truth . . . with exceptions, obviously." He won't say his "home" but "the house in Modesto" or "the house where Laci disappeared," won't call Laci his wife but "the woman I'm married to." At times it seems as if he is choosing his words carefully to leave open every possible avenue of defense. By refusing to admit to Amber that Conner was his son, was he simply revealing the lack of any human connection he felt toward his unborn child? Or was he preserving his ability to argue that Laci may have become pregnant by someone else who did her harm? In Scott's mind, that may have seemed like a viable argument for reasonable doubt, as he was not expecting Conner's body ever to be found and his paternity established.

Rather than directly incriminating facts, most of the evidence in the Peterson case pointed to what is known in legal terms as a "consciousness of guilt"—that Scott knew his wife was dead and was moving on with his life without her. The defense argued that Scott sold Laci's Jeep within weeks of her disappearance, trading it in for a truck for himself, because police had impounded his own, and he needed transportation, both for work and to look for Laci. Besides, according to Jackie Peterson, Laci herself termed the car "a piece of shit" and wanted something safer when the baby arrived. The defense also came up with an excuse for why Scott attempted to put his and Laci's house on the market just as quickly, claiming his wife would never want to live there again after such a traumatic experience (although the kidnapping was supposed to have happened at some location outside the house).

No one attempted an explanation, however, for why he offered to sell their home furnished. Surely Laci would want her furniture, which included expensive Tiffany lamps and other treasured heirlooms from her paternal grandmother.

It is rare, indeed, for families of genuinely missing persons ever to move or change their phone number while a loved one is still missing—in hopes that the person will one day turn up or at least try to call for help. Parents of missing children almost always preserve their child's room both for evidentiary purposes, to preserve articles scent dogs can use for searches, and for sentimental reasons, as a way of freezing time and hanging on to their memories of their lost child.

Marc Klaas and his second wife, Violet, who shared custody of his daughter, Polly, with her mother at the time of her kidnapping, didn't change a thing in Polly's room at their house for five years after her death. "We just couldn't," said Klaas, who has since worked with scores of other families with missing children. "That's how it is for almost every family whose child has been kidnapped."

Peterson did not merely seem as though he couldn't wait to get on with his life: nothing associated with Laci or Conner seemed to hold any sentimental value for him. He continued to talk about a future with Amber "after everything was resolved" with Laci, while at the same time hitting on other women—from Anne Bird's teenage babysitter to the house sitter at the home of Anne's adoptive parents, where he went to lay low after looking for an apartment in the Bay Area under an assumed name. When police served a second series of search warrants six weeks after Laci disappeared, they found wedding photos that had originally been inside his office stuffed unceremoniously into a wastebasket in a rented storage unit. Conner's nursery had basically been turned into a storage room as well, with furniture from Scott's shuttered warehouse and piles of linens crammed willy-nilly into the space.

A separate wiretap that police obtained to listen in on all Peterson's calls captured Scott in early February 2003 telling a supporter that he'd spent the previous four days at a retreat for grief counseling, when in fact he had traveled to Mexico for a fertilizer conference—where detectives feared he might forever flee their clutches.

Scott also did not seem concerned about potential sightings of his wife after she went missing. Around the time of the Mexico trip, a clerk at a grocery store in Washington State reported that a pregnant woman who looked like Laci came into the store claiming to have been kidnapped. Jackie called Scott and left a message urging him to go up and review the store's surveillance tape, offering the name of a relative with whom he could stay in the area. The wiretap picked up Scott chuckling at his mother's message and erasing it midstream.

He was concerned, however, when Modesto police reported in early January that divers using sonar technology detected what they believed might be a body in the bay waters near the Berkeley Marina. Police were exceedingly tight lipped throughout their investigation, but this information they purposely released, making a point of saying that the weather would not permit them to return and attempt to retrieve the possible body for a couple of days. They wanted to turn the heat up on Scott, to see what he would do.

Rather than checking in with police or going to the marina to see firsthand what they had discovered, Scott rented a car and hit the road, covering more than thirteen hundred miles over the next three days. It was one of the rare instances when he actually seemed to be afraid. As when he was forced to "confess" to Amber that he had been married, he wasn't in control of the situation: he didn't know if police had indeed found Laci. Police later reconstructed his movements, based on cell sites he used to make phone calls while on the road. To each and every person he spoke to during that period of time, including his own mother, he lied about his whereabouts, giving everyone a different and apparently randomly selected location hundreds of miles away from where he really was.

It was Sharon Rocha who inadvertently let Peterson know he was in the clear. At that point still believing in his innocence, she called his cell phone to pass along the good news: the murky image picked up by sonar on the muddy bay floor was not a body but an old boat anchor. The wiretap preserved his reaction. As Scott listened to his mother-in-law's message, he let out a whistle of relief. He was back in control.

When the bodies washed up on their own in mid-April 2003—first a baby's and then a woman's, a day later and a mile apart along the East Bay shoreline—Scott once again took flight. During the several days it took for authorities to identify the remains through DNA testing, he never once called police to inquire whether they could be his wife and child or came to the bay to see for himself, even though he told his half sister that he was just forty-five minutes from the scene when she called him with news of the macabre discovery. Instead he drove as far as he could in the opposite direction, to San Diego, where he was just minutes away from the Mexican border.

Scott had by now discovered the secret GPS transmitter police had implanted on his truck. He left the truck with relatives, who drove it around town while he used a car he purchased that week under his mother's name—telling the skeptical seller that the name Jacquelyn Peterson was a "Boy-Named-Sue kind of thing." After several panicked days trying to locate him, surveillance teams finally spotted Scott in his new car. They didn't even recognize him at first, as he had grown a goatee and lightened his hair, beard, and eyebrows to an unnatural orange hue.

On April 18, 2003, the bodies were positively identified as Laci and Conner. As an arrest warrant was being prepared, undercover officers from the California Highway Patrol and the Department of Justice struggled to keep Peterson in their sights as he led them on a wild 170-mile trek over several counties using every evasive driving technique in the book in an attempt to shake his tail—darting across several lanes of traffic to exit the freeway, then pulling right back on; making sudden U-turns in the middle of the street; abruptly pulling over to the side of the road, then getting back on after the cars trailing him were forced to pass. At one point he was driving so fast on a winding road, seventy-five in a thirty-five-miles-per-hour zone, that he caused one of the surveillance cars to fishtail and nearly wreck.

At other times he couldn't resist a display of bravado, flipping the bird at his pursuers, clapping his hands in glee at a particularly clever maneuver, or pulling up alongside one of the unmarked cars and smirking at the driver.

When they finally pulled him over at the entrance to Torrey Pines Golf Course, where he was scheduled to play a round a golf with his family earlier that morning, the officers found evidence that seemed to indicate that Scott was planning a run for the border or some attempt to live off the grid. The car was packed with a huge amount of survival gear, including a tent, water purifier, camp ax, hunting knives, folding saw, cooking implements, and fishing gear. They also found four cell phones, his brother John's driver's license, credit and gas cards belonging to several relatives, and nearly $15,000 in cash. The cash came mostly from Jackie Peterson, who gave a convoluted explanation, claiming that Scott's brother was actually buying the truck from Scott and that she was advancing the money, "accidentally" making a large withdrawal from Scott's account and then a duplicate withdrawal from her own to reimburse him.

He also had with him a stash of Viagra. It seems amazing that Scott could contemplate a game of golf while waiting to find out if life as he knew it was over for him, but the fact that sex was also on his mind at a time like that is probably even more revealing of his ability to compartmentalize and the compulsiveness of his narcissistic drives. Two weeks after his wife went missing, Peterson called his cable company and added the Playboy channel to his subscription. However, that apparently was not enough for him. Four days later he called back, switching to two harder-core pornography channels—which he abruptly had disconnected while police were in the midst of searching his home in mid-February.

Perhaps the most disturbing discovery on the day of his arrest was a map inside the car with directions to Amber's workplace, the result of a MapQuest search Scott had performed that very day. At trial, the defense claimed that Scott was simply planning to return a book to Amber, *The Purpose-Driven Life*, a spiritual book she had sent him in February just before asking him to stop calling her. The gift was a last-ditch attempt on her part to elicit some kind of self-examination from Scott. She had tried to get him to confess to her, had tried to talk him into submitting to a polygraph. With this final gesture she hoped to provoke his conscience.

Unfortunately, psychopaths have no conscience. Scott did try to exploit this last ray of hope from Amber, shape-shifting himself once more in a way that he hoped would impress her. He immediately began using a new e-mail address—purposelife2003@yahoo.com— and writing her claiming he had discovered his life's purpose. He would dedicate himself to his family, which he said would include a wife and child, and strive "to be positive in people's lives."

If Scott was simply planning to mail the book back to her, as the defense contended, why did he print out driving directions? And why did he suddenly decide to do so two months after she broke off contact with him, during what had to be the most stressful week of his life? Police believe he may have been planning to see Amber, perhaps even to do her harm.

Modesto detectives had been so concerned for Amber's safety that they refused to let her meet with him in person. In response to her demands that Scott take a polygraph to prove his innocence, he had finally agreed, but only if it was not administered by the police and if she accompanied him. On the day of the scheduled test, even before he realized that Amber was not coming, he fled after spotting Det. Al Brocchini in a parking lot near the polygrapher's office. He called Amber, angrily accused her of betraying him, of working with the cops to set him up.

In their final conversations, Scott had begun to sound desperate, begging to see her in person. A week after the aborted polygraph, he tried to talk her into meeting him at a remote cabin in the mountains outside Los Angeles. The cabin belonged to Anne Bird's parents, and he had been staying there increasingly since the news of his affair with Amber had broken. He became very emotional, saying he needed to look into her eyes, say things he could not say over the phone.

"There's so many things I want to tell you—God, it's unbelievable," he said, and for once his crying sounded genuine. Worried that his phone was being tapped, he began calling her from pay phones. He offered to send her on a vacation, presumably somewhere he could then show up. On her February 10 birthday, which was also Laci's due date, he left a shopping bag full of presents for her in the parking lot of a children's hospital near her home: a necklace with an amber stone, a decorative box with a moon-and-stars motif reminiscent of their night of stargazing, and the Norah Jones CD *Come Away with Me*.

Was Scott, on his very last day of freedom, going to surprise Amber and try to talk her into "coming away" with him? Or was he planning to make her disappear, too? Other items found in his car at the time of his arrest—rope, duct tape, and a shovel—made detectives worry that he may have had the latter scenario in mind.

———

The words of Scott Peterson himself on the tape recording were the most emotionally powerful part of the case against him. Even though Scott Peterson never took the stand it felt as if he had, and he had only offered lies and obfuscations. But there was also powerful physical and scientific evidence pointing to his guilt.

From the moment Al Brocchini arrived at the Peterson home to investigate a report of a missing wife, he feared that something very bad had happened to her. A mop and bucket propped outside the kitchen door made him wonder if someone had attempted to clean up a crime scene. Scott's explanation that his nearly eight months pregnant wife was mopping the kitchen the day after the maid's visit only made him more suspicious, as did Scott's account of showering and laundering the clothes he had worn that day before reporting his wife missing. Scott's claim of having spent the day fishing in a boat about which none of the dozens of friends and family gathered at the house that night knew anything set his gut on edge even more, as did Scott's showing more concern about the detective's accidentally dinging his car door than he did about his wife and child's being in peril.

Following his instincts, Brocchini asked to see the boat, a task Scott purposely made more difficult by pretending that the power was out in his warehouse where the boat was stored. Forced to use his headlights and a flashlight to illuminate the space while he took some photographs, Brocchini was nonetheless able to preserve two critical pieces of physical evidence.

Unlike the Peterson home, which was neat as a pin, the warehouse was a mess, with white powdery residue spilled all over the top of a flatbed trailer Peterson used as a work surface. When police returned with a search warrant two days later and took a better look at the residue, which turned out to be quick-dry cement, they could make out numerous circular voids or rings that matched up perfectly in circumference with the pitcher Peterson said he used to mold a cement anchor for his boat, then shook out onto the flatbed top. Although he was insistent that he made only one anchor, the rings indicated that he had made at least five—weights that the prosecution argued he used to sink his pregnant wife to the bottom of San Francisco Bay.

Equally significant, the photographs Brocchini shot that night revealed a pair of yellow-handled pliers wedged beneath one of the seats in the boat. This was important because a hair matching Laci's was collected from inside the teeth of those pliers during the search two days later. Laci was never supposed to have been in that boat, so how did some of her hair wind up there? In a tactic reminiscent of the O.J. case, the defense implied that an overzealous Detective Brocchini planted the hair months later after coming to a dead end in the investigation. But photos taken during the search of the warehouse clearly show the hair sticking out of the nose of the pliers.

The victims themselves, however, provided the most unimpeachable evidence of guilt. That their bodies were found within a mile and in the tidal path of where Scott Peterson told police he had gone fishing the day his wife disappeared was so damning that before he was hired to represent Peterson, Mark Geragos declared on Greta van Susteren's *On the Record* that "it would just be the most phenomenal coincidence of all time" if Scott was not their killer.

Two days later, on the day Peterson was arrested, Geragos went even further in an appearance on *Larry King Live*, using words that would come back to haunt him after he decided to mount an all-or-nothing innocence defense.

"The man is a sociopath if he did this crime," Geragos said. "There's no other way to put it. This is his wife, his unborn baby. If he's the one who took the two of them up there and put concrete around them and threw them into the ocean and concocted and went onto Diane Sawyer and gave that impassioned plea with the tears—that's not somebody that generally you're going to give ... manslaughter to."

The only other possible explanation for the bodies ending up in that precise location was for Peterson to have been framed. Who would have a motive to pin the crime on the victim's husband, not to mention the knowledge of exactly where he claimed to have gone fishing, and the means to get her body not only to the bay but out into the water? The defense put forth no viable suspects.

Geragos seemed to rest his entire defense on the scientifically specious theory that Conner had been born alive. If so, Scott was innocent, as he was under near-constant surveillance at the time Laci was scheduled to give birth. He based his contention on a few cobbled-together facts: bone measurements of the corpse, which fell within the range of full-term fetuses, and the pathologist's inability, due to the wet and decomposing condition of Conner's lungs, to rule out that the child had ever taken a breath.

For such a theory to hold up, however, Conner would have had to have been cut out of Laci's womb and kept alive for at least a month and a half until he reached full term, or Laci had to have been held somewhere for a month and a half until she gave birth. Then both mother and son were killed and transported to the bay, even as police divers were searching it on a nearly daily basis, for the sole purpose of pinning the crime on Scott Peterson.

But judging from the markedly more intact condition of Conner's remains as compared to Laci's, Brian Peterson (no relation), the pathologist who performed the autopsy, firmly believed that Conner had been released from his mother's womb only a day or so before he washed ashore. "If he would have spent substantial unprotected time in the water as Laci did, he would have been eaten," Peterson testified. "There simply wouldn't have been anything left."

Laci had been in the water so long that every organ in her body was missing except for her uterus. She had protected Conner from the elements as long as she could, even after death. Her uterus remained enlarged from having been pregnant, but the cervix was still closed, proving that she never gave birth naturally. There were no cuts indicating that she had undergone a cesarean section. Over time, however, animal feeding and tidal action had eroded an opening at the top of her uterus through which, Dr. Peterson believed, the baby emerged.

Furthermore, the pathologist also found meconium in the baby's bowels, a substance that is expelled within a day or two after birth in the child's first stool.

The forensic anthropologist who calculated the fetus's age based on bone measurements conceded that it was difficult to get an accurate measurement, as the marine environment had partially liquefied the corpse.

By the time Geragos put on his own expert, OB-GYN Charles March, the defense was no longer pushing the contention that

Conner had been born at full term, simply that he had lived at least five days past Christmas. March, however, proved to be a terrible witness. After he was eviscerated on cross-examination for basing his methodology on unsubstantiated assumptions about the earliest date Laci could have gotten pregnant, the defense seemed to implode.

It was a shocking reversal of fortune, considering that for the first several months of the trial, most of the media and legal analysts were predicting a defense victory, or at the very least a mistrial. Mark Geragos dominated the courtroom as though he owned it, neutralizing witness after witness with his superb cross-examination skills. He seemed to think that he could bulldoze the prosecution's case by knocking down their witnesses like cascading dominoes. But when it came time to put on his own case, to back up all the allegations and assertions he had gotten in through questions and hearsay, he had nothing to present.

Mark Geragos was one of the most media-savvy attorneys in the country, having represented pop star Michael Jackson, actress Winona Ryder, President Clinton's brother Roger, Whitewater scandal figure Susan McDougal, and former Modesto-area congressman Gary Condit—the latter when he was being investigated regarding the disappearance of a Washington intern he had been secretly dating, Chandra Levy.

Geragos tried the Peterson case as much outside as inside the courtroom, waging criminal defense like a political campaign geared to shaping the news and planting doubt in the minds of potential jurors. When he first assumed the case, he held a press conference outside the Modesto courthouse at which he vowed he would not only "prove" his client's innocence but also find the "real" killer. It was a foolhardy bit of showmanship. The defense doesn't have to prove anything. Why would he offer to take on that burden?

He called a later news conference asking a "mystery witness" to come forward, who he claimed held information that would exonerate Scott, and another to announce adding two of the nation's foremost forensic experts, Henry Lee and medical examiner Cyril Wecht, to the Peterson defense team.

He floated numerous theories in the press about who might have killed Laci: from a Satanic cult to a ring of methamphetamine tweakers, from dark-skinned men seen near a van in the Petersons' neighborhood (who may simply have been a team of gardeners) to a pair of burglars who robbed a home across the street from the

Petersons, from homeless vagrants in the park to an obsessive search center volunteer who seemed to have developed a crush on Scott (but knew neither Scott nor Laci before the crime).

And, as defense attorneys do in cases when all the evidence points to their client, he put the cops on trial—most notably Detective Brocchini, whom he portrayed as a rogue cop hell-bent on convicting Peterson no matter what. A rush-to-judgment defense might have worked against the Los Angeles Police Department in the O.J. Simpson case, where there was a long history of racial animus and community discontent. But who was going to believe that the Modesto police were out to get Peterson, a man they had never heard of until the day his wife disappeared, whom everyone declared to be a perfect husband and model citizen?

Although the prosecutors, who are ethically prohibited from commenting on the evidence, refused to the point of paranoia even to exchange pleasantries with the media during the trial, the ever-charming Geragos wooed and cultivated friendly reporters and legal pundits to disseminate his spin. In an end run around a court-imposed gag order, paid defense experts, including their jury consultant, appeared as guests on TV talk shows during jury selection and while the trial was under way.

The trial reached a "theater of the absurd" stage when Geragos hired one of the trial commentators, who was regularly appearing on MSNBC, the *Today Show*, and other media outlets, to put his client through a mock cross-examination to determine whether Scott should take the stand. A practice cross-examination is commonly done with high-profile cases and was famously done in the Simpson case—where the Dream Team brought in a pair of female defense attorneys to grill Simpson and gauge how he might stand up to prosecutor Marcia Clark.

But a mock cross should always be done in complete secrecy. Michael Cardoza, the former prosecutor Geragos tapped, told Geragos in advance he would agree to the job only if he could disclose that he had done so to his media clients. It was clear that Geragos wanted the information to get out, I can only assume to provide the impression that Scott, as an innocent man, really wanted to testify. But his plan backfired in a way that I think verges on malpractice. If the jury somehow learned about the practice cross-examination, they might have concluded that Scott failed miserably—as rumor has it—and that that is why he failed to take the stand.

The defense sought to portray Amber as a scorned woman out for vengeance, even intimating that she might have had something to do with the murder. But the tapes spoke for themselves. Scott admitted both on the tapes and in media interviews that Amber had no idea he was married when Laci disappeared. (She also passed a polygraph.) She was so expert at getting Peterson to repeat and acknowledge everything he had ever said to her that there was really nothing she testified to that was not backed up by Scott's own words. The anticipated courtroom showdown never materialized. When she finally took the stand, Geragos made no real attempt to impeach her.

In the end, it seemed that both Scott and his attorney shared the same fatal flaw: an inflated sense of hubris. Geragos seemed to possess the same narcissistic belief as his client that he could change reality and sway everyone around him with the magic of his words, that he could make them believe him no matter how the evidence stacked up.

A strategic decision was made to exercise Peterson's right to a speedy trial—a bold but ultimately reckless decision. Typically in a death penalty case, the defense strategy is to delay trial as long as possible because the potential penalty is so draconian. Scott's trial began just a little more than a year after his arrest, practically unheard of in a capital case. Less than two years after his arrest, he was seated on Death Row, bringing his execution date years closer than it needed to be.

Delay is also beneficial in notorious cases, to allow emotions and publicity to die down. The defense must have been hoping to push the state to trial before it had its case ready—and before any more damaging evidence was discovered, such as the cement weights. Geragos believed he could simply out-lawyer the "small-town" prosecutors assigned to the case. Although he succeeded in winning a change of venue, he lost most of the other critical motions, failing in his efforts to keep out the tapes, scientific testimony that genetically linked the hair found in the boat to Laci, and, perhaps most controversially, evidence that a search dog traced Laci's scent from the parking lot at the Berkeley Marina to the end of the public pier where Peterson launched his boat.

Geragos was guilty of the cardinal sin for a defense attorney: promising too much and delivering too little. Rather than merely casting doubt on the prosecutors' case, arguing that they had not met their burden of proving their case beyond a reasonable doubt, he threw down the gauntlet from his opening statement, making the astonishing declaration that the evidence would show "beyond any doubt" that his client was "stone-cold innocent."

The jurors said after the trial that Geragos's opening statement led them to believe he was going to present a whole other theory for the murder, but they got no such thing. All the tantalizing references Geragos made during cross-examination of police witnesses about other suspects, or Laci sightings, or tips he claimed were not followed up, were all left hanging in midair without any substantiation. Neither the promised Henry Lee nor Cyril Wecht ever took the stand. Nor did Geragos put on a single one of the eyewitnesses who claimed to have seen Laci alive after Scott left on his trip to the bay.

His "stone-cold innocence" defense also left him with little to work with when it came to the penalty phase. Geragos acted as if it had never occurred to him that his client might be found guilty. In fact, he was caught so unaware that the day the jury came in he was in Los Angeles and not able to make it back in time for the reading of the verdict. He confessed to the court (and later the jury) that he hadn't prepared anything for the penalty phase, not believing the case would ever get to that stage. Such short-sightedness demonstrated incredible arrogance and recklessness—the legal equivalent of a tree-trimmer cutting off the limb on which he is standing—a failure he himself described to the jury in his final summation as "probably professional malpractice or ineffective assistance of counsel."

The judge had to recess the trial for two weeks in order for Geragos and his team to pull together evidence they hoped would persuade the jury to recommend life over death. They put on thirty-nine witnesses—mostly family members, a few former coaches and co-workers, friends, and employees of the Peterson family, and a neighbor Scott had once helped out when she had a flat tire. Second chair Pat Harris took the lead in this phase, with Geragos believing his standing before the jury was now seriously compromised, but the defense ultimately offered little to mitigate against the heinousness of Peterson's crimes.

Witness after witness simply ignored the verdict, or chastised the jury for arriving at guilt. They continued to contend that Scott Peterson was a great guy, a perfect son and loving husband without a violent impulse in his body. Whereas penalty phase testimony usually focuses on the disadvantages the defendant suffered that led to where he is today—for example, a childhood marred by poverty and abuse—the defense witnesses in the Peterson case went on and on about his privileged upbringing. They talked about country clubs, the fabulous house in Rancho Santa Fe, exotic family vacations to France and Monte Carlo, and golf, golf, and more golf. They seemed bent more on celebrating Scott Peterson's charmed life than on saving him from execution.

The defense had also rested its hopes on the composition of the jury. Both sides relied on top-flight jury consultants to help select the panel, the defense using the same expert the Dream Team used to pick the O.J. jury. From the outside looking in, the twelve jurors that decided Peterson's fate appeared to be as close to a pro-defense panel as Geragos ever could have hoped to find. They included a woman who killed her own child, accidentally running over her twenty-two-month old son when he wandered in front of her car, and another who married a man who was in prison for murder and who was himself murdered while serving his sentence. Another woman on the panel had once worked as a child abuse investigator, which would normally make her seem like a good prosecution juror. But she voiced a strongly negative attitude toward police during jury selection, stating that, in her experience, cops put more effort and interest into investigating an auto accident than a domestic situation.

Of the six men on the jury, one expressed severe qualms about the death penalty and admitted consulting with his priest during jury selection to ask if his faith would allow him to make such a decision. Another had a restraining order taken out against him by a former wife, and said during voir dire that he knew what it felt like to be wrongfully accused. A third was a former cop, but he had been arrested twice—once for assault on a police officer. A fourth had a tangential connection to Scott Peterson. His daughter's fiancé had worked for and now owned the restaurant Scott and Laci had opened in San Luis Obispo.

In the end, the jury members defied the roles that many of the experts and the media had placed on them. Nearly every court watcher considered Richelle Nice to be firmly in the defense camp—because of her nine tattoos and dyed fire-engine-red hair, the fact that her brother had been to prison and her mother was a drug counselor, and because she seemed to laugh broadly at all Geragos's jokes. But she ended up being one of the hardest on Peterson, one of two jurors who held out the longest for a first-degree verdict for the killing of Conner as well as Laci. A mother with four sons of her own, she referred to Conner as "Little Man" and wept when pictures were shown in court of his tiny waterlogged corpse.

"*His daddy* did that," Nice, thirty-four, said after the verdict. "He should have been his protector and instead he took his life."

Although the panelists said it was not one thing that convinced them of Peterson's guilt but rather the totality of evidence, several conceded that they would have set him free had Laci and Conner not turned up in the location they did.

"If those bodies had never been found, or had been found in the desert or Yosemite National Park, we wouldn't be here," said juror Greg Beratlis, forty-six, a youth sports coach.

Even with that evidence, however, Scott Peterson very likely would not have been convicted if one of the jurors originally picked to hear the case had remained on the panel.

Justin Falconer was another juror who defied conventional wisdom. A twenty-eight-year-old airport security screener with both a military and law enforcement background who today works as a deputy sheriff, he seemed like an ideal prosecution juror.

In the third week of trial, Falconer was kicked off the jury after a TV camera captured him exchanging a few words with Laci's brother. The conversation turned out to be innocent, nothing more than Falconer's awkward attempt at a joke when the two found themselves next to each other passing through the courthouse metal detector. But the judge decided to remove him a day later after other jurors complained that he was talking about the evidence presented in the case, and he admitted to discussing media coverage with his girlfriend.

Unabashed at his dismissal, Falconer walked straight out of the courthouse and up to the microphones in the designated press area where he gleefully trashed the prosecutors' case and proclaimed that he would have acquitted Peterson. As reporters and producers shoved their business cards into his hand and offered him everything from free beer to Metallica CDs, limo rides to flights to New York, Falconer basked in the attention like the star of his own reality TV show.

"I wanna do Bill," he shouted over the fray, referring to Bill O'Reilly's Fox talk show. "Greta wants to talk to you," a rival producer quickly interrupted, thrusting her cell phone to his ear. The juror heretofore only notable for never taking notes and for wearing shorts to court became an instant celebrity and "expert" on the case for the remainder of the trial, appearing regularly on all the legal talk shows up to and including verdict day, when he politely but adamantly disagreed with the jury's decision.

Throughout jury selection, Mark Geragos decried what he called "stealth jurors," people with a secret agenda "to send my client to the death chamber." Although Justin Falconer describes himself as a "NASCAR Republican" and strong law-and-order type, he seemed unable to see the case any way but through the eyes of the defendant. The closest in age to Peterson on the panel, and with a similar cocksure swagger about him, he seemed to identify with Scott on a personal level—much like the holdout who caused Richard Crafts's first trial to end in mistrial.

Scott's fishing alibi made sense to him because "when you've got a new toy you want to take it out." Peterson's seeming lack of concern for his missing wife and child did not seem suspicious because "I'm not an emotional person either." Falconer dismissed Scott's statements that he had "lost" his wife to Amber Frey and Shawn Sibley as harmless lies, something a guy says to gain sympathy in order to get a woman to sleep with him.

In his mind, Scott simply could not have killed Laci to be with Amber, whom he viewed as less attractive than Scott's beautiful wife. He referred to Amber as a "side salad"—a meaningless fling. Laci could have been abducted while out walking, as Scott suggested, despite testimony from others that she had stopped exerting herself on doctor's orders. "Pregnant women are crazy," he opined. "One minute they just want to lie on the couch, and the next day they think they're fat and want to run a marathon." He even said he did not believe that a woman's womb could be strong enough to hold a baby inside her and protect him from the marine environment during all those months in the bay.

During voir dire, when potential jurors were questioned one by one to determine whether they could sit on a death penalty case, prosecutor Dave Harris had tried to explain to Justin the nature of circumstantial evidence and how the logical inferences jurors are called on to make between facts in a criminal trial are no different than those they make in everyday life. He used as an example how when someone flips a switch and a light goes on we can assume that the switch controls the electric current without having to personally see all the wiring and circuits. Falconer nodded in agreement, but later he told me he never bought into the concept.

"I thought if you want me to convict him," he said, playing out Harris's analogy, "you have to show me Scott's finger on the switch." Like the Robert Blake jurors, Justin Falconer would never believe Scott Peterson was guilty without seeing a smoking gun in his hand. He impugned his fellow jurors, saying that the fact that some of them published a book after the case was over showed they hoped to profit from the trial. But Falconer himself had asked me right after he was bounced from the panel how he might go about writing a book, even though he had served just thirteen days on the case.

Conclusion
Fixing a Broken System

Ｗith the evolution of laws and public awareness—beginning in the 1960s and culminating in 1994 with the federal Violence Against Women Act and a series of important statements articulating the extent and seriousness of crimes against women worldwide by the United Nations Commission on Human Rights—marriage was no longer supposed to be a shield for domestic violence.

Yet a legal system with an institutionalized punishment discount for men who kill an intimate partner is tacitly condoning the ultimate act of domestic violence. It is telling men that killing a wife or girlfriend is to some degree understandable and justifiable.

We can't even begin to get an accurate assessment of the number of women murdered by a "loving" partner because so many of these cases go undetected or unpunished. Between murders disguised as unexplained disappearances and those staged to look like accidental falls, drownings, suicides, natural deaths, carjackings, or other randomly perpetrated crimes, untold numbers of eraser killings every year are never even recognized as domestic homicides.

An eraser killing is precisely the type of violent crime most likely to fall through the cracks and loopholes in our justice system, whether because of problems with death investigation, the handling of missing persons cases, or other stumbling blocks of legal and police procedure. Although a complete list of reforms and solutions would require a book unto itself, the following are some recommendations for changes that could make it more difficult to get away with murder and, one hopes, prevent at least some future eraser killings.

—◌◌◌—

Reform the death investigation system.

The system for investigating unnatural deaths in the United States is so faulty and antiquated that Michael Baden, one of the top forensic pathologists in the country and the former chief medical examiner for New York City, calls it a "national disgrace." Werner Spitz, another of the nation's preeminent forensic pathologists and editor of the text that is considered the "Bible" on death investigation, has estimated that less than a third of the country has properly trained staff and procedures in place to assess suspicious deaths adequately.

In the United States there is no uniform set of standards or guidelines for investigations either at the scene where the body is found or later at autopsy. Instead, there are fifty different state systems and over three thousand county and regional systems with wildly varying methods and unsettlingly uneven results.

In many jurisdictions, county coroners without any medical or forensic background are the gatekeepers. Although they do not generally perform autopsies themselves, they wield enormous power in determining which deaths merit investigation and which do not, whether an autopsy should even be performed, and what tests should or shouldn't be run, such as X rays that might detect a hidden skull fracture or toxicology screening that could uncover a case of secret poisoning. These coroners are merely elected officials, sometimes with no more than a high school education and a few weeks of on-the-job training. Accountants, gas station attendants, tow-truck drivers, and beauticians have served as county coroners. They alone have the authority to sign death certificates, and because they have no supervision, it can be very difficult to get them to amend the cause or manner of death once officially entered, even if other information comes to light that draws their findings into question.

In some states that rely on the coroner system, which has its roots in twelfth-century England, there is a wide variation from one county to the next in the percentages of deaths that are actually investigated; some counties investigate only 3 or 4 percent of the number of deaths per capita as other counties in the state.

Rather than rising with the murder rate and increasing sophistication of criminals, autopsy rates have actually declined dramatically due in large measure to lack of personnel and funding.

Although many states have reformed and improved their systems of death investigation over the past three decades, there is nothing approaching a national standard for education, testing, and certification for coroners in the way that pharmacists or registered nurses, for example, must be trained at accredited schools and pass standardized national tests for knowledge and competency. It is scandalous that search and cadaver dogs have rigorous testing and certification standards but coroners do not.

Eraser killers already have something of an advantage over investigators because of their ability to alter a crime scene to fit the scenario they want to project, and because they have intimate access to the victim and knowledge of her habits and lifestyle. They control and manipulate the evidence, hoping a lazy or badly trained investigator will swallow their bait. Because an eraser killer usually shares the same abode as his victim or has easy access to his victim's home, he can take all the time he needs to clean up and dispose of the blood, contaminated clothing, rugs, and so forth, an advantage relatively few other types of murderers have. He determines how and where to place the victim's body and whatever props he chooses, such as an open liquor bottle, an unsafe ladder, a bag of fish food, or a gun. He is also the person who controls time. He can make the 911 call or arrange to have someone else find her. He can contact friends and relatives of the victim and put on a show of grief, or he can wait to notify them until the body and other "evidence" have been removed so that they cannot see anything that might lead them to question his carefully staged scenario.

If he places himself at the scene or pretends to have "discovered" his dead wife, he has the enormous advantage of being able to give police and emergency responders the first description of what happened. His version of events—what he saw, what his wife was doing, how she had been behaving prior to her death, his claims of how he desperately tried to revive her—can create a lasting impression in the minds of investigators. In addition to physically setting the stage, the killer is able to provide a verbal narrative that can have a very significant impact on how the death scene is viewed. Even if police later change their minds and become suspicious about his story, the scene where the body was found has almost always been "unsealed" and turned back to its everyday use, destroying or contaminating what little forensic evidence might remain.

When an inexperienced or poorly trained coroner arrives on the scene and sees a dead woman sitting on the sofa with a gun in her lap, as in the case of Barton Corbin's first victim, Dolly Hearn, little if any real investigation may be undertaken. In Dolly's case, sheriff's deputies took pictures at the scene, looked for signs of forced entry, poked around her apartment a bit, and swabbed her hands for GSR. The coroner arrived and spent just a few minutes looking at the body. As soon as he left, the body was removed and the scene released. Dolly's friends and roommate were told they could clean up the blood; it was no longer considered a crime scene worthy of preservation, even though detectives had yet to talk to the scary-acting ex-boyfriend Dolly's roommate told them about, or to her parents and other people who knew she had not been depressed and suicidal.

In the state of Georgia, where Barton Corbin managed to get away with murder for fourteen years, only to be caught when he staged a second intimate partner killing in the same way, staff shortages recently forced the state-run crime lab, where autopsies are actually performed, to temporarily stop accepting bodies after normal lab hours. Because many of Georgia's rural counties lack major hospitals with morgue facilities, some areas had no means of preserving bodies pending an autopsy. One coroner was told by officials in her county to store bodies in refrigerated deer lockers until the lab could take them.

Officials tried to assure an alarmed public that bodies of their deceased loved ones would not be mixed in with deer carcasses, but the strange crisis underscores how fragile and patchwork America's system of death investigation really is. And no investigations are at higher risk of being mishandled or lost in the shuffle than those involving clever cover-ups and staging. No victims are more vulnerable in this process than women killed by the men they have trusted.

Had Barton Corbin been living in one of the poorest counties of Georgia instead of in one of the wealthiest at the time of his second murder, the error-prone coroner system might have made it possible even for a brazen double killer to get away with another eraser killing.

If the scene is staged well and the killer's story is convincing, things may not seem suspicious enough to prompt a forensic autopsy, in which case the eraser is very close to beating the system permanently.

There are no nationally agreed-on standards for medical examiners either, although they are MDs. Even when an autopsy is performed by a well-qualified medical examiner, however, it may not yield enough information medically to bring murder charges—despite strong circumstantial evidence that the death was the result of a homicide.

A North Carolina man named Tim Boczkowski made a 911 call late in 1990 to report that his wife, Elaine, a healthy woman in her mid-thirties, had apparently drowned in their bathtub. He said he found her unconscious with her head underwater, and pulled her out of the tub. The emergency operator immediately dispatched a rescue squad from the nearest fire department, while at the same time giving Boczkowski instructions on how to administer CPR. Very quickly firemen arrived on the scene, followed by a paramedic team equipped with defibulators and other tools used to revive drowning victims. Everything possible was done to get Elaine's heart beating again as they rushed her to the nearest hospital, where the effort to revive her went on into the early hours of the next morning, when she was finally pronounced dead.

The case sounded like an accidental drowning. Tim would later tell friends that Elaine had too much to drink that evening and simply drowned. But the firemen, the paramedics, and a patrol officer who arrived later all noticed one strange fact—the bathtub in which the woman had supposedly drowned before being dragged out by her frantic husband was bone dry, and not a single drop of water had been splashed on the floor. As time went on, the details of what happened that night changed every time Boczkowski related them. Even before a homicide detective was assigned to the case, the uniformed officers involved had determined that this story of a woman drowning in a completely dry bathtub just did not make sense.

Unfortunately, the autopsy carried out on Elaine Boczkowski was inconclusive. The doctor found no water in the lungs to indicate drowning, but also could not find any other immediate cause of death and simply wrote the fateful word "undetermined" in the box under cause of death. It may be surprising to most people, but death due to drowning is extremely difficult to determine with scientific precision. In this case there were simply none of the typical conditions that accompany drowning, but also no other discernable cause for her death. She had some bruises on her body, but those could be explained by the fact that she had been subjected to an extremely long period of vigorous resuscitation efforts. She also had five different bruises on the interior of her scalp, one of which could have been caused by an accidental fall in the tub, but not all five. There was also no alcohol found in her system, despite her husband's contention that she had been drinking in the tub.

Still, because the chief medical examiner who performed the autopsy could not determine what killed her, the case was closed. In that jurisdiction, if the medical examiner could not determine cause of death, there would be no further investigation.

As the staged fishpond "drowning" death of Pam Mead in Salt Lake City demonstrates, there should ideally be a great deal of interaction and communication between homicide investigators and the medical examiner and coroner when the cause of death is ambiguous—and in some states the rate of "undetermined" causes of death among all homicides and suicides is up to 50 percent. But in Greensboro, North Carolina, where Elaine Boczkowski died of no apparent cause, having drowned in a dry, empty bathtub, the homicide investigation was believed to be pointless. Her husband probably never would have been charged with murder—as he was four years later after he moved to Pennsylvania—had his second wife, another perfectly healthy woman, not drowned suddenly and unexpectedly in the family's outdoor hot tub. Mary Ann Boczkowski was still in the tub, floating in water, when emergency responders arrived. Once again, Tim was quick to tell emergency responders that his wife had been drinking alcohol while relaxing in the hot tub—fourteen beers as well as some wine, he said.

This time, however, the medical examiner determined that she had clearly not drowned. She had been strangled to death, and the forensic evidence was unmistakable. (Eerily, she also had five fresh bruises on the interior of her scalp, just as Elaine had.) It appeared that Mary Ann fought hard for her life. Fresh scratch marks were found on Tim Boczkowski's neck, torso, and hand, which he claimed were the result of his wife giving him a "scratch massage."

The determination that his second wife died as the result of homicide triggered a reevaluation and reopening of the unresolved cause of death of his first wife. Murder charges were filed against Boczkowski in North Carolina and Pennsylvania, and juries in both cases found him guilty. He received a life sentence for killing his first wife, death in the second case. The Pennsylvania Supreme Court, however, overturned the death sentence on a technicality and ordered that he be sentenced instead to life in prison for the second murder.

While Boczkowski was in jail in Pennsylvania awaiting trial, his cellmate claimed he boasted about his crimes. When the man asked him why he made the potentially foolish mistake of killing his second wife in a manner so similar to the first, Boczkowski expressed chagrin that he wasn't more creative. "That was stupid, wasn't it?" he reportedly remarked.

What we don't know is how many eraser killers elude detection by murdering just once, establishing no pattern to attract attention. One of the disturbing things that this case demonstrates is that even when an eraser killer makes a major tactical error—forgetting to fill the bathtub to make his drowning story credible—he can still get away with murder. Because death investigation depends for success on highly coordinated and interactive relationships between completely different government entities—an elected coroner's office, an appointed medical examiner, patrol officers, and homicide detectives—the opportunities for fumbles, lack of cooperation, indecisiveness, and slow response times all give an edge to an even moderately intelligent eraser killer who has planned a bloodless soft kill.

Efforts have been made in recent decades to reform, modernize, and establish comprehensive training systems and national qualification standards to address weaknesses in the area of death investigation. Many states have already instituted changes in this direction, and given the leading role that state governments have as the shapers of felony law and criminal administration, the only realistic reform efforts must be aimed at the state level. National movements for improved and standardized practices are likely to come from nongovernmental organizations; the rising prominence of the National Association of Medical Examiners shows how concerned professionals can take the lead in education and training even when government lags behind.

—₩—

Close the "missing persons" loophole.

Eraser killers hope that by making their wife or partner appear to have simply gone missing, she will be forever lost in a vast shadow land of hundreds of thousands of seemingly inexplicable and unsolvable cases.

The truth is that missing adults can be divided into two groups: those whose past history, medical or mental condition, and demonstrated lifestyle make it much more likely that they have only temporarily "gone missing"; and those adults who have none of the conditions or risk factors that might explain a voluntary disappearance, no previous habit of running away or dropping out of sight, and who are highly committed, involved, and responsible in their current lives.

But law enforcement agencies have no national standards to follow, no established procedures that are developed and implemented across the country to quickly and efficiently distinguish those who are voluntarily missing and will soon return home from those who are involuntarily missing, endangered, or very likely already the victim of a homicide. In far too many police departments, missing persons cases—especially those of adults—represent a low priority in terms of the expenditure of manpower and resources.

Many eraser killings simply get shuffled in among the large stack of nondeadly missing persons reports, never advancing to the level of a homicide inquiry or doing so only after the killer has had time to get rid of any evidence linking him to his victim's murder. Thomas DiBiase, former assistant U.S. attorney, is blunt about the need to change police procedures and standards so that camouflaged cases of intimate partner homicide are not simply stuck in a police file waiting for evidence to walk in the door or for the killer to confess. He believes these hidden homicides are so prevalent that missing persons cases need to be triaged to identify those that meet the typical profile of a suspected eraser killing. Those that do should be assigned as quickly as possible to a homicide detective for investigation.

Basing his judgment on almost a decade of prosecuting homicides in one of America's homicide hotspots—our nation's capital—as well as on the unique database he has assembled of virtually every homicide ever brought to trial in the United States in which no body of the victim had been recovered, DiBiase understands how an intimate partner killing often lurks behind the misleading phrase "missing woman."

"Most of the cases I have looked at across decades, where there was no body, it was the boyfriend or husband or ex-husband who killed the woman and pretended that she was missing," he says. "Clearly, there is a pattern here, and the police have to be able to identify the pattern. When there is a woman who has a history of being responsible, a history of being in touch and no history of disappearing or taking sudden trips, homicide detectives should ideally be involved in a matter of days. We should be reacting even faster if the woman is a mother and known to be responsible. That just cannot be called a missing persons case."

Appealing to commonsense notions of human behavior, DiBiase asks, "What mother, unless she is out of town on business or some other trip, does *not* have contact with her children no matter what is happening? After two or three days of not hearing from her, I would argue that there is something very wrong and we need to find out what it is. And it isn't just the women who are mothers. If these women have been known to be responsible, have a history of keeping in contact with people—whether it's Kristin Smart or Chandra Levy—they don't just run away or disappear and cut off contact with the outside world. The pattern here is that when these women are reported missing, they're not just missing; they're dead."

It took several years of highly publicized and emotionally wrenching news stories about "missing" children—especially the stranger-abduction cases that first gained national attention with Adam Walsh and continuing through Polly Klaas—to bring about critical changes in law enforcement strategy based on the cruel fact that if a young child is abducted by a stranger, the chances of finding her or him alive drop dramatically after the first six to twelve hours.

Before the efforts of Marc Klaas and other family members who became advocates for victimized children, and before the media began doing serious, in-depth reporting of the closely linked problem of predatory pedophiles who are repeat offenders, very few people knew that the abduction of young children was a widespread problem that had to be named, defined, and challenged. Those efforts have been extraordinarily successful in many ways. Guidelines have been published for investigating reports of missing children. Forty-eight states have adopted a fairly standard "best practices" set of procedures to issue Amber alerts. Registries for both missing children and sexual offenders have been established. And many states have substantially increased criminal penalties for violent child predators.

Women who have been murdered by their own husband or boyfriend in the supposed safety of their own home, then dumped into the ocean or simply into the trash, have not yet sparked calls for a fresh look at laws relating to violence against women. A significant part of the problem has been the irresponsible and strangely smug backlash by media opinion leaders—the view that missing women are not a legitimate topic of news and investigation.

Media treatment of missing and murdered little girls has fortunately escaped the misplaced scorn and vitriol poured on those in cable news and other media who have believed that they might actually be helping to catch a killer or find a young woman, such as Laci Peterson, Lori Hacking, or LaToyia Figueroa. Media members who took these cases seriously—including Nancy Grace, Greta van Susteren, Catherine Crier, and Dan Abrams—deserve our collective thanks.

Just as recognition of the apparently random, unconnected, and sporadic nature of child abductions by strangers eventually reached a critical mass and their perpetrators acquired a name—violent sexual predators—I hope that the links between apparently unconnected cases of vanishing women will be appreciated and taken seriously by the public, the media, and law enforcement as we learn more about eraser killers.

—∿—

Start the investigation at ground zero.
The most difficult challenge facing police if they do mount a full-scale investigation of a suspicious missing persons case is how to search what is always the most likely scene of the actual crime—the victim's own home.

One of the reasons that eraser killers seem to have such success in committing perfect or nearly perfect murders has to do with the carefully constructed legal safeguards that prevent rapid response by the police to situations that are not clearly identifiable as murders or even crime scenes. When an eraser killer physically eliminates his victim and stages a missing person scenario—even when he does so very crudely by offering no excuses or minimal explanations regarding her disappearance to friends and relatives—it may take many weeks, months, or even years for law enforcement to assemble enough evidence to reach the all-important "probable cause" hurdle needed to get a search warrant.

For eighteen months, Ira Einhorn was able to prevent authorities from searching the Philadelphia apartment he shared with his "missing" girlfriend, claiming he had no idea where thirty-year-old Holly Maddux had gone, while all that time he was hiding her corpse right on the premises, under lock and key.

After a long and tempestuous relationship, Holly had finally decided to break the bond with Ira and move out permanently into an apartment she planned to sublet from another young woman who was leaving on a long trip. Einhorn claimed he had been encouraging her to leave because of her inability to accept his involvement with other women. But he wasn't about to let her go like that.

Einhorn was narcissistic to the point of megalomania. He despised the idea of monogamy, and felt entitled to quench his unceasing sexual appetite with an endless series of willing groupies. He was also frighteningly Machiavellian and probably quite sociopathic. He choked a previous girlfriend into unconsciousness and hit another one over the head with a bottle. His copious journals later revealed a long-festering contempt for women in general. "Violence always marks the end of a relationship," he wrote in one passage. He also once declared that "[w]omen don't leave me; I leave them"—a veritable eraser killer mantra.

He once compared himself in a speech to Charles Manson, saying "Psychopaths like myself emerge when societies are about to change." He helped found Earth Day but he couldn't abide the idea of creating and nurturing a life, forcing Holly to have an abortion when she got pregnant by him, as he had forced several other paramours before her to do the same.

Although she had tried to leave Einhorn several times in the past, Holly was finally both determined and able to make the break. Although she was beautiful and had shown her own brilliance through her school and university work, her self-esteem had taken a beating from her years with Ira. In the process of extricating herself from under Einhorn's shadow—her friends would say from under his thumb—she had fallen in love with a man she had met on a trip to Fire Island in New York. Handsome, suave, gentle, and concerned for Holly's welfare, he was everything that Einhorn was not.

She planned to make the move after spending a few weeks in New York with her new love, sailing on his yacht. But a call from Einhorn made her return hastily. He lured her back to the apartment by threatening to throw all her belongings out on the street.

Although people who knew the troubled nature of the relationship were a little concerned about Holly's making one more attempt to calm Ira down, their closest friends were pleasantly surprised to see them arrive as a couple and enjoy and amicable dinner together on the evening of September 11, 1977. To their dinner companions, Ira seemed positively placid following several days of high agitation about Holly's plans to leave him and about her new love, and Holly appeared equally at ease. That was the last time anyone besides Ira Einhorn ever saw Holly Maddux alive. After that seemingly civilized dinner, she vanished from the face of the earth.

Ira claimed that while he was taking a bath the following day, Holly said she was going to the store and never returned. He said he became worried and began calling around trying to find her, but had no luck. Then two days later, he claimed, she called and told him that she was fine but that she didn't want to see him anymore and asked him not to try to find her. The local Philadelphia police were only contacted when friends of Holly's family back in her hometown of Tyler, Texas, began making long-distance calls and inquiries, including calls to old friends of Holly's from her college days. One of those friends happened to work in federal law enforcement and took it on himself to file a missing persons report with the local police. What the police then did to investigate that report was sadly typical of how investigations into adult missing persons cases are handled. In their eyes, she was a "flower child" who happened to live in a high crime district where the priorities are homicides and other violent felonies. The police made some phone calls, checked her untouched bank account, and talked to Einhorn. The hippie chick had just picked up and left him, was the story he gave the police. He had absolutely no idea where she'd gone; she had just moved on.

Actually, that cursory investigation was probably more atten-tion than most young adult missing persons cases receive. Finding no obvious signs of a crime—other than the fact that a young woman disappeared from the face of the earth—the case was simply filed away.

It was only through the efforts of her parents that any ongoing search was made to find Holly Maddux. As weeks went by and various family birthdays passed without any word from Holly, their worry grew. It was completely out of character for their daughter to suddenly drop all communication—not just with her parents and her sisters but with all her friends, her associates from previous jobs, everyone in the world. They knew something had happened to her, but in order to find out what, they had to hire their own detectives, starting with a street-smart retired FBI agent named J. R. Pearce, who had run the regional FBI office in Texas, but who had set up shop as a private investigator, as many agents do when they hit the mandatory retirement age of fifty-five. Pearce eventually added another retired FBI agent based in Philadelphia.

It was the work of these two former G-men working as private investigators that eventually put the case together. No one in the Philadelphia police force had mustered the resources or the will to push hard on that ephemeral category, the "just another missing person" case.

It took over a year of work—interviewing; tracking down potential witnesses, friends of Holly's, friends of Ira's; gathering reams of information—to finally create the case file that J. R. Pearce turned over to the Philadelphia homicide squad in early 1979. From that point, another half year passed while homicide detectives reinterviewed the witnesses and verified all the information the former FBI agents had uncovered and gathered more evidence on their own.

All of this work was not necessarily intended to effect an arrest of Ira Einhorn but simply to establish enough "probable cause" to get a search warrant to look around the missing woman's own home. In the eighteen months since her disappearance Ira had refused to allow police even a ten-minute "walk-through" of the apartment to look for clues as to where she might be.

As it turned out, Holly Maddux never left home. After crushing her skull with some blunt object that caused her to collapse to the floor with a thud so loud it was heard by a downstairs neighbor, Ira packed his still-breathing girlfriend into a steamer trunk he had recently purchased. He tried to talk several people into helping him get rid of the trunk, claiming it contained top-secret Russian papers the KGB was after, but could find no one to help him. So he kept it inside the apartment, padlocked inside a closet just off a screened in porch.

Ira Einhorn had stood unabashedly on his right not to be subject to unreasonable search and seizure, under the Fourth Amendment, even as he extinguished every human right and every civil right Holly Maddux had—killing her, concealing her body, lying repeatedly to her family and friends, and skipping bail when he was finally charged with her murder.

He was able to hide behind the "protections" of the law even as the smell of decomposition emanated from his apartment, nauseating his neighbors. The smell was accompanied by a dark, unidentifiable liquid oozing down through the floor of the closet into the apartment below.

Within a week and a half of Holly's disappearance, the downstairs tenant, a university student—who had been away for a few days attending a family wedding—returned to find what he called an "overpowering stench" so noxious that it made the kitchen unusable. The student enlisted some brave friends who worked for days using every cleaning agent available to counter the smell, but to no avail.

The landlord was called in. A roofer was called in. Over and over again, Ira Einhorn said that he had no odor problem in his apartment and that if any repair work was needed it had to be done without anyone going near the closet on the back porch. Every time he had guests over, from the day Holly went missing, he ordered them, sometimes startling them, not to go near the porch. It was dangerous, he said.

Horrifically, when police finally got the warrant that allowed them to enter the apartment and force open the trunk, they found Holly's partially mummified body with one hand raised in a clawlike position—as if she had been trying to push open the lid or claw her way out of the trunk when she finally succumbed.

Einhorn reacted to the discovery with neither fear nor alarm.

"You found what you found," was all he said.

The cases in the files I have compiled over these last five years of investigations into missing women are voluminous, and the stories all follow the same pattern. It took police four and a half years to get a warrant to dig up the backyard of Navy Lieutenant Commander

Leonard Eddington, whose estranged twenty-nine-year-old wife, Vickie, "went missing" in 1987—despite the fact that neighbors had seen Eddington running an earthmover in the yard right after his wife vanished. Sure enough, her skeletal remains were there all along, her skull bashed in by a vicious bludgeoning. After a jury found that he had staged his wife's murder to look like a random kidnapping, punching a hole in his wife's tire and leaving her car on the side of a highway four miles from their home near San Diego, Eddington still maintained his innocence, claiming that he could not understand how the discovery of his wife's corpse in their backyard had led to his conviction.

New York City police had to wait until Robert Bierenbaum moved out of his Manhattan apartment—five years after his twenty-nine-year-old wife, Gail, disappeared—before they could conduct a forensic search, because they were never able to obtain a warrant. During the first three months after he reported Gail missing, the Manhattan surgeon allowed police into their apartment, but only after imposing extraordinary conditions. They could look for fingerprints and at his wife's diary and address book, but they could not search for blood or other forensic evidence.

Authorities were unable or unwilling to push the matter in order to get a warrant to force a more thorough search. They suspected Bierenbaum was responsible for his wife's disappearance, but they had no proof that she was dead and no idea what he might have done with her body. He had refused to answer their tougher questions about prior violence in the relationship, and had retained an attorney and refused to cooperate any further. The district attorney felt that the case was too weak to charge, and after nine months the investigation was dropped. Fifteen years would pass before Bierenbaum would stand trial for his wife's murder.

Bierenbaum had told police that his wife left home on the morning of July 7, 1985, to go sunbathing in Central Park, scantily clad in shorts, a halter top, and sandals but wearing $10,000 worth of jewelry—as patently ludicrous a cover story as ever conceived by an eraser killer, as this was something a native New Yorker like Gail Katz-Bierenbaum would never do in a park known as a paradise for muggers and deviants. He claimed that he waited at home all afternoon and that when she did not return, he went to a birthday party at his sister's home about twenty miles away in Montclair, New Jersey.

What he repeatedly failed to mention when asked by authorities to detail everything that happened that day was that he had rented a small plane at an airport just a few miles from his sister's house and gone out for a two-hour solo flight that afternoon, returning the plane just minutes before showing up for the birthday party.

The couple's two-and-a-half-year marriage was extremely volatile. Bierenbaum was jealous and controlling, and was violent with Gail on at least one previous occasion. Two years before she disappeared, Gail told friends and relatives and reported to the police that Bob had strangled her into unconsciousness. The report simply languished. No investigation was ever performed, and Bierenbaum was never arrested for the assault.

Bob begged his wife for forgiveness and promised her it would never happen again. Gail, who was herself training to be a therapist, demanded he go into counseling, and Bob eventually agreed. But psychiatrist Michael Stone was so disturbed by what Bierenbaum told him that he felt obligated to send Gail a letter warning her that he believed she was in great danger from her husband. Bob was unrepentant about his violent impulses, describing the episode with Gail without apology and admitting that he had choked a previous girlfriend as well, causing her to break off their engagement. He also admitted to strangling his previous fiancée's cat to death, and said he attempted to kill Gail's cat in the same way because it "didn't listen" to him and was "ungrateful"—exactly the way the therapist believed Bierenbaum felt toward his wife.

Stone, a professor of psychiatry at Columbia University's College of Physicians and Surgeons and the author of one of the standard texts on abnormal personalities, later devised his own classification system for different types of murderers. He put Bierenbaum under the same rubric as Jeffrey MacDonald, Charles Stuart, Richard Crafts, and others as psychopaths who killed someone, generally their wife, whom they viewed as in their way.

The day before Gail disappeared, she told a friend that she was about to tell her husband she wanted a divorce. She borrowed money to get her own place and began looking for an apartment. Gail was afraid of her husband, but she mistakenly believed that the letter the psychiatrist had written provided her with some protection, or at least leverage. She told friends that if he did not agree to a divorce settlement she would reveal the letter's contents to his colleagues. She also threatened to expose his and his father's involvement in what she said was a multimillion-dollar Medicare fraud scam.

After reporting Gail missing, Bierenbaum seemed uninterested in any efforts to find his wife. He called police only once to check on the progress of their investigation, failed to return their phone calls to him, spent no time of his own looking for her, and began dating other women within weeks of her disappearance. Four months after his wife went missing, he moved a new girlfriend, a medical student, into their apartment.

He was irritated when police woke him up one night and asked him to come see a woman they had picked up whom they believed resembled his wife.

"I doubt it's Gail," he coolly told his new live-in girlfriend, when she asked if she should collect her things and move out while he went to the police station.

Over the years he came up with innumerable explanations for his wife's absence. He claimed that Gail's therapist told him she was depressed and suicidal, though the therapist had said no such thing. He charged that she was into drugs, speculated that she was killed by a disgruntled dealer or that she had run off with a boyfriend to the Caribbean, and even joked that she was on an extended shopping spree at Bloomingdale's. He claimed to have hired a private detective who found her working as a waitress in California. Others times he said that his wife was seen walking around Central Park in a fugue state.

Four years after Gail went missing, a partially decomposed torso washed up on the shore of Staten Island. The corpse had been clearly disarticulated: the head and each of the limbs were cut off with some kind of tool. Although there was little left with which to identify the remains, it was determined that the torso belonged to a woman of the same size and age range as Gail. When some, but not all, irregularities in the bones were matched to known X rays of Gail, a death certificate was issued in her name, and her family was given the torso to bury as their daughter. Because the body was deemed to have been in the water for only about six months, Bob Bierenbaum seemed to be in the clear.

Gail's family was still nagged by doubts. They later had the body exhumed and the bones tested for DNA, but the samples were too degraded to get a reading. Her parents died without ever finding out that the woman they had buried was not their daughter. Gail's sister, Alayne, continued on her own to investigate the case and keep the heat on Bob, knocking on doors and sending letters about Gail's disappearance to his neighbors and colleagues.

Haunted by the resurgence of news about his missing wife and his sister-in-law's ongoing campaign, Bierenbaum left New York, relocating to Las Vegas, where he established a lucrative cosmetic surgery practice specializing in breast augmentation and reconstruction. He drove a sports car with the personalized license plate "NIPNTUK," dated numerous women, then seriously began looking for another wife—getting engaged to several different women but breaking it off when he found something he didn't like about them.

He believed he had put the stain of his past behind him. No one in Las Vegas knew about his missing wife, and he wanted to keep it that way. When a woman he was seeing asked him if he'd ever been married, he refused to answer the question. To break the awkwardness, she tried a joke: "What did you do, kill her?"

Bierenbaum looked stricken, his skin flushing red. "What do you *know*?" he demanded, over and over again.

That woman and a friend of hers who had also briefly dated Bierenbaum became suspicious and began looking into his background, jokingly dubbing themselves the "Harriet-the-Spy Club." What they learned horrified them. Word quickly spread around Las Vegas. The doctor had always forbidden his office staff to open his mail and had refused to advertise his practice. Suddenly things that had just seemed strange began to seem sinister. Was "Dr. Bob" a man on the run?

Bierenbaum picked up and moved again, marrying an OB-GYN and following her to North Dakota, where she had been offered a job. Once again, he thought he could start over in anonymity. But a year later, in 1997, the district attorney's office decided to reopen the Bierenbaum case, largely as a favor to one of the office's top investigators who was about to retire and did not want to leave feeling that Gail's killer had gotten away with murder. Alayne Katz gave permission for the body she had been told was her sister's to be exhumed once again for further DNA testing, which this time ruled conclusively that the torso did not belong to Gail.

Alayne was disconsolate. Bob was no closer to being arrested, and now she didn't even have the comfort of believing her sister was at rest.

As the authorities began reinvestigating the case, however, they found a few more damning facts. Another former girlfriend of

Bierenbaum, who had done some of her own poking around after learning about his missing wife, discovered that he had altered his flight log on the day Gail disappeared. They also learned that Bierenbaum had sent out the living room rug to be cleaned right after his wife went missing.

The case was still wholly circumstantial. There was no body, no proof of death, no forensic evidence. But the political will was now there to take the case to trial, to put the evidence before a jury and let the chips fall where they may.

The theory advanced by the prosecution was that Bierenbaum killed his wife in the apartment the day he said she went missing. Using his surgical skills, he dismembered her five-foot three-inch, 110-pound body and packed her remains into a suitcase or flight bag, which he dropped into the ocean during the plane flight he had kept hidden from authorities. Like that in the Peterson case, much of the evidence dealt with consciousness of guilt, the myriad lies Bierenbaum told as well as the omission of crucial facts.

In November 2000 he was convicted of second-degree murder and sentenced to twenty years to life in prison. Second-degree murder does not require a showing of premeditation, but one of the most chilling facts in the case seemed to indicate that Bierenbaum had considered in advance how to kill his wife without leaving any trace of evidence.

Years before she disappeared, Gail and Bob happened to see something on television about the murder trial of Claus von Bülow, a socialite who was accused of putting his wife, Sonny, into an irreversible coma by injecting her with insulin. Von Bülow was convicted of attempted murder, but the verdict was overturned, and he was acquitted at a second trial.

As Gail related the story to a relative, Bierenbaum remarked, "The problem with Claus von Bülow is that he left evidence. I would not leave evidence."

———

No real investigation of a missing person can begin until and unless the spouse or partner gives permission for a thorough search of the house or apartment in which she or he or both of them have been living. To use legal blockades to prevent police from carefully investigating the very epicenter of a disappearance is to admit that the partner has no serious interest in finding out what happened to the "missing" woman. The point here is not to dismantle the Fourth Amendment, but rather to allow the moral claim that one ought to permit, and can be expected to cooperate with, the kind of intensive investigation that every missing adult and missing child case demands.

Allowing eraser killers to block the ability of police to conduct a search at "ground zero" is to make the twisted claim that the Constitution was meant to provide a moat around a killing field.

The need for extremely rapid response is something no one doubts when children are abducted by predators. Former prosecutor DiBiase believes that police, district attorneys, and judges need to view warrants as a necessity when a woman's life is at high risk.

"Ideally, you get permission to search," he says, "but if the person won't give permission, then by the end of one week, you have to be able to get that search warrant. When I look at these cases where it took months or even years to get a search warrant, I just think it's a tragedy."

DiBiase believes that when investigators are faced with a case of a suspiciously missing woman who has no known risk factors pointing to a voluntary disappearance, and whose partner or husband appears to be sandbagging the legitimate requirements of a missing and endangered person search, then the requirements of "probable cause" must be altered to reflect new realities. He believes that when asked to grant a search warrant, judges should consider not just the individual facts of the case at hand but what we have learned in recent years about similar planned and staged disappearances.

"We have a history of these cases, and we should be able to give a judge the argument that there is a pattern here, from Chandra Levy to Laci Peterson and many others. We need a search warrant because these women do not just disappear. They are crime victims. They are likely to be murder victims. This involves change in the way people look at these cases, but now is the time for the change. It may involve educating judges, helping them to understand that they should take into account the history of all of these women who seem to have disappeared, but who have really been murdered. They are not your ordinary missing persons case, and time is very critical."

This is not to presume in any way that all husbands or all partners of women who disappear are or ought to be murder suspects. But as every detective who handles cases of suspiciously missing children and adults will tell you, the only viable way to proceed with an investigation is to eliminate as suspects family members and whomever was the last person known to have seen the missing individual alive.

John Walsh, the relentless anticrime crusader who successfully fought for what became the first round of stronger child protection measures, describes what he and his wife had to go through in order to be completely cleared as possible suspects when their six-year-old son, Adam, disappeared in the toy department of a suburban Florida Sears store. "They took my wife and I into separate rooms in the police department for almost twelve hours, cross-examining us separately. And we took polygraphs repeatedly, two polygraphs each, to dispel any doubt, any innuendo even that could hang over us. That's because you have to eliminate the immediate family or friends when there's a missing kid who has been abducted."

Marc Klaas, whose life was forever changed by the stranger abduction of his little girl, who, like Adam Walsh, was eventually found murdered, accepts and understands what the police must do to eliminate the suspects who are closest at hand—clearing, in effect, anyone who was at the "ground zero" of the crime. As part of his life's mission in fighting for better systems and methods of protecting children, he has dealt with many people in the midst of a missing persons investigation involving a loved one and always urges them to provide full and complete cooperation.

"I took a polygraph," said Klaas about the investigation into his daughter's kidnapping. "You don't want to. It's intimidating. You hear defense attorneys say it is so discredited and unreliable that you think you're going to be the guy who gets a false reading. But I put her needs ahead of mine. I had to eliminate myself in the eyes of police so Polly could be found." He also answered every question police asked him throughout their investigation. "They said 'The more you tell us, the more we have to work from.'"

Klaas strongly recommended the same course of action to Scott Peterson when he spoke to his sister Susan Caudillo during the first week of the search for Laci. "I told her to make sure everybody cooperates with police and that you don't put lawyers between you and police. And she said 'We've already got a lawyer lined up for Scott.'"

Many of the cases explored in this book are, indeed, resolved. Although the fate of the victims is immutable, at least justice is often able to prevail—sometimes against astonishing odds. But too many cases still go unnoticed, uninvestigated, uncharged, and without a killer's ever facing his day in court.

"The men who do this, who plan these crimes and carry them out, they are getting creative," warns DiBiase. "This is very, very serious." The question for the rest of us is whether we too can become more creative. I believe we can begin by naming those who violently erase women who loved and trusted them with a label that casts light on everything they attempt to hide from the world. They are eraser killers. And by understanding the dark triad of traits that lie behind the crime, perhaps we can someday confront the problems of what Robert Hare calls "the psychopaths among us" without having to have another dead or vanished woman to alert us to the danger.

⸺ᵥᵥ⸺ Bibliographical Sources

This book is a result of five years of research into the psychological etiology, the legal challenges, the criminal characteristics, and the history and magnitude of the vexing social problem of eraser killing. My research has been guided by a search for "motive" in a kind of crime that often seems to have no real motive or to which have been attached such all too simplistic motives as "he wanted freedom" or "he didn't want to share his money." The research is also an attempt to answer questions that began with, then transcended, the legal challenge presented by seemingly normal men who kill their wives or girlfriends and attempt to get away with murder by committing their crimes in the most deceptive and secretive fashion. Although many men (and women as well) desire personal freedom, want to escape or avoid permanent obligations, and attach extraordinary importance to wealth, very few commit murder in acting on such motives. Fewer still attempt to kill in total stealth and "erase" someone they claimed to love, as if their victim had never existed.

What puzzled so many people about Scott Peterson was not only how someone so successful, engaging, and seemingly normal could brutally take the life of his wife and child, but also how he was able to carry out all the gruesome tasks needed to plan the murder and dispose of his wife's pregnant corpse and lie to everyone he knew without a glimmer of conscience or remorse. The deadly twins—lack of remorse and lack of empathy for the pain and suffering of others—are the most decisive indicators of psychopathic personality, and several commentators in the broadcast media were quick to notice this fact.

But I puzzled over what this kind of diagnosis might really mean. Classic psychopaths were people who shared this lack of remorse and empathy, but they usually exhibited great criminal versatility and had long histories of violence by the time they were as old as Scott Peterson. Were there varieties of psychopaths who could be just as emotionless in their remorse and empathy deficits, but who were highly functional in other aspects of their lives? Whereas some, like Scott Peterson, seemed driven by a need for approval (and endless female attention), others, like Barton Corbin, seemed driven by a more classic need to control.

—*√√√*—

Although I interviewed hundreds of individuals, ranging from witnesses, attorneys, forensic experts, and police to psychologists, psychiatrists, prosecutors, and criminologists, this section on bibliographical sources will focus primarily on books, papers, research, and other works that are available to anyone. Because the core of my book involves weaving together strands from diverse threads in psychology, criminology, case law, and law enforcement, I believe I have an obligation to provide the information and resources for other people interested in exploring these issues. My intent here is to reference those materials that have been most pivotal and essential in my work in order to acknowledge my debt to these writers and researchers and to encourage further research into this very costly and troubling area of psychology and human behavior. In many cases, the most formative books and research that underlie much of what I have done do not give rise to direct citations. But I want to acknowledge the research, investigation guides, and resources on which I have relied in order to provide the most open access for others.

—*√√√*—

To understand the psychology of these killers, I began researching the major theories and approaches to psychopathy, all of which build on the life's work of one man: Dr. Hervey Cleckley. A professor of psychiatry and neurology in Georgia who began his work in the field in the 1930s, Cleckley published his landmark work in 1941 as *The Mask of Sanity*, the founding text on the study of psychopaths. *The Mask of Sanity* went through many editions and revisions over several decades and is still regarded as an essential text. It was Cleckley who took the old ill-defined idea of "moral insanity" and attempted to analyze a set of individuals who everyone agreed were psychopaths, even if there wasn't yet agreement on exactly what that meant. I have relied on the last major revision of Cleckley's book, the fifth edition, published by Mosby in 1982.

Cleckley's work began with people, predominantly men, who were confined in institutions. He discerned ten common behavioral characteristics and began to turn what had been a vague notion into a first brilliant attempt at an empirical definition. He thus founded the science of studying this strangest of personality disorders, one in which people are quite sane—that is, able to distinguish reality from unreality, right from wrong—but also very deceptive in their appearance of normality.

The ten characteristics Cleckley found in his psychopaths included a high level of selfishness or egocentricity; an inability to form any real bond of love with another person; frequent and sometimes uncontrollable lying; a superficial kind of charm; and, perhaps most important, a complete lack of guilt or remorse no matter what the person might have done, coupled with an utter lack of empathy for others. After the initial publication of his book, Cleckley was continuously bombarded with urgent requests to study, analyze, or explain the strange behavior of dozens, then hundreds of psychopaths referred by mental institutions, wives, families, hospitals, prisons, and lawyers from around the world.

Cleckley's work provided the starting point for the person who is now regarded as the second great researcher in the field of psychopathy: Dr. Robert Hare at the University of British Columbia. Hare systematized the concept and through years of research and testing developed and revised what is now the internationally accepted test for identifying psychopaths. Although there are other approaches to psychopathy, I have relied very heavily on the ideas first advanced by Hare in some of his key research papers, including those in which he partnered with the growing number of scientists who use his core methodology:

Hare, R. D. "Psychopathy, Affect and Behavior." In D. Cooke, A. Forth, and R. D. Hare (eds.), *Psychopathy: Theory, Research and Implications for Society*. Dordrecht, the Netherlands: Kluwer Academic, 1998.

Hare, R. D. "Psychopaths and Their Nature: Implications for the Mental Health and Criminal Justice Systems." In T. Millon, E. Simonson, M. Burket-Smith, and R. Davis (eds.), *Psychopathy: Antisocial, Criminal, and Violent Behavior*. New York: Guilford Press, 1998.

Hare, R. D., Hart, S. D., and Harpur, T. J. "Psychopathy and the DSM-IV Criteria for Antisocial Personality Disorder." *Journal of Abnormal Psychology*, August 1991, *100*(3), 391–398.

Hare, R. D. "Psychopathy: A Clinical Construct Whose Time Has Come." *Criminal Justice and Behavior*, 1996, *23*(1), 25–54.

Hare, R. D. "Psychopathy: A Clinical and Forensic Overview." *Psychiatric Clinics of North America*, 2006, *29*(3), 709–724.

Hare has also written very useful popular books expanding his research to look at broader problems of crime and deviant behavior, most notably:

Hare, R. D. *Without Conscience: The Disturbing World of the Psychopaths Among Us.* New York: Simon & Schuster, 1993.

Because the core set of cases on which Cleckley developed his concept of the psychopath were primarily men in involuntary mental institutions, and Hare's research was initially based only on psychopaths in prison populations, I looked for research that might be more relevant to the kind of killers I was examining: men who were very unusual in that they had not previously led lives of crime. This was an important puzzle to solve, because psychopaths who would "only" murder a wife but otherwise generally lead law-abiding lives are fairly anomalous.

What I wanted to find were descriptions and research on individuals who evidenced the key characteristics of lack of remorse and empathy but who were also "high functioning," typically white collar, and who had little or no previous contact with law enforcement. It was this search that led me to work done by a colleague of Robert Hare at the University of British Columbia, Professor Delroy Paulhus, who heads the Paulhus Personality Lab at the university.

Although he is a prolific researcher and covers twelve separate specialties, Paulhus has spent much of his professional career studying such characteristics as human deception, the ways in which people present themselves to others to achieve certain ends, and what he calls self-enhancement. What drew me to Paulhus's work was that he was studying forms of "deviant" behavior not among hard-core, repeat felons but among college students and other "normal" people who sometimes lie, cheat, misrepresent themselves, and manipulate others. In a way, he seemed to be studying the high-functioning, well-educated, and polite-society segment of the population who share much of the same criminal pathology Hare had originally studied.

As I was researching this book, Paulhus and his colleagues Craig Nathanson and Kevin M. Williams began publishing a series of important papers casting light on questions I had been asking. In them they articulated a theory on what Paulhus calls the Dark Triad—the closely related but distinct personality characteristics of psychopathy, narcissism, and Machiavellianism. I have relied on all the key papers published thus far in this area of research, including the following:

Paulhus, D. L., and Williams, K. M. "The Dark Triad of Personality: Narcissism, Machiavellianism, and Psychopathy." *Journal of Research in Personality*, 2002, *36*, 556–563.

Williams, K. M., and Paulhus, D. L. "Factor Structure of the Self-Report Psychopathy Scale (SRP-II) in Non-Forensic Samples." *Personality and Individual Differences*, 2004, *33*, 1520–1530.

In addition to interviewing Paulhus on the subject of the Dark Triad, I have also drawn on a number of unpublished papers and presentations by Paulhus and his collaborators. I should add that the application of the concept of the Dark Triad to the cases in this book is in no way part of Paulhus's own research project. Although he has looked at the three factors all within what he terms "the normal range," I am looking at cases that fall between the lifelong criminal careers of the traditional psychopath population and the groups primarily studied by Paulhus—the relatively well-functioning narcissists, Machiavellians, and people who do not rank in the highest percentiles on the psychopathy scale.

But I believe that in using the tools that have been developed to study what Paulhus calls clusters of aversive traits, I am following a trend in psychopathy research that is now being used to cast light on what many are calling the white-collar psychopath—the ones who are successful, or seemingly successful, who avoid arrest or at least manage to do so for a long period of time, and who may do great damage to the lives of others but are extremely adept at getting away with their misdeeds.

Robert Hare has recently joined with longtime organizational psychology researcher Paul Babiak in producing an extremely useful book in this area:

> *Snakes in Suits: When Psychopaths Go to Work* (New York: HarperCollins, 2006).

Hare and Babiak have discovered that the modern corporation presents the moderate- to high-level psychopath with a wide range of opportunities to manipulate and exploit others with virtual impunity.

In other related research, psychologist John McHoskey has proposed that Machiavellianism, an often neglected concept in analyzing antisocial behavior, is in fact the most useful key for explaining and understanding traits that overlap considerably with psychopathy but do not rise to the level of the true clinical psychopath:

> McHoskey, J. W., Worzel, W., and Szyarto, C. "Machiavellianism and Psychopathy." *Journal of Personality and Social Psychology*, Jan. 1998, *74*, 192–210.

Many psychologists have researched the forms narcissism takes when this perfectly normal characteristic is a dominant aspect of someone's personality. Otto Kernberg, a Freudian-oriented psychiatrist, offers insights into pathological narcissism and its relationship to the kind of psychopathy described earlier by Cleckley in his *Aggression in Personality Disorders and Perversions* (New Haven, Conn.: Yale University Press, 1992), which examines violence and criminality from the psychoanalytic perspective. Kernberg also describes the particularly violence-prone, deadly form of narcissism he calls malignant narcissism, a term sometimes used more broadly by more recent writers.

———

Because of the staging involved and the lengths to which eraser killers go in order to cover up their tracks, it takes thorough and rigorous police work to solve these crimes. Detectives and the first officers on the scene will be well equipped for the task if they have been trained in the methods presented by the dean of homicide investigation, Vernon Geberth, a legendary detective and retired lieutenant commander in the New York City Police Department, who literally wrote the book on police investigation. Geberth's simple motto is "Do it right the first time. You only get one chance." Readers of my book will understand how absolutely critical this advice is for investigators approaching what appears to be a missing persons case or an accident, apparent suicide, or sudden but natural death but that may actually be a disguised homicide. I have relied on Geberth's massive *Practical Homicide Investigation: Tactics, Procedures, and Forensic Techniques*, 4th ed. (Boca Raton, Fla.: Taylor & Francis Group, 2006) to provide a template of how, ideally, investigations of suspicious deaths and homicides should proceed.

In my research, I came to see eraser killings as a clearly defined and particularly nefarious subset of the larger problem of intimate partner homicide or intimate "femicide." An interesting exploration of intimate femicide has been developed by Gregory Kerry, a psychologist and a researcher within Canada's federal correction system, whose doctoral dissertation involved a unique and in-depth process of questioning and interviewing men who were convicted of having killed their wives. (In the study of both intimate partner homicide and the psychological factors I believe underlie eraser killing, Canadian researchers utilize their access to convicted killers for more direct study than do their American counterparts and thus are leading the way in many important areas pertinent to this subject.)

Although I do not follow the specific analytical typology Kerry proposes, his study "Intimate Femicide: An Analysis of Men Who Kill Their Partners" (Carleton University) includes a wealth of information primarily on how men who killed their wives, often in a fit of rage, commit their crimes and act afterward. Although one might assume that all killers take pains to get away with murder, his research shows how very different the "typical" domestic homicide is from the highly planned, carefully executed, and extremely stealthy and secretive acts of the eraser killer.

A series of annual studies published by a Washington-based research group, the Violence Policy Center, titled *When Men Murder Women*, provides an extremely useful summary of the crime statistics collected by the FBI and teases out the data specifically related to the killing of women by men. Another annual publication offering a gold mine of research to those interested are the Web-published proceedings of the Homicide Research Working Group (www.icpsr.umich.edu/HRWG), which include very useful additions to research on femicide in each edition.

While researching and writing this book, I learned how the actual process of building a case, getting an indictment, and successfully prosecuting eraser killers involves overcoming endless hurdles, from police procedure to juror and media misunderstanding of circumstantial evidence. After studying key court rulings, including those in the L. Ewing Scott case—America's first prosecution for a homicide with no body, no confession, and no physical evidence—I became fascinated by the legal issues and debates. Some key articles in law journals proved very enlightening in this quest, especially Francis Paul Greene's "I Ain't Got No Body: The Moral Uncertainty of Bodiless Murder Jurisprudence in New York after People v. Bierenbaum," *Fordham Law Review*, May 2003; and Rollin Perkins's "The Corpus Delicti of Murder," *Virginia Law Review*, Mar. 1962.

My analysis of the Peterson case is also based on five years of research and reporting. I attended every day of the preliminary hearing, pretrial motions, jury selection, and trial; listened to all the testimony; reviewed all the evidence and exhibits presented; traveled to all the relevant locations in the case for firsthand observations and investigation; and conducted hundreds of interviews with police, friends, family members, witnesses, search team members, divers, and experts in forensics, psychology, and other aspects of the case.

My reporting on the other individual cases presented in this book is drawn from personal interviews and investigation, trial transcripts, appellate decisions when applicable, police records and documented evidence, daily news coverage, historical research, and other sources.

The following books were helpful to me and provide a fuller explication of some of the cases discussed in this book: Ann Rule's *And Never Let Her Go* (on Thomas Capano); Kieran Crowley's *The Surgeon's Wife* (Robert Bierenbaum); Joe McGinniss's *Fatal Vision* (Jeffrey MacDonald); Craig Brandon's *Murder in the Adirondacks* and Joseph Brownell and Patricia Enos's *Adirondack Tragedy* (Chester Gillette); Diane Wagner's *Corpus Delicti* (L. Ewing Scott); Arthur Herzog's *The Wood Chipper Murder* (Richard Crafts); Sherrie

Gladden-Davis's *My Sister Is Missing* (John David Smith); Ann Rule's *Too Late to Say Goodbye* and John Glatt's *The Doctor's Wife* (Barton Corbin); Howard Lemcke's *Death in a Fishpond* (David Mead); Steven Long's *Every Woman's Nightmare* (Mark Hacking); Joe Sharkey's *Deadly Greed* (Charles Stuart); Michael Finkel's *True Story* (Christian Longo); Corey Mitchell's *Dead and Buried* (Rex Krebs); Fannie Weinstein and Ruth Schumann's *Please Don't Kill Mommy!* (Tim Boczowkski); and Steven Levy's *The Unicorn's Secret* (Ira Einhorn).

Because news coverage is often incomplete or inaccurate and many true crime books are written very rapidly to meet the demands of publishers who specialize in the field, it is inevitable that inaccuracies sometimes appear in print. Rather than rely on other books for reporting, I chose to follow the facts of the cases as presented in the actual trial transcript or as recapitulated in the opinions of appellate courts reviewing the cases, because of the enormous care taken in the preparation of these documents and court rulings. Some of the appellate court rulings—such as those in the Bierenbaum case in New York, the Einhorn case in Philadelphia, and the L. Ewing Scott case in California, present rich tapestries of legal reasoning as judges grapple with the most fundamental concepts of our legal system and the challenge presented by men who specifically intend to thwart justice.

———

The problem of America's faulty death investigation system is a theme running throughout my research and is explicitly covered in the final chapter. An invaluable overview of the complexity and anachronistic nature of the U.S. system is provided by Andrea Tischler's "Speaking for the Dead: A Call for National Coroner Reform," in the *Southwestern University Law Review*, 2004, *33*(4), 553–572. The sometimes disastrous consequences of the current system are highlighted in Mark Hansen's "Body of Evidence: When Coroners and Medical Examiners Fail to Distinguish Accidents from Murders and Suicides," in the *ABA Journal*, June 1995.

My research in this area has been aided enormously by the groundbreaking work of sociologist Stefan Timmermans and his intensive "embedded" investigation of a major urban medical examiner's office, the findings of which are published in *Postmortem: How*

Medical Examiners Examine Suspicious Deaths (Chicago: University of Chicago Press, 2006). Timmermans explains every stage in the investigation of suspicious deaths—including homicides, suicides, staged killings, accidents, poisonings, and others—and his effort is aimed not at showing how death investigation is supposed to happen but at how it really does happen. Short of getting permission to witness several hundred autopsies and eavesdrop on the medical examiner's discussions of suspicious deaths, Timmermans offers the closest view anyone outside the profession is likely to get. Anyone who has followed lengthy testimony by medical examiners in a case where the charge is homicide will benefit enormously by reading Stefan Timmermans's brilliant book.

When I needed to find out the medical reasoning behind the investigation of such things as arsenic poisoning or suspicious drownings in the bathtub, I have relied on the standard reference work edited by the esteemed forensic pathologist Dr. Werner Spitz, titled *Spitz and Fisher's Medicolegal Investigation of Death: Guidelines for the Application of Pathology to Crime Investigation, Fourth Edition* (Springfield, Ill.: Thomas, 2006). This massive tome includes contributions by dozens of specialists—including such familiar names as Michael Baden and Henry Lee—and is filled with hundreds of images portraying vivid examples of the kinds of deaths and evidence with which medical examiners are faced in their work. It's authoritative, exhaustive in its coverage, and, like Geberth's *Practical Homicide Investigation*, not intended for casual perusal.

I must emphasize that although I have drawn on a wide range of theories and research—especially in the fields of psychopathy and the "Dark Triad," my application of these theories to a newly identified group of domestic homicide perpetrators is entirely my own. Whatever strength there is in the resulting thesis can be credited to the original researchers in these fields, but any errors are mine alone.

FOOTNOTES

Some facts and quotations in this book that relate to data, specific studies, or the work of others deserve more formal attribution than was necessary or elegant to include in the text:

3   *Usually domestic homicides are preceded by years of physical abuse:* Campbell, J. C., and others. "Risk Factors for Femicide in Abusive Relationships: Results from a Multisite Case Control Study." *American Journal of Public Health*, July 2003, *93*(7), 1089–1097.

7   *His sister-in-law remembered Barton remarking one day that Peterson got caught "because he couldn't keep his mouth shut":* Rule, A. *Too Late to Say Goodbye*. New York: Free Press, 2007.

27   *Young women, and especially young pregnant women, are most in danger from the men they love:* Shackelford, T. K. "Cohabitation, Marriage, and Murder: Woman-Killing by Male Romantic Partners." *Aggressive Behavior*, 2001, *27*, 284–291. Also see Shackelford, T. K., Buss, D. M., and Peters, J. "Wife-Killing: Risk to Victims as a Result of Age." *Violence and Victims*, Fall 2000, *15*(3), 273–282; Rennison, C. M., and Welchans, S. *Intimate Partner Violence*, a Bureau of Justice Statistics special report. Washington, D.C., May 2000, revised Jan. 2002.

27   *More than a thousand women a year are murdered in America by an intimate partner:* Violence Policy Center. *When Men Murder Women: An Analysis of 2004 Homicide Data*, an annual report. Washington, D.C., Sept. 2006.

27   *Many of those women, about seven in ten, bear the scars of male rage:* Campbell, J. C., and others. "Risk Factors for Femicide in Abusive Relationships: Results from a Multisite Case Control Study." *American Journal of Public Health*, July 2003, *93*(7), 1089–1097.

27   *eighteen hundred women in the United States were murdered by men, more than half of those by a current or former husband or boyfriend:* Violence Policy Center. *When Men Murder Women: An Analysis of 2004 Homicide Data*, an annual report. Washington, D.C., Sept. 2006. The figures cited here are based on homicide data submitted annually from police departments across the nation to the FBI. Although this is the most accurate "official" figure we have, it excludes killings involving multiple victims, such as a wife or girlfriend and one or more of her children, murders for hire planned and arranged by an intimate partner but carried out by someone else, as well as cases in which the perpetrator has not been identified or charged at the time that the reports are filed with the FBI. See also U.S. Department of Justice. *A Study of Homicide in Eight U.S. Cities*, a National Institute of Justice intramural research project, Nov. 1997. This in-depth study of homicide in eight large American cities—Atlanta; Detroit; Indianapolis; Miami; New Orleans; Richmond, Virginia; Tampa; and

Washington, D.C.—from 1985 to 1984 also found that about half of female homicide victims were killed by an intimate partner. Other researchers estimate that from 40 to 70 percent of female murder victims are killed by a husband or boyfriend. See Bailey, J. E., and others. "Risk Factors for Violent Death of Women in the Home." *Archives of Internal Medicine*, April 14, 1997, *157*(7), 777–782.

27   *less than 5 percent of male murder victims are killed by their wife or girlfriend:* Campbell, J. C., and others. "Risk Factors for Femicide in Abusive Relationships: Results from a Multisite Case Control Study." *American Journal of Public Health*, July 2003, *93*(7), 1089–1097. That figure has remained consistent. In 1998, only 4 percent of murdered men were killed by an intimate partner. See Rennison, C. M., and Welchans, S. *Intimate Partner Violence*, a Bureau of Justice Statistics special report. Washington, D.C., May 2000, revised Jan. 2002. A CDC study from 1991 to 1998 found that just 5 percent of male murder victims were killed by an intimate partner. See Centers for Disease Control. "Surveillance for Homicide Among Intimate Partners—United States, 1981–1998." *Morbidity and Mortality Weekly Report*, Oct. 12, 2001.

28   *An analysis of five years of death records in Maryland revealed that a pregnant or recently pregnant woman is more likely to die from homicide than any other cause whatsoever:* Horon, I. L., and Cheng, D. "Enhanced Surveillance for Pregnancy-Associated Mortality: Maryland 1993–1998." *Journal of the American Medical Association*, 2001, *285*, 1455–1459.

28   *Homicide was discovered to be the single biggest cause of injury-related death among pregnant and postpartum women in New York City and Cook County, Illinois, and among women up to a year after giving birth in the state of Georgia:* Dannenberg, A. L., and others. "Homicide and Other Injuries as Causes of Maternal Deaths in New York City, 1987–1991." *American Journal of Obstetrics*, May 1995, *172*, 1557–1564; Fildes J., and others. "Trauma: The Leading Cause of Maternal Death." *Journal of Trauma*, 1992, *32*, 643–645; Dietz, P. M., and others. "Differences in the Risk of Homicide and Other Fatal Injuries Between Postpartum Women and Other Women of Childbearing Age: Implications of Prevention." *American Journal of Public Health*, 1998, *88*, 641–643.

28   *A 2005 study that attempted to look at the problem nationally found homicide to be the second leading cause of injury death in pregnant and postpartum women:* Chang, J., Berg, C. J., Saltzmann, L.,

and Herndon, J. "Homicide: A Leading Cause of Death Among Pregnant and Postpartum Women in the United States, 1991–1999." *American Journal of Public Health*, Mar. 2005, 95(3), 471–477.

28   *Researchers reviewing eight years of autopsy records of reproductive-age women in the District of Columbia found murder to be the second most common cause of death among pregnant women, just one death behind medical complications related to pregnancy:* Krulewitch, C. J., and others. "Hidden from View: Violent Deaths Among Pregnant Women in the District of Columbia, 1988–1996." *Journal of Midwifery and Women's Health*, Jan./Feb. 2001, 46(1), 4–10.

28   *But Isabelle Horon and Diana Cheng, authors of the Maryland study, believe that the national study seriously undercounted the number of pregnancy-associated homicides:* Horon, I. L., and Cheng, D. "Underreporting of Pregnancy-Associated Deaths." Letter to the editor of *American Journal of Public Health*, Nov. 2005, 95(11), 1879.

29   *an estimated two to four million American women are physically assaulted by their partner every year:* The low-end figure, two million, was derived from the first National Family Violence Survey, conducted in 1976 by prominent researchers Richard Gelles, Murray Strauss, and Suzanne Steinmetz, published most notably in Straus, M. A., Gelles, R. J., and Steinmetz, S. K. *Behind Closed Doors: Violence in the American Family*. Garden City, N.Y.: Anchor Books, 1980. The survey asked respondents if they had been physically abused by their husband in the previous year. But because of the huge number of respondents not willing to disclose abuse and because the survey did not ask about violence from an ex-husband or ex-boyfriend, the three authors estimated that the true number of victims of intimate partner violence was as high as four million a year. A 1993 national survey on women's health by the Commonwealth Fund estimated that 4.4 million women a year are assaulted by an intimate partner. See Commonwealth Fund. *Violence Against Women in the United States: A Comprehensive Background Paper*. Commission on Women's Health, Columbia University, New York, 1994; and Plichta, S. B. "Violence and Abuse: Implications for Women's Health." *The Commonwealth Fund Survey*, 1996, 237–270. A 2003 study by the CDC put the figure as high as 5.3 million intimate partner victimizations per year: Centers for Disease Control. *Costs of Intimate Partner Violence Against Women in the United States*, March 2003.

29   *the rate of homicide just within families in this country is higher than the total homicide rates in most other Western industrialized nations:* Saunders, D. G., and Browne, A. "Intimate Partner Homicide." In R. Ammerman (ed.), *Case Studies in Family Violence.* (2nd ed.) New York: Plenum Press, 2000; Browne, A., Williams, K. R., and Dutton, D. G. "Homicide Between Intimate Partners: A Twenty-Year Review." In M. D. Smith and M. A. Zahn (eds.), *Homicide: A Sourcebook of Social Research.* Thousand Oaks, CA: Sage, 1999.

29   *A recent Canadian study found that half of men who had killed their intimate partners contemplated killing themselves afterward, and up to 40 percent of the men claim they tried to kill themselves.... [This figure is] validated by numerous studies both in the United States and Canada:* Kerry, G. P. "Understanding and Predicting Intimate Femicide: An Analysis of Men Who Kill Their Intimate Female Partners." Unpublished doctoral dissertation, Carleton University, Ottawa, Ontario, Department of Psychology, 2001. See also Lewandowski, L. A., McFarlane, J., Campbell, J. C., Gary, F., and Barenski, C. " 'He Killed My Mommy!': Murder or Attempted Murder of a Child's Mother." *Journal of Family Violence*, Aug. 2004, *19*(4), 211–220; Frye, V., and others. "Femicide in New York City: 1990 to 1999." *Homicide Studies*, 2005, *9*(3), 204–228; Lund, L. E., and Smorodinsky, S. "Violent Death Among Intimate Partners: A Comparison of Homicide and Homicide Followed by Suicide." *Suicide and Life-Threatening Behavior*, 2001, *31*, 451–459; Dawson, M. "Intimate Femicide Followed by Suicide: Examining the Role of Premeditation." *Suicide and Life-Threatening Behavior*, 2005, *35*, 76–90; Cooper, M. *Wasted Lives: The Tragedy of Homicide in the Family.* Vancouver, B.C.: Institute on Family Violence, 1994.

35   *"The* real *Scott Peterson . . . can be appreciated":* Babiak, P., and Hare R. D. *Snakes in Suits: When Psychopaths Go to Work.* New York: HarperCollins, 2006, p. 65.

39   *"I lie like I breathe, one as much as the other":* Hare, R. D. *Without Conscience.* New York: Guilford Press, 1993, p. 40.

39   *"rework the facts so that they appear to be consistent with the lie":* Hare, *Without Conscience*, p. 46.

39   *"[W]e are dealing here not with a complete man at all":* Cleckley, C. *The Mask of Sanity.* New York: Mosby, 1982, p. 228.

45   *"psychopaths are more concerned with the inner workings of their cars than with the inner worlds of their 'loved' ones":* Hare, *Without Conscience*, p. 45.

48 *"by what their beloved does for them"*: Fox, J. A. "Murderers Not Like the Rest of Us." *Boston Globe*, Feb. 22, 2006.

48 *"Never underestimate the overconfidence of a narcissist"*: Fox, "Murderers Like the Rest of Us."

60 *"Dreiser wants us to believe that Clyde didn't mean to kill Roberta"*: Gordon, M. *Good Boys and Dead Girls*. New York: Viking, 1991, p. 11.

60 *Dreiser himself later reflected on the novel and the real-life murder*: Dreiser, T. "I Find the Real American Tragedy." *Mystery Magazine*, Feb. 1935. Reprinted in Dreiser, T. *Theodore Dreiser: A Selection of Uncollected Prose*. Detroit, Mich.: Wayne State University Press, 1977.

60 *"the young ambitious lover of some poorer girl"*: Dreiser, "I Find the Real American Tragedy."

61 *"who cannot master his fate"*: Gordon, *Good Boys and Dead Girls*.

65 *stated his personal belief that Gillette really was just planning to take Grace Brown to some kind of home for unwed mothers*: Brandon, C. *Murder in the Adirondacks*. Utica, N.Y.: North Country Books, 1986.

83 *Scott confessed to Diane Wagner, a journalist who was writing a book on the case*: Wagner, D. *Corpus Delicti*. New York: Martins/Marek, 1986. Given the vagueness of Scott's claim and the long lapse in time, there is no way of confirming his claim, but Wagner did find it credible.

104 *Elizabeth Rapaport refers to this phenomenon as the domestic discount*: Rapaport, E. "Capital Murder and the Domestic Discount: A Study of Capital Domestic Murder in the Post-Furman Era." *Southern Methodist University Law Review*, July-Aug. 1996.

104 *In a study she conducted of all men sentenced to death in six states*: Rapaport, "Capital Murder and the Domestic Discount."

110 *they have difficulty learning from or adapting to changes in the complex world outside themselves*: Patrick, C. J. (ed.), *Handbook of Psychopathy*. New York: Guilford Press, 2006.

137 *psychopaths see children as an inconvenience*: Hare, *Without Conscience*, p. 63.

138 *the unborn baby may be perceived as a direct threat and as a rival*: Bacchus, L., Mezey, G., and Bewley, S. "A Qualitative Exploration of the Nature of Domestic Violence in Pregnancy." *Violence Against Women*, 2006, *12*(6), 588–604.

139   *Recent research indicates that between 20 and 35 percent of men who kill their pregnant partners had no previous history of violence:* Nicolaidis, C., and others. "Could We Have Known? A Qualitative Analysis of Data from Women Who Survived an Attempted Homicide by an Intimate Partner." *Journal of General Internal Medicine*, 2003, *18*, 788–794.

175   *In a book published by seven of the jurors after the trial, they said they based their second-degree verdict in the killing of Conner on a lack of evidence of premeditation and malice:* Beratlis, G., and others. *We, the Jury: Deciding the Scott Peterson Case.* Beverly Hills, Calif.: Phoenix Books, 2006.

288   *a "national disgrace":* Hansen, "Body of Evidence." *ABA Journal*, June 1995, *81*, 60–67.

288   *less than a third of the country has properly trained staff and procedures in place to adequately assess suspicious deaths:* Hansen, "Body of Evidence," p. 63.

— About the Authors

Marilee Strong is an award-winning journalist who specializes in the coverage of psychological and social issues. She is the author of *A Bright Red Scream* (Viking, 1998) on the aftereffects of childhood abuse and trauma. She has also written widely for newspapers and magazines on such topics as child kidnappings, women in prison, gang violence, hate groups, and psychological treatment for sex offenders. A graduate of Columbia University's Graduate School of Journalism, she was the recipient of a Pulitzer Fellowship to cover the civil war in Mozambique. She lives in Oakland, California.

Mark Powelson is an editor and researcher who was editor of San Francisco's award-winning city magazine and vice president of the PBS affiliate KQED.

Index